SHARI'AH GOVERNANCE IN ISLAMIC BANKS

Edinburgh Guides to Islamic Finance
Series Editor: Rodney Wilson

A series of short guides to key areas in Islamic finance, offering an independent academic perspective and a critical treatment.

Product Development in Islamic Banks
Habib Ahmed

Shari'ah *Compliant Private Equity and Islamic Venture Capital*
Fara Madeha Ahmad Farid

Shari'ah *Governance in Islamic Banks*
Zulkifil Hasan

Islamic Financial Services in the United Kingdom
Elaine Housby

Islamic Asset Management
Natalie Schoon

Legal, Regulatory and Governance Issues in Islamic Finance
Rodney Wilson

Forthcoming
Islamic and Ethical Finance in the United Kingdom
Elaine Housby

www.euppublishing.com/series/egif

SHARI'AH GOVERNANCE IN ISLAMIC BANKS

Zulkifli Hasan

EDINBURGH
University Press

© Zulkifli Hasan, 2012

Edinburgh University Press Ltd
22 George Square, Edinburgh EH8 9LF
www.euppublishing.com

Typeset in Minion Pro by
Servis Filmsetting Ltd, Stockport, Cheshire, and
printed and bound in Great Britain by
CPI Group (UK) Ltd, Croydon CR0 4YY

A CIP record for this book is available from the British Library

ISBN 978 0 7486 4558 9 (hardback)
ISBN 978 0 7486 4557 2 (paperback)
ISBN 978 0 7486 4559 6 (webready PDF)
ISBN 978 0 7486 6837 3 (epub)
ISBN 978 0 7486 6838 0 (Amazon ebook)

CONTENTS

TABLES

FIGURES

STATUTES

Bahrain

Anti Money Laundering Law 2001
Central Bank of Bahrain and Financial Institutions Law 2006
Commercial Companies Law 2001
Commercial Law 1987
Companies Registration Act 1983
Financial Trust Law 2006
Law of Civil and Commercial Procedure 1971
Law on the Establishment of the Bahrain Monetary Agency 1973
Stock Exchange Law 1987

Kuwait

Central Bank of Kuwait Law No. 32 of 1968 as Amended by Law No. 130 of 1977
Civil Code Law 1980
Commercial Code 1981
Commercial Companies Law 1980
Kuwaiti Constitution 1962

Lebanon

The Establishment of Islamic Banks in Lebanon Law No. 575 of 2004

Malaysia

Banking and Financial Institutions Act 1989 (Act 372)
Central Bank of Malaysia (Amendment) Act 2003 (Act A1213)
Central Bank of Malaysia Act 2009 (Act 701)
Federal Constitution 1957
Islamic Banking Act 1983 (Act 276)
Securities Commission Act 1993 (Act 498)
Takāful Act 1984 (Act 312)

Qatar

Civil and Commercial Procedure Code Law No. 13 of 1990
Qatar Financial Centre Law No. 7 of 2005
Qatar Financial Market Authority Law No. 33 of 2005

Saudi Arabia

Banking Control Law 1966
Basic Law of Rule of 1992
Capital Markets Law 2003

United Arab Emirates

Civil Court Procedures Law of Abu Dhabi No. 4 of 1987
Civil Procedure Law of Abu Dhabi No. 3 of 1970
Dubai International Financial Centre Law No.13 of 2004
Federal Law No. 10 of 1973
Federal Law No. 6 of 1985
Federal Law No. 11 of 1992

Federal Law No. 18 of 1993
Union Law No. 10 of 1980

United Kingdom

Companies Act 2002

ACKNOWLEDGEMENTS

In the name of Allah, The Most Compassionate, The Most Merciful. All praise be to Allah who is Most Praiseworthy, Most High, may His peace and blessings be upon our beloved Prophet Muhammad *Sallāhualaihiwasallam* and upon his family, His companions and all his sincere followers after them. My utmost thanks to Allah for His blessings and for granting me the patience and the endurance to complete this book successfully.

I would like to express my gratitude and heartfelt thanks to my distinguished supervisor, Professor Rodney Wilson, whose precise and precious guidance propelled me towards the completion of this book. My deepest appreciation is also due to Dr Mehmet Asutay, my second supervisor, for his valuable guidance, intellectual stimulus and encouragement.

My gratitude also is extended to the respondents in Malaysia, GCC countries and the UK for their cooperation in answering the questionnaires. Special thanks to Mr Mazdlan Mohammad Hussein of the IFSB, Mr Ismail Nik of the BNM, Mr Nick Nadal and Jahanara Sajjad Ahmad of the Hawkamah, the Institute for Corporate Governance and Mr Syamsulfaiz Zainuddin of Messrs Habib Mulla & Co for their assistance in conducting the study.

I would like also to take this opportunity to thank to my beloved wife, Hanani Harun and my dearest children, Muhammad Al Ameen, Iffah Madiehah and Izzah Maisarah, who never fail to provide me with love and warmth and have helped to lessen the pressure of the task of accomplishing this book. My heartfelt gratitude goes to my parents, Haji Hasan Yeen and Hajjah Rabeah Khalid and my parents-in-law, Haji Harun Said and Hajjah Nik Marathiah Nik Man for their sacrifice, encouragement and prayers for my success. Last but not least, I would like to thank everyone who has directly or indirectly contributed to the successful accomplishment of this book.

I owe you a great debt of appreciation.

To my dear parents:
Haji Hasan Yeen
&
Hajjah Rabeah Khalid

To my beloved wife:
Hanani Harun

To my dearest children:
Muhammad Al Ameen
Iffah Madiehah
Izzah Maisarah

INTRODUCTION

The main aim of corporate governance is to ensure transparency, fairness and accountability. An efficient corporate governance framework is therefore vital to any organisation as it plays a significant role in resolving the agency's problems as well as promoting transparency, fairness, integrity, credibility and accountability. In Islamic financial institutions (IFIs), another component of corporate governance, namely *Shari'ah* governance, is the very essence of Islamic financial practice in building and maintaining the confidence of the shareholders and other stakeholders, assuring them that all transactions, practices and activities are in compliance with *Shari'ah* principles.

In view of the tremendous growth and sophistication of the Islamic finance sector,[1] *Shari'ah* governance now has a profound influence on the day-to-day practice of IFIs. Realising the importance of *Shari'ah* governance, each jurisdiction has adopted different approaches to developing and nurturing its *Shari'ah* governance framework. It is very important to understand and appreciate the pluralistic approaches to *Shari'ah* governance across jurisdictions, so as to identify and highlight best practice. It should be noted that, from a regulatory point of view, Malaysia represents the most regulated *Shari'ah* governance model, followed by Brunei, Pakistan and Sudan respectively, whilst Gulf Cooperation Council (GCC) countries and the UK prefer less regulatory interference.

Malaysia   has   developed   both   regulatory   and non-regulatory aspects of its *Shari'ah* governance infrastructure and architecture.[2] In fact, a special endowment fund of USD 60 million has been allocated by the government of Malaysia to promote the development of *Shari'ah* compliance and governance in the Islamic financial services sector. IFIs in GCC countries,[3] namely countries in the Arabian Gulf including Saudi Arabia, Kuwait, Bahrain, Qatar and the UAE, have their own framework of *Shari'ah* governance which is different from that of Malaysia. Saudi Arabia treats IFIs as equal to their conventional counterparts and therefore allows the market to develop its own *Shari'ah* governance system. On the other hand, Kuwait, Bahrain, Qatar and the UAE allow slight regulatory intervention in their *Shari'ah* governance framework by issuing several directives in the form of rulebooks, as well as adopting the Accounting and Auditing Organization for Islamic Financial Institutions (AAOIFI) governance standards. The *Shari'ah* governance framework in the UK[4] is aligned with that of the Financial Services Authority (FSA), and is unregulated by specific legislation. The establishment of a *Shari'ah* board is due to market factors and not because of regulatory requirements in the UK.

In view of the lack of an intensive and in-depth book in the area of *Shari'ah* governance, this book provides comprehensive information on the extent of *Shari'ah* governance practices. It aims to provide useful information on the frameworks and practices of *Shari'ah* governance of IFIs, particularly on the aspects of design and implementation, strategy and framework at the institutional, national and international levels; the role of the regulatory authority in improving the standards and best practices and the role of *Shari'ah* board practices. The book consists of six chapters which are divided into four parts, as follows. Part 1: Theoretical concept of corporate governance; Part 2:

Theoretical concept of *Shari'ah* governance; Part 3: State of *Shari'ah* governance practices; and Part 4: Concluding remarks.

Part 1 of the book comprises two chapters. Chapter 1 discusses a conceptual framework of corporate governance from a Western perspective. This includes conceptual definition, roles, models and institutions of corporate governance, particularly within the context of the financial services sector. References are made to famous Western academic concepts of corporate governance, namely 'shareholder value' and 'stakeholder value' models. Chapter 2 provides a comprehensive analysis of the concept and theoretical context of corporate governance from Islamic perspectives. This chapter briefly analyses a few models of corporate governance in Islam and explains its fundamental principles in the context of the financial services industry.

The discussion on the conceptual definition and theoretical framework, as well as the comparative overview of corporate governance from both conventional and Islamic perspectives in Chapters 1 and 2 is very important for the purpose of enlightening the relevancy of *Shari'ah* governance as part of the corporate governance in IFIs. The faith-based epistemology of corporate governance in Islam, which is inclined towards a stakeholder-oriented system, means that IFIs require additional measures to address specific issues pertaining to Islamic rules and principles in the form of *Shari'ah* governance.

There are two chapters in Part 2. Chapter 3 constructs a theoretical concept of *Shari'ah* governance whereby it discusses the conceptual definition of *Shari'ah* governance, roles and models of the *Shari'ah* board, the development of the *Shari'ah* governance system, and its process and guidelines. The book also highlights issues and challenges pertinent to the *Shari'ah* governance system, as practised by

IFIs in cross-border jurisdictions. Chapter 4 focuses on the regulatory frameworks of the *Shari'ah* governance system in Malaysia, GCC countries and the UK. The book identifies five *Shari'ah* governance models in the context of regulatory perspectives.

Part 3 interestingly illustrates the state of *Shari'ah* governance practices in IFIs. Chapter 5 discusses the actual practice of *Shari'ah* governance in Malaysia, Kuwait, Bahrain, UAE, Qatar, Saudi Arabia and the UK through the analysis of questionnaires. In addition, Chapter 6 elucidates the extent of disclosure of *Shari'ah* governance practices via analysis of annual reports, financial statements and websites.

Part 4 provides the overall findings, policy recommendations and conclusions. Chapter 7 offers details of specific policy recommendations for the purpose of enhancement and improvement of *Shari'ah* governance. This chapter concludes by summarising the entire book's findings, the extent of its contribution, and highlighting the book's limitations.

The aim of this book is to provide an in-depth understanding of the topic of *Shari'ah* governance. To achieve this, the book emphasises the regulatory and non-regulatory aspects of *Shari'ah* governance, and these include *Shari'ah* governance approaches, regulatory and internal frameworks, roles of the *Shari'ah* board, attributes of the *Shari'ah* board with respect to independence, competency, transparency and confidentiality, operational procedures, and assessment of the *Shari'ah* board. With significant numbers of *Shari'ah* boards in numerous IFIs in Malaysia, GCC countries and the UK, it is undeniable that there are distinctive models and practices of *Shari'ah* governance in these three jurisdictions. This diversity actually reflects the beauty and blessing of Islam because it provides an opportunity to study comparatively the *Shari'ah* governance practices with the purpose of identifying gaps, shortcomings and weaknesses, and highlighting the best practices for possible recommendations. It is a strong belief that some common elements underlying and promoting good governance and best practices can be drawn together to facilitate the creation and optimisation of a healthy and viable environment for *Shari'ah* governance without impeding further growth of the industry, to ensure optimal *Shari'ah* governance in IFIs.

Notes

1. Mackinsey and Co. estimates that the value of assets managed by IFIs will grow 33% from USD 750 billion in 2006 to USD 1 trillion this year (Reuters 2009). *The Banker* reported that the total value of *Shari'ah*-compliant assets managed by the top 500 IFIs in 2009 is about USD 822.1 billion (*The Banker* 2009: 26).

2. As of March 2010, the assets of Islamic banking in Malaysia total approximately USD 72.5 billion, representing 19.6% of the total banking sector (Parker 2010).

3. As of November 2009, the GCC countries still dominate the Islamic finance industry with *Shari'ah*-compliant assets of USD 353.2 billion, representing 42.9% of the total global aggregate; Saudi Arabia represents the largest share with 36.2% of the total aggregate, followed by UAE (23.8%), Kuwait (19.1%), Bahrain (13%) and Qatar (7.8%) (*The Banker* 2009: 26).

4. *The Banker* (2009: 26) reports that the *Shari'ah*-compliant assets of IFIs in the UK total approximately USD 19.5 billion, representing 2.3% of the total global aggregate.

CHAPTER 1

CORPORATE GOVERNANCE: A CONVENTIONAL PERSPECTIVE

1.0 Introduction

Corporate governance is one of the vital elements in any corporation. There has been much debate and discourse on the issue of corporate governance for many years. The concept of corporate governance is becoming much more popular since there have been more corporate failures due to ineffective governance. Basically, there is no consensus on the definition and concept of corporate governance. This is due to the different understandings of the goals of corporations with respect to different models of corporate governance, as well as a large number of distinct economic systems. As a result, there are various definitions and concepts of corporate governance propounded by different parties that basically reflect their special interest in the field.

Iqbal and Mirakhor (2004: 43–4) argue that the increased attention focused on the issue of corporate governance is due to the growth of institutional investors, the weaknesses and defects of a 'shareholder model' of corporate governance, a shift away from the traditional shareholder value system to a stakeholder model, and the impact of globalisation of the financial market. Recognising all these aspects, this chapter explores the theoretical foundation of corporate governance from a conventional perspective, in general, and tries to conceptualise its framework in the context of the financial-services sector. The aim of this chapter is to build a basic understanding of corporate governance in conventional literature so as to enable this book to construct and develop the concept of corporate governance within the Islamic paradigm that will be discussed in Chapter 2.

1.1 Conceptual definition

The discourse on corporate governance as a discipline in its own right is relatively new and has evolved over centuries (Cadbury 1999: 3). There are various definitions of corporate governance and the absence of any real consensus on its actual meaning leads to various interpretations.

Literally, the word 'corporation', as defined in the *Oxford English Dictionary* (1989), is derived from the Latin word *corpus* which means 'a group of people authorized to act as an individual and recognized in law as a single entity'. In terms of the legal definition, *Blacks' Law Dictionary* (2009) legally defines a corporation as 'an artificial person or legal entity created by, or under the authority of, the laws of a state'. In short, these different definitions lead to a similar conclusion: that a corporation can be defined as a form of organisation that represents a group of people as a single entity for certain purposes.

The term 'governance' originates from a Latin word, *gubernare*, which means to steer or to govern (Cadbury 2002: 1). Lewis (2005: 5) also mentions that the word governance comes from the Greek word *kybernan* which means to steer, to guide or to govern.[1] The *Oxford English Dictionary* (1989) provides a wider meaning of governance as to include any 'act or manner of governing'. All of these definitions present a very wide meaning of governance as the term may cover areas of politics, economics, social justice and public administration. In other words, the term governance in a general sense means the style or way an organisation, institution or corporation is guided, steered and controlled.

From the above definitions of corporation and governance, the meaning of corporate governance can be categorised into two senses, namely a narrower sense and an expansive term. The former considers it a formal system of accountability between the shareholders and their agent, such as the Board of Directors (BOD) and senior management, and the latter refers to it as the entire network of formal and informal relations involving a large group of stakeholders in the firm, such as shareholders, management, employees, the community and the environment.

1.2 Defining corporate governance in the financial-services sector

A concept of corporate governance in the context of the financial-services sector presents its own distinct characteristics and features. Basically, it requires additional measures and greater concerns as compared to the firms in other sectors as it involves a larger group of stakeholders. The Organisation for Economic Co-operation and Development (OECD 2004: 11) provides a general definition of corporate governance as 'a set of relationships between a company's management, its board, its shareholders, and other stakeholders'. This definition nevertheless does not specifically differentiate the nature of corporate governance in the financial-services sector.

The Basel Committee for Banking Supervision (BCBS), in *Enhancing Corporate Governance for Banking*

Organizations, specifically explains corporate governance from a banking-industry perspective, which involves

> the manner in which the business and affairs of individual institutions are governed by their BOD and senior management affecting how a bank sets its corporate objective, daily business, interest of the stakeholder, to align corporate activities operate in a safe and sound manner and to comply with laws and regulations, and to protect the interest of depositors. (BCBS 1999: 3)

Here, the BCBS expands the term 'stakeholders' to include employees, customers, depositors, suppliers, supervisors, government and the community. In explaining corporate governance in the context of the financial-services sector, Arun and Turner (2003: 6) specifically mention the importance of ensuring capital and investment return and protecting depositors as well as shareholders. On the whole, corporate governance in financial institutions is to a certain extent different to that in other types of business organisation, as it involves a larger group of stakeholders. With this position, financial institutions are much more regulated as compared to other commercial entities.

1.3 Role of corporate governance

If we refer to early academic discussion on corporate governance in the case of the United States, it is found that the main function of corporate governance is to reduce agency costs due to conglomerate mergers and hostile takeovers; it then evolves into other areas, including the role of institutional investors as corporate monitors to control managerial shirking and to maximise shareholder value (Macey 2004: 580). This is affirmed by Scott (2003: 527), who explains the objective function of a corporate governance system as a set of legal rules, incentives and behaviours that support the reliance by investors in order to maximise the economic efficiency of the firm. Several studies affirm the positive correlation between corporate governance behaviour and firms' performance. In the UK, companies with good governance posted 18 per cent higher returns than those with poor governance, while in Russia it is predicted that it may significantly increase a firm's value and in Korea firms with good governance have been found to trade at a premium of 160 per cent to poorly governed corporations (IFC and Hawkamah 2008: 12).

In the context of the financial-services sector, Claessens (2003: 14) considers that corporate governance is very important, particularly in determining a firm's performance in terms of ability to facilitate access to external finance, to lower cost of capital, to improve operational performance, to mitigate the operational risk, and to achieve better relationships amongst the stakeholders. In this aspect, a clear and precise corporate governance framework will stimulate the bank's efficiency which may contribute towards better performance, avoid unnecessary agency cost, and resolve the agency problem (Hart 1995: 678).

Another key function of corporate governance is the promotion of corporate fairness, transparency and accountability (Wolfensohn 1999). Corporate governance requires financial institutions to be more transparent and to ensure fairness not only to shareholders but also to other stakeholders. Having greater transparency and more accountability as an element of best corporate governance practice will positively affect growth as well as improve a firm's stability, efficiency and trustworthiness (Grais and Pellegrini 2006c: 5).

To sum up, corporate governance plays an essential

role in meeting the specific goals and objectives of a corporation. The distinct function of corporate governance in the financial-services sector is mainly focused on the determination of policies, a set of legal rules and managerial behaviours amongst the shareholders, the managers, the BOD, the depositors and other stakeholders. The complication and sophistication of the financial-services sector with a larger group of stakeholders affects the scope and framework of the corporate governance system in financial institutions. These factors also lead to the need for distinctive codes and guidelines to promote best practice of corporate governance in the financial-services sector.

1.4 Corporate governance systems

It is imperative to conduct a worldwide survey of the international corporate governance system and how it is practised. Shleifer and Vishny (1997) provide a comprehensive survey of corporate governance, centring on the essence of legal protection of investors and ownership concentration in the governance system. The underlying problem of corporate governance, as recognised by a long tradition of scholars such as Berle and Means (1932), Marshall (1920) and Smith (1993), lies with the issue of separation of beneficial ownership and executive decision-making (Keasey *et al.* 1997: 528).

Corporate governance has emerged for several reasons, including corporate fraud and corporate collapse. All these events have led to corporate governance reforms in the form of governance codes, rules and guidelines as to how companies can be best managed and controlled. Becht and Barca (2001) provide a literature review of a number of quantitative corporate governance models as a possible means to resolve the issue of the collective action problem among dispersed shareholders. These models comprise: the takeover model; block holder model; delegated monitoring and large creditors; board models; executive compensation models; and multi-constituency models. Another interesting examination can be found in Lewis (1999: 33–66), where he examines six different models of corporate governance, namely the Anglo-Saxon model, the European model, the Japanese model, the Latin model, the Confucian model and the Islamic model. This book chooses this classification by Lewis (1999) to explain the differences of corporate governance models by focusing on the main two dominant systems, that is, the Anglo-Saxon and the European models.

1.4.1 The Anglo-Saxon model

The Anglo-Saxon model is also known as a market-based, shareholder value or principle-agent system and is considered the most dominant theory of corporate governance. This is demonstrated by the practice of numerous corporations all over the world, such as in the United States and the UK.[2] This corporate governance system is relatively important for corporations in these jurisdictions as it sets a clear and very objective corporate goal of maximising shareholders' profit.[3]

Although the corporate governance theory has been discussed for centuries, there has been no formal or serious discussion on the approach or model of corporate governance. The extensive discourse on corporate governance began in the 1970s when a group of American financial economists developed the agency theory as a basis of a corporate governance system (Lazonick and O'Sullivan 2000: 14–17). This agency theory was formulated with the sole motivation of maximising shareholder value and it suggests legal rules and policies to be imposed on the BOD and executive officers which require them to act in the best interest of the shareholders.

Mallin (2007: 12) states that one of the advantages of the agency theory is that it 'identifies the relationship where one party, the principal, delegates work to another party, the agent'. She mentions that the BOD plays a role as an essential monitoring device to minimise any principal-agent relationship problems (Mallin 2007: 13). In addition, Hart (1995: 678) considers that corporate governance is very important to resolve the agency problem either in the form of cost of business or conflict of interest.The agency theory influences the corporate governance structure in the Anglo-Saxon model of corporation where the BOD and senior managers act as agents to protect the interest and rights of investors or shareholders.

1.4.2 *The European model*
Since the publication of Berle and Means (1932), many have believed that there are significant problems with the share-holder value system of corporate governance. This model is viewed as inferior by some scholars because it does not effectively address the agency problems (Macey and Miller 2004: 552). This modern tendency has led to a formula-tion of another corporate governance system known as stakeholder theory.

A different perception of corporation in the European countries results in another approach to corporate govern-ance which is based on the stakeholder-oriented model. Initial studies on the stakeholder theory of corporate govern-ance have been conducted by Clarkson (1995) and Donaldson and Preston (1995), who claim that the interests of all the stakeholders have intrinsic value and that one set of inter-ests is not supposed to dominate the others (Yamak and Suer 2005: 113). The efficiency of this model is proven by referring to the successful corporations and industrial societies that have developed a reputation for the ethical treatment of suppliers, clients and employees and that are able to build up trusting relationships, which support profitable investments and mutually beneficial exchanges (Jones 1995: 404).

As a basic premise, the stakeholder theory rejects propositions of the shareholder value model and enhances the corporate governance framework by which stakeholders have a governance right to participate in corporate decisions; it is the manager's fiduciary duty to protect the interests of all stakeholders and the corporation's objective to promote the interest of all stakeholders and not only the shareholders (Iqbal and Mirakhor 2004: 46). Mallin (2007: 16) states that 'stakeholder theory takes into account a wider group of constituents rather than focusing on shareholder'. In explaining the term stakeholders, Freeman (1984: 46) defines it as a group of constituents who have a legitimate claim on the corporation or a person who contributes directly or indirectly to the firm. In addition, Lepineu classifies the stakeholders into shareholders, internal stakeholders (employees and labour unions), operational partners (customers, suppliers, creditors and contractors), and the social community (state authorities, trade union, non-governmental organisations and civil society; Pesqueux and Salma 2005: 7).

In terms of corporate governance structure, the special attribute of the European model of corporate governance is the practice of the two-tier system, comprising a supervisory board of outside directors and a separate management board of executive directors, in which structure the two boards meet separately (Dignam and Galanis 2009: 269–74). There is much literature examining and discussing the role of firms, which is contrary to the understanding of the Anglo-Saxon corporate governance model, particularly in

Germany. The concept of corporate personality or '*Verbands Personlichkeit*' affects the German view of a corporation as it constitutes part of the social and economic structure within the community and has its own function towards society at large (Kay and Silberston 1995: 88). Mallin (2007: 162) states that the philosophy of the German approach to corporate governance emphasises a wider set of stakeholder interests and this includes the employees and customers.

1.5 Corporate governance in the financial-services sector

Corporate governance is crucial in the financial-services sector. History has witnessed the corporate collapse and malpractice of several financial institutions because of weak corporate governance frameworks, such as the cases of BCCI, Barings and Equitable Life with mortgage endowment mis-selling, split-cap investment trust opacity and a spate of money laundering failures (Schachler *et al.* 2007: 628). There are various significant issues of corporate governance in the financial-services sector that affect its structure and approach, such as the opaqueness of the banks, heavily regulated and impeded natural corporate governance mechanisms and government ownership, which alter the corporate governance equation (Caprio and Levine 2002: 11–18).

Financial institutions are more opaque than other sectors of the economy. In this regard, the government or regulatory authority normally imposes certain regulatory requirements upon banks, such as restrictions on shareholders, rules on deposit insurance and restrictions on certain activities. In addition, there are differences in some key corporate governance variables in the financial-services sector, particularly in terms of board size and composition, board activity, CEO compensation, and ownership and block share ownership. These unique characteristics imply the need for distinctive and effective corporate governance measures for financial institutions. This is affirmed by Macey and O'Hara (2003) who conducted a study on corporate governance for the Federal Reserve Bank of New York and highlighted the need for additional measures on corporate governance in the financial-services sector.

In view of the unique features of corporate governance in the financial-services sector, the BCBS has taken the initiative to issue guidelines on enhancing corporate governance for banking organisations in order to foster safe and sound banking practices. Unlike the OECD *Principles of Corporate Governance*, which are more general and applicable to any type of corporate entity, the BCBS guidelines address specific corporate governance issues exclusive to financial institutions. The BCBS (1999) stresses the importance of an environment supportive of sound corporate governance, the role of supervisors and the significance of other stakeholders.

The above corporate governance studies imply that the multiple approach to corporate governance models is necessary within the context of the financial sector. The diversity in the financial sector as compared to other types of corporate entity stems mainly from the presence of various stakeholders, such as shareholders, investors, depositors and regulators (Yamak and Suer 2005: 112). This condition entails that the BOD and managers are assumed to have a duty to all stakeholders and it needs a distinctive corporate governance system as a mechanism of control. Yamak and Suer (2005: 114–15) identify and classify major stakeholders in financial institutions into the owners, the managers, the depositors, the borrowers and the regulators. The shareholders and the owners expect profit maximisation, the managers assume they will obtain monetary and non-monetary compensation as stipulated in their contracts, the depositors expect a return on their deposits, the borrowers are concerned with fair and non-discriminatory treatment by the banks, and the regulators are interested in the compliance to the laws and regulations by all the stakeholders. Recognising all the stakeholders' interests and rights, the corporate governance model in the financial-services sector seems to be more complicated than in other types of corporation and it implies the need for a specific and distinctive model.

1.6 Conclusion

This chapter has attempted to explore the conceptual dimension and theoretical framework of corporate governance from conventional perspectives by referring to the two main dominant corporate governance systems of the Anglo-Saxon and the European models. The Anglo-Saxon model, which is formulated on the basis of agency theory, represents the shareholder value system, while the European model, which is constructed on the basis of stakeholder theory, seems to offer remedies for the defects of the shareholder model by promoting the stakeholder value orientation system. In the context of financial services, the OECD *Principles of Corporate Governance* and the BCBS *Enhancing Corporate Governance for Banking Organisations* seem to bridge the gap between these two models by acknowledging the essence of the shareholders' value and at the same time recognising the large stakeholders' interest. In this regard, the BOD, the supervisory board, the managers, the shareholders, the depositors and the regulatory authorities are the key participants in corporate governance in the conventional financial-services sector.

The model of corporate governance system from a conventional perspective raises an issue of the design of an efficient corporate governance structure of IFIs within an Islamic paradigm. It is very important to identify characteristics, values, norms and behaviour of corporate governance from an Islamic perspective. As an observation, the initial study finds that the corporate governance model in Islam is inclined towards the stakeholder value orientation, where its governance style aims at protecting the wider group of stakeholders. This book further explores the conceptual and foundational dimensions of corporate governance in Islamic literature and further highlights its differences and diversities in Chapter 2.

Notes

1. *The Macquarie Encyclopedic Dictionary* (1990), states that the etymological root of governance is from the Greek to the Latin *gubernare* and to the Old French *governer* (Lewis 2005: 25).

2. The concept of enlightened shareholder value is clearly enshrined in section 172 (1) of the Companies Act 2006. With the recommendation of the Law Review Committee Steering Group, section 172 (1) provides that 'directors owe their fiduciary duty only to the shareholders generally, rather than a range of interest groups, but seeks to provide a broader context for fulfilling that duty' (Andrew 2007: 579).

3. Although the UK and the United States corporate governance models share many similarities, there are several differences in their actual practices such as the board structure and the roles of Chairman, CEO and executive directors. It is reported that the Chairman and the CEO of 75% of the S&P500 in the United States are the same person, while in the UK the roles are separated (Keenan 2004: 173). In addition, unlike in the UK, it is a rare practice in the United States to appoint additional executive directors on top of the Chairman, CEO and Chief Financial Officer (Keenan 2004: 173).

CHAPTER 2

CORPORATE GOVERNANCE IN ISLAMIC FINANCIAL INSTITUTIONS

2.0 Introduction

This book classifies the existing literature on corporate governance in IFIs into three main phases, namely the first phase (pre-1980s), the second phase (1980s–1990s) and the third phase (post-2000s). The first phase shows an absence of studies on corporate governance and the subject has not been given due concern in mainstream research. This is affirmed by the surveys of Siddiqi (1981), Mannan (1984) and Haneef (1995) of the contemporary literature on Islamic economics.

Specific studies on the issue of corporate governance of IFIs began in the second phase (1980s–1990s). For example, Aboumouamer (1989) conducted a survey on the role and function of *Shari'ah* control in Islamic banks and Banaga *et al.* (1994) carried out research on external audit and corporate governance in Islamic banks. However, both studies were carried out by a single individual and only addressed the issues of *Shari'ah* control and audit.

In view of several corporate failures of IFIs in the 1990s and 2000s, including the closures of Ihlas Finance House in Turkey, the Islamic Bank of South Africa and Islamic

Investment Companies of Egypt, a significant number of studies on corporate governance were then carried out by different individuals, organisations and institutions in the third phase (post-2000s). One of the most significant studies on corporate governance in IFIs was carried out by Chapra and Ahmed (2002), who discussed the issue of the roles and functions of the *Shari'ah* board, auditing, accounting and the general framework of corporate governance. Other studies were conducted by Al-Baluchi (2006), on corporate disclosure practices of IFIs, and Al-Sadah (2007), on the corporate governance of Islamic banks, its characteristics, its effect on stakeholders and the role of Islamic bank supervisors. In 2008, the Islamic Financial Services Board published a *Survey on* Shari'ah *Boards of Institutions Offering Islamic Financial Services across Jurisdictions* (IFSB 2008b) and this was followed by Faizullah (2009), who discussed issues of governance, transparency and standardisation of Islamic banks.

Based on the above development, undeniably, corporate governance is one of the vital components in IFIs as it plays a role in designing and promoting principles of fairness, accountability and transparency. In fact, it is an even bigger challenge to IFIs due to their additional risk when compared to the conventional banking system. Therefore, it is strongly indicated that IFIs need to have a sound governance system and appropriate strategies that will promote the adoption of strong and effective corporate governance within the Islamic paradigm. This chapter attempts to provide an overview of the foundational dimension of corporate governance from an Islamic perspective, with special emphasis on the governance framework of IFIs. It also aims at constructing a basic understanding of corporate governance in Islam and clarifying any issues involved so as to differentiate its value and features from its Western counterpart. The initial study submits that Islam presents distinctive values and special characteristics of corporate governance with the aim to uphold and maintain the principle of social justice not only to the shareholders of the firm but to all stakeholders.

2.1 Conceptual framework of corporate governance from an Islamic perspective

Basically, the concept of corporate governance from an Islamic perspective does not differ much from the conventional definition as it refers to a system by which companies are managed, directed and controlled with the purpose of meeting the corporation's objective by protecting all the stakeholders' interests and rights. Uniquely, the context of corporate governance within the Islamic paradigm presents certain exceptional characteristics and features in comparison with Western theories.

Choudhury and Hoque (2006) discuss the faith-based theoretical framework of corporate governance in Islam and they consider it as a theory pertaining to decision-making processes that employ the premise of the Islamic socio-scientific epistemology of *Tawhīd*. The practical implications of the Islamic idea of corporate governance are immense, especially when they are related to transaction cost minimisation in decision-making environments and achieving the aims and objectives of the corporation within the boundary of *Shari'ah* rules and principles (Choudhury and Hoque 2006). Therefore, it is essential to understand and refine the conceptual definition of corporate governance from an Islamic point of view in order to enlighten any further discussion on the subject of *Shari'ah* governance.

From an Islamic perspective, corporate governance can be defined as a set of organisational arrangements as to how a corporation is directed, managed, governed and controlled, which provides the governance structure through which all stakeholders' interests are protected, the company's objective is achieved, social responsibility is upheld and the principles of *Shari'ah* are complied with. This is in parallel with the definition of corporate governance in IFIs of the *Guiding Principles on Corporate Governance for Institutions Offering Only Islamic Financial Services (Excluding Islamic Insurance (*Takāful*) Institutions and Islamic Mutual Funds)* (hereafter termed IFSB-3).[1]

IFSB-3 defines corporate governance as

> a set of relationships between a company's management, its BOD, its shareholders, and other stakeholders which provides the structure through which the objectives of the company are set; and the means of attaining those objectives and monitoring performance are determined.

In addition, IFSB-3 further characterises corporate governance in IFIs to encompass

> a set of organizational arrangements whereby the actions of the management of IIFS are aligned, as far as possible, with the interests of its stakeholders; provision of proper incentives for the organs of governance such as the BOD, *Shari'ah* board, and management to pursue objectives that are in the interests of the stakeholders and facilitate effective monitoring, thereby encouraging IFIs to use resources more efficiently; and compliance with Islamic *Shari'ah* rules and principles. (IFSB 2006b: 33)

This definition concludes that there are two main elements of corporate governance in IFIs, namely the governance structure and framework through which all stakeholders' interests and rights are protected and the requirement of compliance with the *Shari'ah* rules and principles.

2.2 Role of corporate governance in IFIs

With several corporate failures of IFIs, such as the closures of Ihlas Finance House in Turkey, the Islamic Bank of South Africa and the Islamic Investment Companies of Egypt, and corporate difficulties, as in the case of the Dubai Islamic Bank and Bank Islam Malaysia Berhad, the need for a good and efficient governance system is considered as a crucial part of corporate governance. All these cases indicate that IFIs are not immune from crisis and failures due to governance issues and conundrums. Table 2.1 summarises and highlights the corporate governance issues that contributed to the corporate difficulties and the closure of these IFIs.

The role of corporate governance in IFIs is to promote corporate fairness, transparency and accountability. In the context of IFIs, the requirement of *Shari'ah* compliance as part of its corporate governance framework signifies the essence of maintaining the relationship between the different stakeholders as well as the relationship with God. In this aspect, IFIs require the additional framework of *Shari'ah* to safeguard and maintain not only the relationship with God but to include other human beings and the environment.

Basically, there are three main roles of corporate governance that are exclusive to IFIs. Firstly, corporate governance plays a role to reassure stakeholders that their activities are fully compliant with *Shari'ah* principles. Secondly, the stakeholders also need to be assured that IFIs aim to maintain and improve growth and are able to prove their efficiency, stability and trustworthiness (Grais and Pellegrini 2006b: 2). Corporate governance therefore has the role of harmonising these two functions so as to meet the requirement of *Shari'ah* and to satisfy the natural aim of the corporation of maximising profit without violating stakeholders' rights and interests.

Table 2.1 *Corporate difficulties of IFIs due to corporate governance issues*

IFIs	Corporate governance issues
Ihlas finance in Turkey	Ihlas Finans in Turkey was closed on 10 February 2001 due to financial distress and weak corporate governance. Ali (2007) reported that the closure of Ihlas Finans was mainly due to the failure of corporate governance and internal checks and balances. It was found that the bank was run without proper systems of internal control, the management was not preparing any changing circumstance regulations and the scope of regulations was unclear.
Islamic Bank of South Africa (IBSA)	The IBSA was closed in November 1997 with debts of between R50 and R70 million due to a lack of supervision by the regulatory authority, bad management, weak risk management and numerous loans to insiders (Okeahalam 1998: 37–8). It is sad to mention that the IBSA was unable to compensate all of the depositors, mostly Muslims saving specifically towards performing the pilgrimage to Mecca.
Islamic Investment Companies of Egypt (IICE)	The closure of the IICE in 1988 was due to weak corporate governance, irresponsible management and improper regulatory frameworks as well as engagement in *Shari'ah* non-compliant activities (Zuhaida 1990). Over 1 million small investors lost their investments when the IICE and other investment companies collapsed. The IICE was an investment company that offered services free from interest.
Dubai Islamic Bank (DIB)	This refers to a fraud case involving USD 501 million. Seven individuals have been charged including two DIB former executives (Morris 2009). This was the biggest case in the Dubai Court of First Instance, in terms of amount of financial irregularities (Za'za 2009).

Table 2.1 *(continued)*

IFIs	Corporate governance issues
Bank Islam Malaysia Berhad (BIMB)	The BIMB declared losses totalling RM 457 million in 2005 mainly due to the provisioning of RM 774 million as a result of bad financing and investments incurred by its Labuan branch (Parker 2005). The composition of the board was not appropriate, as there were no board members who were familiar with the banking sector, and no proper credit and debt collection (Parker 2005).

Thirdly, corporate governance in IFIs is important as a means to address risk, particularly governance risk. Iqbal and Mirakhor (2007: 227–50) define governance risk as 'the risk arising from failure to govern the institution, negligence in conducting business and meeting contractual obligations and from a weak internal and external environment'. They further classify the governance risk into operational risk, fiduciary risk, transparency risk, *Shari'ah* risk and reputation risk (Iqbal and Mirakhor 2007: 242–6). With the complexity and some exclusive characteristics of risks in IFIs, unlike their conventional counterparts, a sound and efficient corporate governance system must be in place in order to mitigate those kinds of risk.

The special characteristic of IFIs of needing to comply with *Shari'ah* rules and principles in all their activities requires a specific kind of governance. IFIs should avoid any involvement with all kinds of *Shari'ah* prohibitions, such as *riba* (interest), *gharar* (uncertainty), speculation and *maysir* (gambling), stay away from investing in any unlawful activities, and observe the principles of Islamic morality or the Islamic ethical code. In this respect, corporate governance in Islam is an obligation not only to IFIs to foster and gain the confidence of the stakeholders but also to the general

public that all products, operations and activities adhere to
Shari'ah rules and principles.

2.3 The development of corporate governance in IFIs

This section briefly discusses the development of corporate governance in IFIs by revisiting the historical development of financial institutions from the early stages of Islam
until today. This book classifies the development of corporate governance in IFIs into two main phases, namely pre-
twentieth century and post-twentieth century. The second
phase is further subdivided into two stages: the first stage
(pre-1970s) and the second stage (post-1970s).

2.3.1 *Phase I (pre-twentieth century): absence of corporate governance in traditional IFIs*

The term 'bank'[2] is alien to the early Muslim period where
the term *bayt al-māl* is extensively used. *Bayt al-māl* could
be considered a state-owned bank; it played the role of an
agricultural credit bank, commercial bank and clearing
house for merchants to facilitate commercial activities from
the time of Umayyad (Imamuddin 1997a: 132). In the eighth
and ninth centuries, financiers were known as *ṣarrāf*[3] and
jahbadh and functioned as modern bankers in pre-modern
Islam. *Ṣarrāf* provided financing facilities primarily on the
basis of *mudhārabah* and *mushārakah*, negotiable instruments and trade facilities by cashing cheques, and issued
promissory notes and letter of credits (Chapra and Ahmed
2002: 3). They also provided banking facilities to the public
as well as the private sector, while *jahbadh* served mainly
the public sector.[4] *Ṣarrāf* as financiers were owned by the
individual, family or tribe, whereas *jahbadh* were owned
by the state. Neither institution, however, was a bank, as

they did not receive deposits or issue cheques as normal modern banks do; therefore Udovitch prefers the term *ṣarrāf* to mean bankers without a bank rather than the bank as financial intermediary (Chapra 2007: 328).

Corporate governance was not an issue at all in *ṣarrāf* or *jahbadh*, since neither institution was classified as a corporate legal entity. Interestingly, even without any sort of corporate governance framework, the so-called banking institutions during that time, in the form of *ṣarrāf* and *jahbadh*, were able to effectively facilitate economic activities both locally and internationally. Although there is no appropriate data available to prove the efficiency of such a financial system, historical evidence in many works of literature provides its clear indication.[5]

2.3.2 Phase II (post-twentieth century): the emergence of corporate governance in modern IFIs

Stage I: pre-1970s
At the end of the nineteenth century, the Muslim role in *ṣarrāf* business was radically reduced by the increase in non-Muslim *ṣarrāf* families and the emergence of modern banks, established largely by Europeans and by Armenian and Greek *ṣarrāf* such as such as the Deutsche Orient Bank, the Deutsche Bank, the Crédit Lyonnais and the Banque Ottomane (Saeed 2002). The colonisation of the majority of Muslim countries further affected the existing Islamic financial system and hence it was replaced with Western modern banking, an interest-based financial system. Not until the 1950s were there efforts to establish IFIs, such as in Pakistan, on the notion of inserting a clause to ban interest into the constitution and the establishment of a local Islamic bank that provided financing mainly for the poor.[6] This was followed by the opening of the Mitr Ghams Savings Bank on

23 July 1963 and the Nasser Social Bank in 1972 (Harun 1997: 3). The establishment of the Mitr Ghams Savings Bank and the Nasser Social Bank in Egypt demonstrates the potential of the Islamic financial system in the modern economic infrastructure.

The success of the earlier Islamic banks, although a partial breakthrough, was discussed extensively by many scholars, particularly the aspects of operations, procedures, activities, performance, nature of financing facilities and socio-legal matters. Nevertheless, corporate governance was not given due concern and there was no specific discourse or initiatives on it. This is because all of those Islamic banks were incorporated in the form of either cooperative societies or social banks. The modes of financing activities were also very limited and only attempted to redress social and small community needs. Corporate governance is less relevant to this kind of business organisation.

Stage II: post-1970s

The period between 1975 and 1990 was the most crucial period in the development of the Islamic financial sector. The establishment of several Islamic banks, in the form of corporations such as the Dubai Islamic Bank, Faisal Islamic Bank and the Kuwait Finance House including the Islamic Development Bank in Jeddah, triggered the need for a specific corporate governance system. Due to several corporate failures and difficulties of IFIs in the 1990s and 2000s, a few international infrastructure institutions were established with the purpose of supporting the Islamic financial sector to enhance and strengthen the corporate governance framework; these include the Accounting and Auditing Organization for IFIs (AAOIFI), the International Islamic Financial Market (IIFM), the International Islamic Rating Agency (IIRA) in Bahrain, the General Council of Islamic

Banks and Financial Institutions (CIBAFI) and the Islamic Financial Services Board (IFSB) in Malaysia. The AAOIFI and the IFSB were established inter alia to address issues pertaining to corporate governance in IFIs by issuing governance standards and guidelines of best practice while the rest of the institutions provide infrastructure support to the implementation of Islamic finance. In addition, the Hawkamah, the Institute for Corporate Governance based in Dubai, also used its own initiative by setting up a specific task force and working committee on corporate governance for Islamic banks and financial institutions with the purpose of studying and developing best practice for corporate governance in the regions of the Middle East and North Africa.

To date, the AAOIFI has issued seven governance standards: Shari'ah *Supervisory Board: Appointment, Composition and Report*; Shari'ah *Review*; *Internal* Shari'ah *Review*; *Audit and Governance Committee for IFIs*; *Independence of* Shari'ah *Supervisory Board*; *Statement on Governance Principles for IFIs*; and *Corporate Social Responsibility* (AAOIFI 2005a–e). Similarly, the IFSB has issued seven guidelines on governance, disclosure and supervisory review processes for IFIs: *Guiding Principles on Governance for Islamic Collective Investment Schemes; Guidance Note In Connection with the Capital Adequacy Standard: Recognition of Ratings by External Credit Assessment Institutions (ECAIs) on* Shari'ah-*Compliant Financial Instruments; Guidance on Key Elements in the Supervisory Review Process of Institutions offering Islamic Financial Services (excluding Islamic Insurance (*Takāful*) Institutions and Islamic Mutual Funds); Disclosures to Promote Transparency and Market Discipline for Institutions offering Islamic Financial Services (excluding Islamic Insurance (*Takāful*) Institutions and Islamic Mutual Funds); Guiding Principles on Corporate Governance for Institutions Offering Only Islamic Financial*

*Services (Excluding Islamic Insurance (*Takāful*) Institutions and Islamic Mutual Funds)*; *Guiding Principles on Conduct of Business for Institutions offering Islamic Financial Services*; *Guiding Principles on Governance for* Takāful *Operations*; and *Guiding Principles on* Shari'ah *governance System for Institutions offering Islamic Financial Services.*

2.4 Corporate governance model from an Islamic perspective

In view of the distinctiveness of the underlying principles and paradigm of corporate governance in Islam compared with the Western model, there are several studies that attempt to construct an Islamic model of corporate governance.[7] Unlike the Western concept of corporate governance, which is based on Western business morality that derives from 'secular humanism', this book discovers that Islamic corporate governance is founded on the epistemological aspect of *Tawhīd* and the embedded *Shari'ah* rules and principles, where the former refers to the principle of consultation in which all stakeholders share the same goal of *Tawhīd* or the oneness of Allah (Choudhury and Hoque 2004; 2006) and the latter concerns an adoption of the stakeholder-oriented value system (Iqbal and Mirakhor 2004; Chapra and Ahmed 2002). Safieddine (2009) extends the existing literature by highlighting variations of agency theory in the unique and complex context of Islamic banks. At this point it is worth discussing the foundational dimension and main arguments of the Islamic corporate governance model, as identified in the literature, which are based on the four fundamental principles of *Tawhīd*, *shura*, property rights and commitment to contractual obligation that govern the economic and social behaviour of individuals, organisations, society and state.

2.4.1 Tawhīd and shura-based model

It is settled law that the concept of *Tawhīd* is the basis of everything in this world and this includes the philosophical pillars of corporate governance. As the foundation of Islamic faith is *Tawhīd* (Al-Faruqi 1982), the basis for the corporate governance framework also emanates from this concept. In other words, the Islamic corporate governance approach is premised on the *Tawhīd* epistemological model, in which the functional roles of the corporation are working via *Shari'ah* rules. The principle of *Tawhīd* leads to the important concepts of vicegerency (*khilāfah*) and justice or equilibrium (*al-adl wal ihsān*[8]). The stakeholders, as vicegerents of Allah, have a fiduciary duty to uphold the principles of distributive justice via the *shuratic* process. Chapra (1992: 234) highlights that the practice of *shura* is an obligation in any decision-making process and the inclusion of *shura* denotes the widest participation of the stakeholders.

Allah says in *al-Qur'an*

> Men who celebrate the praises of Allah, standing, sitting, and lying down on their sides, and contemplate the (wonders of) creation in the heavens and the earth, (with the thought): 'Our Lord! Not for naught Hast thou created (all) this! Glory to Thee! Give us salvation from the Penalty of the the Fire (3: 191).[9]

The praise by Allah upon the believers that remember Him standing, sitting, lying down, and contemplate the wonders of creation indicates the *Tawhīd* paradigm. Another verse of *al-Qur'an* (51: 56) further points out the *Tawhīd* dimension in Islam as Allah says 'I have only created Jinns and men, that may serve Me'. Both these verses indirectly provide the fundamental principles of governance, where everything created by Allah has a purpose and a human being is created to be the vicegerent of God on earth towards the Unity of God. By putting His trust in mankind as a vicegerent, Allah plays an active role in monitoring and being involved in every affair of human beings and He is omnipresent and a knower of everything (Chapra 1992: 202).

Allah states in *al-Qur'an* (31: 16)

> O my son! (said Luqman), if there be (but) the weight of a mustard seed and it were (hidden) in a rock, or (anywhere) in the heavens or on the earth, Allah will bring it forth: for Allah understands the finer mysteries, (and) is well acquainted (with them).[10]

As Allah knows everything and all mankind is accountable and answerable to Him, the *Tawhīd* paradigm therefore enhances the scope of a firm's obligation and objectives to include a large group of stakeholders rather than the shareholders alone. Furthermore, it also denotes the concept of accountability, or *taklīf*, indicating that everyone is accountable to God for his own deeds. As such, the principle of *taklīf* that is derived from the supreme concept of *Tawhīd* should be the foundation of corporate governance in Islam.

Inspired by the paradigm of *Tawhīd*, which acknowledges the stakeholders as vicegerent, the shareholders, the management, the BOD, the *Sharī'ah* board, the employees and the communities have a fiduciary duty to uphold the principle of distributive justice[11] via the *shuratic* process.[12] In determining the scope of *Sharī'ah*, the institution of the *Sharī'ah* board comes into the picture and plays a crucial role to ensure that all corporation activities are in line with the *Sharī'ah* rules and principles. In addition, the shareholders also have a responsibility as active participants and conscious stakeholders in the process of decision-making and policy framework by considering the interests of all direct and indirect stakeholders rather than only maximising their profit. The other stakeholders, including the community, should also play their roles to provide mutual cooperation to protect the interests of all stakeholders and to stimulate the social wellbeing function for social welfare. All of these processes are centred on fulfilling the ultimate objective of Islamic corporate governance of complementing the private and social goals via upholding the principle of distributive justice (Choudhury and Hoque 2004: 85–8)

In deconstructing the foundational paradigm of corporate governance in Islam, Choudhury and Hoque (2004) summarise their model of *Tawhīd* and the *shuratic* process by referring to four principles and instruments governing Islamic corporate governance: unity of knowledge, the principle of justice, the principle of productive engagement of resources in social welfare, and the principle of economic activities and recursive intention. These principles are the main premises of Islamic corporate governance, in which *Shari'ah* rules embedded in *al-Qur'an* and *al-Sunnah* make the Islamic corporation market-driven and at the same time uphold the principles of social justice (Choudhury and Hoque 2004: 57–83). Lewis (2005: 16–18) seems to support this approach by mentioning the essence of *Tawhīd* and the institution of a *shuratic* decision-making process and explaining how decision-making in business and other activities can meet Islamic moral values. He mentions that all resources are from Allah, ownership of wealth belongs to Allah and the individual is only a trustee who is accountable and answerable to Allah. The ultimate ends of business and economic activities, including the aims of the business organisation, shall be in the direction of upholding the principle of *Tawhīd*.

The *Tawhīd* and *shura*-based approach provides the epistemological foundation of corporate governance. However, it is unclear and ambiguous as to how this approach could be adopted and implemented in the current corporate governance system. Moreover, the practice shows that major corporations, including IFIs, tend to adopt the existing corporate governance model, which is founded on the episteme of rationalism and rationality. This triggers the need for further research and empirical rather than theoretical studies to examine the operational aspects of this *Tawhīd* and *shura*-based approach.

2.4.2 *Stakeholder value approach*

Iqbal and Mirakhor (2004) and Chapra and Ahmed (2002: 14) argue that the corporate governance model in Islam refers to a stakeholder-centred model in which the governance style and structures protect the interests and rights of all stakeholders rather than the shareholders per se. This stakeholder value model is preoccupied by the two fundamental concepts of *Shari'ah* principles of property rights and contractual obligation.

The principle of property rights in Islam formulates a framework as to how to identify and then protect the interests and rights of all stakeholders. The majority of jurists agreed that usufructs (*manafi'*) and rights (*huquq*) are considered as property[13] and they must be protected and safeguarded. Islam guarantees the protection of property rights, be it in the form of *manafi'* or *huquq*, and these include right of ownership, acquisition, usage and disposition. In terms of right of ownership, Islam declares that Allah is the sole owner of property and a human being is just a trustee and custodian in whom it implies the recognition to use and manage the properties in accordance with *Shari'ah*, as property is given as *amanah* (trust) to individuals. There are numerous verses of *al-Qu'ran* referring to the principle of property rights, such as 'Believe in Allah and His Messenger and spend (in charity) out of the (substance) whereof He has made you Heirs. For those of you who believe and spend (in charity) for them is a great reward' (*al-Qur'an* 57: 7) and 'It is He who hath created for you all things that are on earth, then he turned to the heaven and made them into seven firmaments and all of things he hath perfect knowledge' (*al-Qur'an* 2: 29). The implied meaning of these verses lays down the foundational principle and the effect of property ownership where mankind is only regarded as a trustee of God.

Azid *et al.* (2007: 7) considers that property rights in Islam guarantee individuals as well as corporations 'the right to own private property and economic resources, to make a profit, to expand jobs, to boost investment and to increase prosperity'. This implies the recognition of individual ownership or corporation. While acknowledging the right to property of an individual or firm, Islam at the same time provides guidelines on how to deal with property ownership via *Shari'ah* principles. *Shari'ah* requires the enjoyment of rights to property by either individuals or corporations to be balanced with the rights of the community at large. This property rights principle is a vivid recognition of Islam that the corporation should not concentrate on protecting the interests of certain organs of governance in the corporation, particularly shareholders, but should include other stakeholders. In summary, the concept of property rights in Islam is based on three fundamental principles: the right to property is subjected to *Shari'ah*; the enjoyment of the right to property is balanced with the rights of society and the state; and individuals, society and the state are stakeholders and the rights of stakeholders are recognised by Islamic law (Iqbal and Mirakhor 2004: 54).

The contractual framework is also unique in Islam. In *al-Qur'an*, *Surah* 5: 1, Allah clearly reminds the Muslims of the principle of fulfilling each of their contractual obligations where He says: 'O you who believe! Fulfil (all) obligations'. This verse presents a basic foundation for the principle of contract, that every individual, society, corporation and the state are bound by their contracts. In relation to the issue of corporate governance, each stakeholder has a duty to perform his contractual obligations in accordance with the terms stipulated in the contract. While Islam guarantees the freedom of contract within *Shari'ah* parameters, the parties to any transactions are bound to fulfil their contractual obligations.

This contractual framework enhances the scope of the firm's stakeholders, as it is not necessary to refer to the shareholders alone but also involves those who have active and non-active participation in the firm. Iqbal and Mirakhor (2004: 58) formulate two tests to determine whether any individual qualifies as a stakeholder: firstly, whether the individual or group has any explicit and implicit contractual obligations; and, secondly, whether they are someone whose property rights are at risk due to business exposure of the corporation.[14] As such, all parties who are directly or indirectly affected by the firm's business are considered as the rightful stakeholders. In this regard, each stakeholder has its own function: the shareholders have a duty to provide business capital, the management to manage and run the business, the employees to perform their respective duties and the regulators to ensure enforceability of the contracts. All these duties arise through the contractual framework and provide vivid evidence that the Islamic corporate governance model is inclined towards the stakeholder-oriented approach.

The overall arguments on stakeholder value orientation as the ideal model of corporate governance in the Islamic economic system indicate that the corporate goal of Islamic firms should be a balance between the aim of maximising profit and a duty to observe social justice by protecting the rights, interests and welfare of all stakeholders. It is observed nevertheless that, contrary to its ideal framework, the main objective of many corporations, including the so-called Islamic corporations, is to maximise the shareholders' profit. This implies that, in actual practice, many Islamic corporations adopt the shareholder model of corporate governance rather than the stakeholder value orientation. The World Bank's note on risk analysis for IFIs states that the existing corporate governance in IFIs is modelled along the lines of shareholder value orientation (Greuning and Iqbal 2008: 185). This is affirmed by a study conducted by Lim (2007: 737–8) on corporate governance reform in Malaysia, which found the majority of companies prefer to adopt the Anglo-Saxon model of corporate governance as a benchmark rather than the stakeholder value model.

2.5 Conclusion

It is worth mentioning that this chapter does not intend to discuss in detail every single issue of corporate governance; it only aims at providing its conceptual framework and theoretical foundation. The foundational paradigm of corporate governance from an Islamic perspective, then, would be able to enlighten the concept of *Shari'ah* governance in IFIs. In summary, the corporate governance system in Islam has its own unique features and presents distinctive characteristics. This chapter summarises the diversities of the Western models of corporate governance.

With respect to epistemological method, Islam rejects rationality and rationalism as the sole episteme of corporate governance and replaces it with the episteme of *Tawhīd*. While the shareholder model prioritises the shareholders' value alone and the stakeholder value orientation protects all the stakeholders' interest and rights, the corporate governance objective in Islam balances the corporate goal of maximising the profit with the duty to uphold the principle of social justice and *maqāsid Shari'ah* and this entails the notion of protecting the interests and rights of all stakeholders within *Shari'ah* rules.

The nature of management of the corporate governance model is premised by the fundamental principles of *shura*, with the *Shari'ah* board playing a significant role in supervising and overseeing the overall corporate activities so as to ensure they comply with *Shari'ah* principles. In contrast to the Western concept, the nature of ownership structure in corporate governance considers the shareholders and the investment account holders (IAHs) as the rightful owners, rather than the shareholders alone. The distinct features and characteristics of corporate governance combine the elements of *Tawhīd*, *shura*, *Shari'ah* rules and Islamic morality to maintain the private goal without ignoring the duty of social welfare.

On the whole, unlike the Western model of corporate governance, the foundational dimension of Islamic corporate governance is rooted in the fundamental principles of *Tawhīd*, the *shuratic* process, property rights and contractual obligation. Based on this aspirational foundation, key participants in corporate governance in Islamic corporations, particularly IFIs, such as the BOD, the shareholders, the depositors, the managers and particularly the *Shari'ah* board, play significant roles in ensuring the *Shari'ah* objectives and the firm's goal are both realised within the parameters of *Shari'ah* and Islamic values and ethics. As a matter of fact, the spread of Islamic banking business and strong growth of the Islamic finance sector, along with the increasing numbers of IFIs, require a specific organisational arrangement in the form of '*Shari'ah* governance' as part of an Islamic corporate governance framework.

Notes

1. See also (hereafter termed IFSB-6), *Guiding Principles on Governance for Collective Investment Schemes* (IFSB 2009a) and IFSB-8, *Guiding Principles on Governance for* Takāful *(Islamic Insurance) Undertakings* (IFSB 2009b).

2. The term bank originates from the Italian word *banco*, which means 'table' as in the past moneychangers from Lombardy used to place money on a table (Baldwin and Wilson 1988: 178). The first modern bank was started in Venice in 979h or 1584CE and was known as *Banco di Rialto* (Imamuddin 1997b: 153).

3. In the Ottoman Empire, *ṣarrāf* were moneylenders, brokers and pawnbrokers; many *ṣarrāf* became large financiers with well-recognised international connections and played a significant role in the economy and politics of the Ottoman Empire (Saeed 2002). *ṣarrāf* also functioned as moneychangers to provide facilities of currency exchange (Imamuddin 1997a: 134) and played a role in determining the relative value of coins (Cohen 1981: 315–33).

4. The *jahbadh* played its role as an administrator of deposits and as a remitter of funds from place to place through the medium of the *ṣukk* and especially of the *suftadja* (Fischell 2002).

5. Udovitch writes that the Islamic modes of equity financing were able to mobilise the resources of the Islamic world for financing of agriculture, crafts, manufacturing and international trade (Chapra 2007: 328). Cohen (1981: 315–33) illustrates the monetary system in Egypt at the time of the Crusades and the reform of *Al-Kamil* and mentions that there was a sophisticated system of exchange during that time.

6. The experiment was, however, unsuccessful; it faced a lot of

operational problems, was short of funds and had weak governance (Wilson 1984: 33).

7. There are at least three different underlying ethical principles of Western corporate governance that are inappropriate to Islam. Firstly, the Western concept of corporate governance is derived from a secular humanist perspective. Secondly, the Western concept remains rooted in a self-interest paradigm. Thirdly, the theoretical model of Western corporate governance is based on the agency theory rather than stewardship theory (Iqbal and Lewis 2009: 272).

8. Naqvi (1994: 27–8) defines *al-adl wal ihsān* as a state of social equilibrium, which means the best configuration of production, consumption and distribution activities where the needs of all members in the society have priority over the individual.

9. Translations of *Qur'anic* verses throughout this work are from Abdullah Yusuf Ali (2004), *The Meaning of the Holy Qur'an*. Beltsville, MD: Amana Publications.

10. See *al-Qur'an* 99: 7–8: 'So, whosoever does good equal to the weight of a speck of dust shall see it. And whosoever does evil equal to the weight of a speck of dust shall see it.' The verse reminds the human being that Allah knows everything and this invokes the principle of accountability in which all groups of stakeholders are answerable to God.

11. Islam clearly emphasises the principle of distributive justice, where Allah says 'We sent Our Messengers with clear signs and sent down with them the Book and the Measure in order to establish justice among the people' (57: 25). See also 16: 90 and 5: 8.

12. Allah says in *al-Qur'an* (3: 159) 'So pass over (their faults), and ask for (Allah's) forgiveness; for them; and consult them in affairs (of moment). Then, when thou hast taken decision, put thy thrust in Allah. For Allah, loves those who put their trust (in Him).' Based on this verse, in explaining as to how important the concept of *shura* is, Chapra (1992:

234) mentions that the practice of *shura* is not an option but rather an obligation.

13. *Manafi'* refers to the ostensible benefits taken out of material things by way of their utilisation, such as rental payment from a leasing contract, and *huquq* means something that can be justly claimed such as right of ownership, right of easement and right of acquisition (Islam 1999: 361–8).

14. This is in line with the saying of the Prophet: 'A Muslim is the one from whose hand others are safe' (*Sahih Bukhari*, Vol. 1, Book 2, No. 10).

CHAPTER 3

THE *SHARI'AH* GOVERNANCE SYSTEM IN ISLAMIC FINANCIAL INSTITUTIONS

3.0 Introduction

With the lessons from the failure and financial scandals of several IFIs and the huge potential implications of *Shari'ah* non-compliance risks, the need for a good and efficient *Shari'ah* governance system is considered a crucial part of corporate governance. As one of the essential key participants of corporate governance in IFIs, the institution of the *Shari'ah* board plays an essential role in the aspect of *Shari'ah* supervision, monitoring, auditing and issuing legal rulings. The *Shari'ah* board has become the central part of the *Shari'ah* governance system that has a profound influence on the day-to-day practice of finance in providing advisory and consultative services to IFIs. With the aim of providing an overview of the *Shari'ah* governance system and its related issues, this chapter is organised into ten sections, comprising an introduction, conceptual framework, historical development, objective of *Shari'ah* governance system, roles of *Shari'ah* board, models of *Shari'ah* board, international standard-setting agency, *Shari'ah* governance process, issues and challenges, and a conclusion.

3.1 Conceptual framework of *Shari'ah* governance systems

Until the issuance of the IFSB *Guiding Principles on Shari'ah governance Systems in Institutions Offering Islamic Financial Services* (hereafter IFSB-10; IFSB 2009d), there was no formal or proper definition of a *Shari'ah* governance system. The AAOIFI Governance Standards No. 1–5 (AAOIFI 2005a–e) were also silent on its actual definition. In fact, the existing literature, as discussed in this chapter, seems to provide definitions of corporate governance rather than *Shari'ah* governance in particular. Furthermore, neither the AAOIFI nor the IFSB have provided a proper definition of the existing governance standards. This leads to uncertainty and different understandings as to what is meant by a *Shari'ah* governance system. Because of this, it is very important to clarify the term '*Shari'ah* governance system' and to have a sound understanding of its actual concept and meaning.

Perhaps, the best definition of *Shari'ah* governance can be found in IFSB-10.[1] IFSB-10 defines the *Shari'ah* governance system as

> a set of institutional and organizational arrangements through which IFIs ensure that there is effective independent oversight of *Shari'ah* compliance over the issuance of relevant *Shari'ah* pronouncements, dissemination of information and an internal *Shari'ah* compliance review. (IFSB 2009a: 2)

To understand further, this definition can be divided into three essential components:

1. The set of institutional and organisational arrangements. This refers to the *Shari'ah* board and its related

institutions, such as an internal audit department and *Shari'ah* division.

2. Effective independent oversight of *Shari'ah* compliance. This indicates the aims and objectives of the *Shari'ah* governance system to provide efficient mechanisms for the purpose of *Shari'ah* compliance.

3. *Shari'ah* pronouncements, dissemination of information and an internal *Shari'ah* compliance review. This involves the overall *Shari'ah* governance processes that cover both *ex ante* and *ex post* aspects of the *Shari'ah* compliance framework.

This definition implies that the institution of the *Shari'ah* board is crucial to the *Shari'ah* governance system as an authoritative body to ensure *Shari'ah* compliance in IFIs. The AAOIFI Governance Standard No.1 defines a *Shari'ah* board as 'an independent body entrusted with the duty of directing, reviewing and supervising the activities of IFIs for the purpose of *Shari'ah* compliance and issuing legal rulings pertaining to Islamic banking and finance' (AAOIFI 2005a: 4). A similar definition is given by the IFSB-10, which refers to 'a body comprised of a panel of *Shari'ah* scholars who provide *Shari'ah* expertise and act as special advisers to the institutions' (IFSB 2009d: 1). In carrying out this duty, the *Shari'ah* board needs a clear framework and structure to ensure its effectiveness, particularly with respect to its independence, the binding force of its rulings, its objectivity and its full mandate. On this basis, any formal or informal arrangement as to how the *Shari'ah* board is directed, managed, governed and controlled for the purpose of *Shari'ah* compliance is also part of the *Shari'ah* governance system.

Shari'ah governance is a unique kind of governance in financial architecture as it is concerned with religious aspects of the overall activities of IFIs. To illustrate the rationale of the *Shari'ah* governance system in the existing corporate governance framework, Table 3.1 provides an illustration as to how *Shari'ah* governance complements the existing corporate governance framework in IFIs.

Table 3.1 initially indicates that IFIs and typical financial institutions share common institutional arrangements for their corporate governance framework, particularly in the aspects of governance, control and compliance. The only element that differentiates corporate governance in IFIs is the institutional arrangement for their *Shari'ah* governance mechanism. IFIs require another set of organisational arrangements in the form of a *Shari'ah* board, an internal or external *Shari'ah* review and an internal *Shari'ah* compliance unit to meet the religious requirement of *Shari'ah* compliance in all aspects of their business transactions and operations.

In terms of governance structure, the *Shari'ah* governance system adds an additional layer of governance to the existing corporate governance structure. Figure 3.1 simply demonstrates the unique corporate governance structure

Table 3.1 *Institutional arrangement in the* Shari'ah *governance system*

Functions	Typical financial institutions	Exclusive to IFIs
Governance	BOD	*Shari'ah* board
Control	Internal auditor/ external auditor	Internal *Shari'ah* review unit/external *Shari'ah* review
Compliance	Regulatory and financial compliance officers/unit/ department	Internal *Shari'ah* compliance unit

Source: IFSB (2009c: 4).

48

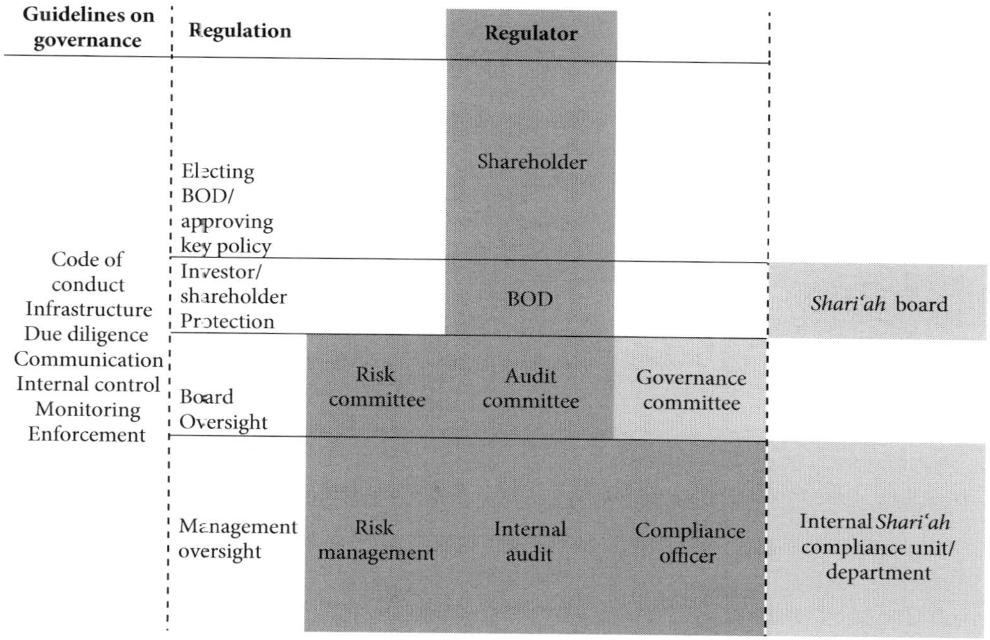

Guidelines on governance | **Regulation** | **Regulator**

Electing BOD/approving key policy — Shareholder

Code of conduct
Infrastructure
Due diligence — Investor/shareholder Protection — BOD

Communication
Internal control
Monitoring
Enforcement — Board Oversight — Risk committee | Audit committee | Governance committee

Management oversight — Risk management | Internal audit | Compliance officer

Shari'ah board

Internal Shari'ah compliance unit/department

Figure 3.1 *Corporate governance structure in IFIs. Source: modified from Stanley (2008).*

in typical IFIs, in which the *Shari'ah* board and internal or external *Shari'ah* review are the additional institutions that oversee the *Shari'ah* compliance aspects. This is actually based on the AAOIFI governance standards, which put the *Shari'ah* board on a par with the BOD in the corporate governance structure and, therefore, subject directly to the shareholders. The IFSB-10 approach, on the other hand, places the *Shari'ah* board either as parallel or subordinate to the BOD. Both the AAOIFI and IFSB guidelines nevertheless agree that the *Shari'ah* board must be independent of the BOD and be accountable not only to shareholders but to all stakeholders.

With regard to the scope of the *Shari'ah* governance framework, it covers *ex ante* and *ex post* aspects of *Shari'ah* compliance, of which the former refers to issuance of *Shari'ah* rulings and dissemination of *Shari'ah*-related information and the latter to the periodic and annual internal *Shari'ah* review process. Figure 3.2 illustrates the scope of the *Shari'ah* governance system in the two phases, *ex ante* and *ex post*. It is worth noting that the process outlined here only illustrates the generic process for the approval of Islamic financial products and this process can differ from one IFI to another. Figure 3.2 only attempts to provide a general idea of the *Shari'ah* governance process and its framework in typical IFIs.

Figure 3.2 illustrates the scope of the *Shari'ah* governance framework in IFIs. It involves a systematic process and requires involvement of numerous organs of governance. In phase 1, processes 1–6, the diagram illustrates *ex ante Shari'ah* compliance aspects, which include a product proposal, legal documentation, *Shari'ah* review, and procuring and dissemination of *Shari'ah* rulings. In phase 2, processes 7–8, the diagram demonstrates the *ex post* processes, which involve the periodic and annual *Shari'ah*

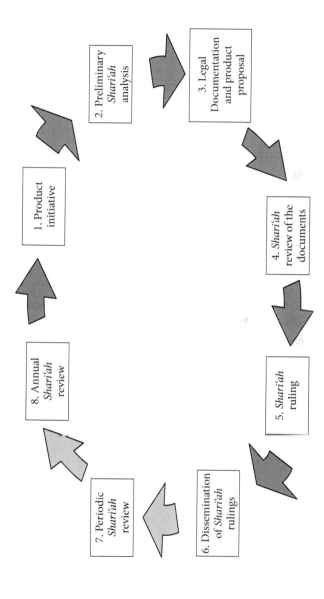

Figure 3.2 *Scope of the Shari'ah governance framework. Source: modified from Dar (2009).*

reviews. The *Shari'ah* board plays a central role in ensuring the legitimacy of the products and services and this can only be achieved by having sound *Shari'ah* coordination and an efficient internal *Shari'ah* review unit. The *Shari'ah* coordinator acts as a liaison officer or coordinator to the *Shari'ah* governance process from product initiation to annual *Shari'ah* review.

This section attempts to provide the conceptual framework of *Shari'ah* governance in IFIs from three main aspects, namely its definition, institutional arrangement and scope of the *Shari'ah* governance system. In summary, the *Shari'ah* governance system refers to a set of institutional arrangements for the purpose of *Shari'ah* compliance and this involves *ex ante* and *ex post Shari'ah*-compliant processes, such as *Shari'ah* pronouncements, dissemination of information and an internal *Shari'ah* compliance review. The institutional arrangement in *Shari'ah* governance places the *Shari'ah* board as the backbone of the system. The formation of a *Shari'ah* board has become an integral part of the *Shari'ah* governance system in IFIs. In light of this conceptual framework, this book attempts to explore various practices of *Shari'ah* governance in IFIs with the *Shari'ah* board as the focus point.[2] It highlights the different governance structures and processes across jurisdictions, including issues and challenges, with an objective of identifying and promoting best practices of *Shari'ah* governance.

3.2 Objectives of the *Shari'ah* governance system

The objectives of the *Shari'ah* governance system lie in the very reason for its existence, that is for the sake of *Shari'ah* compliance as inspired by its philosophical foundation. It involves numerous processes and procedures which incur cost and involvement of various organs of governance in IFIs. Despite the extra cost, time and effort, IFIs still favour having *Shari'ah* governance, at least with the establishment of the *Shari'ah* board. This raises another very significant issue as to what extent is the *Shari'ah* governance system relevant and important for IFIs? To address this issue, it would be better to understand the objectives and instrumental functions of *Shari'ah* governance in IFIs, including legitimacy of the product, promotion of moderation and justice in financial transactions, confidence and trust of stakeholders, and as part of the risk management tools exclusive to IFIs.

Islamic financial products must be genuinely legitimate and comply with *Shari'ah* principles. In this respect, IFIs are in need of a specialised body who are expert in *Shari'ah,* particularly *fiqh al muāmalāt* and *usul al fiqh*, to assist them in determining the legitimacy of certain Islamic financial products. In view of the numerous issues involved in this process, such as the independence, qualifications, reporting structure, accountability and transparency of the *Shari'ah* board, the *Shari'ah* governance system is very important to maintain the credibility of the *Shari'ah* board as well as to ensure the legitimacy of the products.

The *Shari'ah* governance system is also important in promoting moderation and justice in financial transactions (Wilson 2009b: 61) and, therefore, enhancing public confidence in IFIs in the aspect of compliance in its application of *Shari'ah* principles. The objective of IFIs is not to satisfy the shareholders alone but to inculcate the confidence and trust of the public and community, who rely on the services provided by them. In the absence of any control mechanism or governance system, public confidence in the legitimacy and legality of the products may be impaired.[3] The *Shari'ah* governance system, which consists of *ex ante* and *ex post Shari'ah* compliance processes, would enhance the credibility of IFIs.

The *Shari'ah* governance system is meant to address a specific type of risk exclusive to IFIs, known as *Shari'ah* non-compliance risk. IFSB-3 defines *Shari'ah* non-compliance risk as 'the risk that arises from IFIs' failure to comply with the *Shari'ah* rules and principles determined by the *Shari'ah* board or the relevant body in the jurisdiction in which the IFIs operate' (IFSB 2006b: 26). Delorenzo (2007: 398–407) illustrates *Shari'ah* non-compliance risk by referring to the risk of *fatwa* rejection and differences as a form of operational and regulatory risk. In addition, Iqbal and Mirakhor (2007: 245) classify *Shari'ah* risk into two types, namely the risk due to non-standard practices of Islamic financial products and the risk due to non-compliance with *Shari'ah*.

The significance of *Shari'ah* non-compliance risk to the Islamic finance industry can be illustrated in the cases of falling *sukuk* issuance due to a statement made by the chairman of the AAOIFI *Shari'ah* board, the OIC Fiqh Academy declaration on the impermissibility of *tawarruq*,[4] the Malaysian High Court judgment on the issue of *Al-Bai' Bithaman Ajil* (BBA) and the dispute in the case of *The Investment Dar Company KSCC* v. *Blom Developments Bank Sal* (2009) EWHC 3545 (Ch) (Hasan 2011). Despite other factors that affect *sukuk* issuance worldwide, undeniably the statement of 85 per cent of potential *Shari'ah* non-compliance *sukuk* being in the Gulf, by Sheikh Muhammad Taqi Usmani, has negated some of the public confidence in the legitimacy and Islamicity of the *sukuk*.[5] Also, the declaration of the impermissibility of *tawarruq* has potentially huge implications for IFIs, since the *tawarruq* financial instrument is widely offered in the market. Similarly, in the case of BBA in the Malaysian High Court, the learned judge declared that the profit portion derived from the BBA facility was illegitimate. This nearly caused panic in IFIs as more than 80 per cent of Islamic financing facilities in Malaysia are based on the BBA concept.

All of these major cases indicate the significance of the *Shari'ah* governance system as a risk-management tool to mitigate the *Shari'ah* non-compliance risk. If other kinds of risks, such as credit, equity investment, market, liquidity and rate of return risks, are quantifiable, the *Shari'ah* risk on the other hand is difficult to manage. Furthermore, there is no specific risk-management model to address the *Shari'ah* non-compliance risk which is unique to IFIs. The IFSB Guiding Principles on Risk Management (IFSB-1) specifically classify the *Shari'ah* risk as part of the operational risk which can be managed through a sound and proper *Shari'ah* governance system. The *Shari'ah* governance system would help IFIs to mitigate the *Shari'ah* non-compliance risk that could incur unimaginable loss and negate IFIs' credibility.

3.3 Institutionalisation of the *Shari'ah* board

Although *Shari'ah* governance is relatively new to any discourse on *fiqh al muāmalāt*, the notion of market regulation and enforcement through the institutionalisation approach has been implemented since pre-modern Muslim societies and is known as the institution of *hisbah*.[6] The *hisbah* was instituted for the purpose of supervising public morals, where markets were regulated and monitored by its executor or the *muhtasib*.[7] Traditionally, the functions of *hisbah* include duties related to transgressing physical boundaries, such as music-related offences and the public display of wine (Klein 2006: 46–50). On top of that, the jurisdiction of *hisbah* also covered matters inside the private domain, such as offences inside homes, cemeteries and wailing practices, the instruction of children, and proper functioning of the mosque (Klein 2006: 50–8). The most important function of *hisbah* in the context of the economic welfare of the people was supervision of market affairs and this included control of scale and prices, protection of measures and standards of weight, accurate valuation of coins used in the market and prevention of fraud (Wittmann 2006: 115–22).

In view of some similarities of the institution of *hisbah* with *Shari'ah* governance, particularly to their objectives and functions, the institutionalisation of the *Shari'ah* board can be considered as a new concept of the *muhtasib* in modern Muslim societies. The adoption of this modified *hisbah* model is very important to ensure all activities, transactions and operations of IFIs meet the principles of *Shari'ah* and Islamic morals. The *Shari'ah* board, particularly at the national or regulatory level, is the ideal institution to function as *muhtasib*, as the institution of *hisbah* within the context of IFIs. As with the notion of the *hisbah* institution in pre-modern Muslim societies commanding right and forbidding wrong, the spread of Islamic banking business and the strong growth of the Islamic finance sector require a specific organisational arrangement to provide a standard of appropriate behaviour, guidelines and code of conduct for IFIs. At this juncture, it is worth briefly exploring the historical development of the institution of the *Shari'ah* board and the *Shari'ah* governance system in IFIs.

The establishment of the *Shari'ah* board in IFIs is relatively new. The idea of setting up the *Shari'ah* board as part of the governance structure of IFIs is considered to be the initiative of Sheikh Saleh Kamel when he founded the Dallah Al Baraka Group (Abdul-Rahman 2010: 76). In 1976, the first formal *Shari'ah* board was instituted by the Faisal Islamic Bank of Egypt (Kahf 2004: 17–36). In the early period of Islamic finance practice there was no special body responsible for advising Islamic banks on *Shari'ah* matters. The formations of the Mitr Ghams Savings Bank on 23 July 1963, the Nasser Social Bank in Egypt in 1972 and the Dubai Islamic Bank in 1975 were made without setting up any *Shari'ah* body as part of their governance structures. Although lacking such *Shari'ah* supervisory boards, it is observed that the activities of IFIs did conform to the spirit of *Shari'ah*.

The setting up of the institution of the *Shari'ah* board began in 1976 when the Faisal Islamic Bank of Egypt was established. It was the first to have a formal *Shari'ah* board consisting of selected *Shari'ah* scholars in Egypt (Kahf 2004). This practice was then followed by the Jordan Islamic Bank and the Faisal Islamic Bank of Sudan in 1978, the Kuwait Finance House in 1979, the Bank Islam Malaysia Berhad in 1983, and the Dubai Islamic Bank in 1999. Interestingly, the Japan Bank for International Cooperation also set up its own *Shari'ah* board in May 2006 (JBIC 2007: 5). The Islamic Development Bank (IDB) had no formal *Shari'ah* supervisory board or an appointed *Shari'ah* council during its early establishment but it has started establishing relationships with several *Shari'ah* scholars by inviting them for consultation, seeking *fatwa* on *muāmalāt* issues (Kahf 2004: 17–36). The IDB also then established its own internal *Shari'ah* board which was appointed by the IDB Board of Executive Directors.

Besides this, the International Association of Islamic Banks (IAIB) also set up its own *Shari'ah* board. The IAIB, however, was replaced with the CIBAFI in 1999. In the meantime, the Organization of the Islamic Conference (OIC) countries acknowledge the Council of the Islamic *Fiqh* Academy based in Jeddah as having the authority to issue *fatwa* rulings including matters related to Islamic banking and finance. To date, the majority of IFIs, including some of the well-respected central banks, have established their own *Shari'ah* boards.

There are a few independent international entities established to support the Islamic finance sector on the aspect of governance, such as the AAOIFI and the IFSB. The AAOIFI has developed seven governance standards, of which five relate specifically to *Shari'ah* governance. Similarly, the IFSB has issued seven guidelines on governance, disclosure and the supervisory review process and IFSB-10 specifically addresses issues to promote best practice for the *Shari'ah* governance system. At the national level, the Bank Negara Malaysia (BNM) issued the BNM/GPS1 in December 2004 and *Shari'ah* governance framework for IFIs in April 2010, as well as the State Bank of Pakistan issuing the *Instruction and Guidelines for Shari'ah Compliance in Islamic Banking Institutions* in 2008 (SBP 2008). In addition, Bahrain formally acknowledged the adoption of the AAOIFI governance standards, and the Dubai International Financial Centre and the Qatar Financial Centre have each issued a rulebook on the Islamic Financial Business Module, which specifies, among other things, the requirements of *Shari'ah* governance.

Regardless of the positive development of *Shari'ah* governance in IFIs, it is observed that there are a few significant issues that need addressing, particularly with respect to the *Shari'ah* governance process, such as the *Shari'ah* board's independence, competence, conflict of interest, confidentiality, transparency and disclosure, the issue of *Shari'ah* compliance and *Shari'ah*-based products, and the remit of the *Shari'ah* boards. With the diversity of *Shari'ah* governance approaches in IFIs, a high standard of *Shari'ah* governance practice should be implemented to ensure that the institution of the *Shari'ah* board can play its role effectively.

3.4 Models of *Shari'ah* boards

Banaga and Tomkins (1994: 10) describe three main types of *Shari'ah* board: that which is composed of *Shari'ah* scholars, the judicial advisors who are authorised to deal with *Shari'ah* issues; an in-house *Shari'ah* department staffed with *Shari'ah* experts, who provide professional services in relation to *Shari'ah* matters; and a *Shari'ah* board that allows individuals other than *Shari'ah* scholars to be appointed as its members, as in the case of the SBP and BNM. This book offers a further classification of *Shari'ah* board into internal and external *Shari'ah* boards, where the former refers to the in-house *Shari'ah* board of IFIs and the latter to the *Shari'ah* boards at national and international levels, *Shari'ah* advisory firms and individuals undertaking *Shari'ah* advisory services. In addition, there are standard-setting agencies that do not issue *fatwa* but play a role in developing *Shari'ah* standards and issuing guidelines on *Shari'ah* governance, namely the AAOIFI and the IFSB.

3.4.1 *Internal* Shari'ah *boards*

(a) *Shari'ah* boards at individual IFI level

This model is the most prevalent practice of IFIs. Generally, an IFI is required to establish its *Shari'ah* board as stipulated in the article of association.[8] The internal *Shari'ah* board structure may vary from one board to another. The objective of the establishment of the *Shari'ah* board, as stated in the article of association, determines the nature of its governance structure. This model lets an individual IFI establish its own *Shari'ah* board, regardless of its parent or group companies. For instance, HSBC Amanah has a different *Shari'ah* board in each of its subsidiaries to suit the legal environment of the local market.[9]

(b) Central *Shari'ah* board for the whole group

Unlike the former model, this model centralises the *Shari'ah* board for a whole group of companies. Although IFIs of this model are involved in cross-border transactions, there is one central *Shari'ah* board that undertakes responsibility for matters pertaining to *Shari'ah* compliance. This model is practised by the Dallah al-Baraka Group. It nevertheless seems to be inefficient in most jurisdictions, since a single *Shari'ah* board is incapable of handling numerous *Shari'ah* issues from various jurisdictions at one particular time.

3.4.2 *External* Shari'ah *boards*

External *Shari'ah* boards can be further classified into national *Shari'ah* boards, *Shari'ah* boards at international level, *Shari'ah* advisory firms and individuals undertaking *Shari'ah* advisory services.

(a) National *Shari'ah* boards

There are a few *Shari'ah* boards established by governments, particularly at the national level, either by the central bank or securities commission, such as in Malaysia, Indonesia, Brunei, Pakistan and Sudan, or by other government agencies such as the Ministry of *Awqaf* in the case of Kuwait. Another form of national *Shari'ah* board refers to the practice in Iran by which the Council of Guardians plays a role as the only institution that deals with Islamic banking and finance matters (Dar and Azami 2010: 184). Unlike the model in Malaysia, Brunei, Pakistan and Sudan, which also allows the establishment of *Shari'ah* boards at the institution level, the practice in Iran recognises the Council of Guardians as the sole *Shari'ah* authority for IFIs. All these national *Shari'ah* boards nevertheless have common functions as the highest *fatwa* authority for IFIs and aim at harmonising and standardising *Shari'ah* practices and all their decisions are final and binding.

(b) *Shari'ah* boards at international level

A *Shari'ah* board at international level normally refers to an independent *Shari'ah* body established by the mutual cooperation of several Muslim countries, such as the AAOIFI and the IDB. The AAOIFI *Shari'ah* board has different functions from the internal and national *Shari'ah* boards as it plays a role in developing *Shari'ah* standards and promoting uniformity of *Shari'ah* governance practice (AAOIFI 2008). The IDB *Shari'ah* board provides internal *Shari'ah* advisory services to the IDB as well as being involved in developing the governance standards of IFIs. Usually, the AAOIFI and the IDB are comprised of the most eminent *Shari'ah* scholars in the world from diverse backgrounds. All of these scholars are considered as the leading experts in *fiqh al muāmalāt* and enjoy high authority in the *Shari'ah* aspect of Islamic finance.

(c) *Shari'ah* advisory firms

A *Shari'ah* advisory firm is an organisation which offers *Shari'ah* services, either as a supervisory or consultative function, such as the Institute of Islamic Banking and Insurance (IIBI), the International Institute of Islamic Finance Incorporated (IIIF), the Islamic Banking and Finance Institute of Malaysia (IBFIM), Yasaar Limited (YL), the Minhaj *Shari'ah* Financial Advisory (MSFA), Failaka International (FI), BMB Islamic (BMBI) and *Taqwaa* Advisory and *Shari'ah* Investment Solutions (TASIS). These organisations are business entities and not part of any IFIs as they provide consultative and supervisory services for various aspects of banking and finance including matters related to *Shari'ah*. In terms of ownership, the current practice shows that *Shari'ah* advisory firms are either owned by independent parties (e.g. IIBI), IFIs (e.g. BMBI and IBFIM), legal firms or even by *Shari'ah* scholars themselves (e.g. FI, YL, IIIF and MSFA).

All of the above entities provide various *Shari'ah* consultancy services such as *Shari'ah* reviews, auditing and product endorsement. The nature of these *Shari'ah* advisory firms' roles and responsibilities is more towards providing *Shari'ah* compliance and consultancy services. The IFIs that seek their services have to pay consultancy and other related fees based on the degree and extent of the services rendered. The decisions or rulings made by the *Shari'ah* advisory firms nevertheless are not binding upon the IFIs since their roles are merely advisory.

(d) Individuals undertaking *Shari'ah* advisory roles

This form of *Shari'ah* advisory services is rarely utilised by IFIs. In the absence of an internal *Shari'ah* board, instead of hiring a *Shari'ah* advisory firm, IFIs may seek *Shari'ah* advisory services from individual *Shari'ah* experts. This model is more prevalent in the case of Islamic windows, IFIs in non-Muslim countries or small scale companies. For instance, Islamic Financial Securities and Co. of Qatar (IFSC) appoints Sheikh Walid bin Hadi as the only *Shari'ah* expert for *Shari'ah* advisory and consultancy services (IFSC 2009).

3.5 Role of the *Shari'ah* board

The role of the *Shari'ah* board varies from one board to another and it depends upon the nature, extent and degree of *Shari'ah* compliance. Inspired by its foundational dimension and stakeholder value orientation, the *Shari'ah* board has fiduciary duties towards all stakeholders of the IFIs. Moreover, the integrity of IFIs is greatly dependant on the status of *Shari'ah* compliance, the impact of products, professional competence and behaviour towards observance of *Shari'ah* norms (Ayub 2007: 467). In this aspect, the *Shari'ah* board plays a fundamental role in ensuring and enhancing the credibility of IFIs[10] as well as having the authority to issue *fatwa* via collective *ijtihād*.[11]

As a general observation, the *Shari'ah* board plays a role as a control mechanism to monitor the IFI's activities and operations for the purpose of *Shari'ah* compliance including assuring *zakah* obligation (Briston and El-Ashker 1986). This is affirmed by Dawud (1996), who mentions that the *Shari'ah* board's objective is to guide IFIs in the setting of policies and regulations according to *Shari'ah*, in approving their financial transactions from the legal side and in preparing their contracts for future transactions according to Islamic law. In addition, Aboumouamer (1989) describes the role of the *Shari'ah* board as being proactive rather than reactive and mentions that the *Shari'ah* board has fiduciary duties to force the management of IFIs to disclose and dispense revenue from any unlawful transaction to charity as well as to conduct audits on *zakah* funds. Abdallah (1994) seems to agree with the contention that the *Shari'ah* board must be proactive rather than reactive. He suggests that the *Shari'ah* board should set up accounting policies to assure that the formula used in allocating profit between shareholders and account holders is fair and that all revenues are generated from lawful transactions, to ensure *zakah* funds are properly calculated and to influence the IFIs to perform their social responsibilities towards the community and other stakeholders (Abdallah 1994).

Banaga *et al.* (1994), on the other hand, detail the *Shari'ah* board's responsibilities from an auditor's perspective as including answering enquiries, issuing legal opinions, and reviewing and revising all business transactions and operations to ensure they are in compliance with *Shari'ah* principles. This is affirmed by Grais and Pellegrini (2006a: 4), who summarise the functions of the *Shari'ah* board into five main areas, namely *ex ante* audit, *ex post* audit, calculation and distribution of *zakah*, disposing of non- *Shari'ah*-compliant earnings, and advising on the distribution of income and expenses.

Unlike Aboumouamer (1989), Dawud (1996), Banaga *et al.* (1994), Abdallah (1994), Briston and El-Ashker (1986) and Grais and Pellegrini (2006), who are not *Shari'ah* scholars, it is worth referring to a *Shari'ah* scholar's views on the functions of the *Shari'ah* board. Sheikh Yusuf Talal De Lorenzo, a prominent *Shari'ah* advisor, describes the functions of the *Shari'ah* board in IFIs; these include assisting IFIs in the product pre-certification stage, such as product development and structuring, certifying products by means of *fatwa,* and ensuring *Shari'ah* compliance throughout the financial product's life cycle (Delorenzo 2007: 399–400). In another paper, Delorenzo (2000: 3–11) further explains the functions of the *Shari'ah* board in the context of the Islamic mutual fund and these include consumer advocacy, fiscal and moral portfolio purification, portfolio purification with regard to screening stocks, portfolio monitoring of management, fees, funds, documentation, industry, product development and *zakah*. Based on all these descriptions from various works of literature, the ideal functions of the *Shari'ah* board can be summarised as overseeing the *ex ante* and *ex post* aspects of the business transactions, activities and operations of IFIs for the purpose of *Shari'ah* compliance and these include advisory, approval and audit roles.

Despite numerous descriptions of the roles of the *Shari'ah* board in the existing literature, they fail to differentiate the diverse functions of various models of *Shari'ah* advisory services. Even though the majority of the *Shari'ah* boards share common objectives and responsibilities, it is very important to identify and understand their different functions. For this reason, the roles of the *Shari'ah* board can be divided into three different levels, namely international, national and individual IFI levels.

The international level institutions refer to entities such as the AAOIFI and the IDB. The AAOIFI has laid down the objectives of its *Shari'ah* board and these include duties in realising harmonisation and convergence in the concepts and application amongst *Shari'ah* supervisory boards of IFIs so as to avoid contradiction or inconsistency between *fatwa*. The AAOIFI *Shari'ah* board is also involved in the development of *Shari'ah*-approved instruments, examining any inquiries they receive, and reviewing the standards the AAOIFI issues in accounting, auditing and codes of ethics and related statements to ensure that these issues are in compliance with the rules and principles of *Shari'ah* (AAOIFI 2008). The AAOIFI *Shari'ah* board mainly functions as a body to harmonize *fatwa* and to develop, examine and review the *Shari'ah* standards. It does not have power to enforce its rulings or decisions upon any IFIs. The IDB *Shari'ah* board acts as an advisory body to the IDB by issuing *Shari'ah* opinions and it is also involved in developing the governance standards of IFIs together with the IFSB.[12]

At the national level, there are five jurisdictions that have established *Shari'ah* boards at the central bank or regulatory authority level, namely Malaysia, Indonesia, Brunei, Pakistan and Sudan. Basically, a national *Shari'ah* board plays a role as the authority to establish a *Shari'ah* governance framework and to formulate national policy and rulings for the industry. This is affirmed by the IFSB survey on the practice of *Shari'ah* governance in sixty-nine IFIs from eleven countries, namely Bahrain, Brunei, Indonesia,

Iran, Jordan, Malaysia, Pakistan, Qatar, Sudan, the UAE and Bangladesh, which indicates that the primary role of a national *Shari'ah* authority is to establish the *Shari'ah* governance framework and not as a body for specific rulings for IFIs (IFSB 2008b: 17). Despite the above findings, *Shari'ah* boards at the national level also play a significant role in respect of harmonisation and standardisation of *fatwa*, and act as the highest authority for IFIs.[13]

Basically, the *Shari'ah* board at the individual IFI level has a range of responsibilities and these include participation in product development and structuring activities; reviewing and approving matters related with *Shari'ah*; issuance of *fatwa*; *Shari'ah* auditing; issuance of an annual certification of *Shari'ah* compliance (McMillen 2006: 141); ensuring the *Shari'ah* compliance of IFIs' investment in shares, equities, *sukuk* and other business avenues (Ayub 2007: 363); and computation of *zakah*. Provisions on the duties and objectives of the *Shari'ah* board in individual IFIs can be found in the article of association, the AAOIFI governance standards and the IFSB guidelines. For instance, clause 2.4 of the Islamic Bank of Britain's article of association specifies its *Shari'ah* board's function as ascertaining the bank's activities to be in conformity with *Shari'ah* principles (IBB 2008).

To sum up, the *Shari'ah* board is normally involved in three main areas of *Shari'ah governance*: the issuance of *fatwa* via collective *ijtihād*, supervision (*raqabah*) and review (*mutābaah*). The *Shari'ah* board at the individual IFI level has a key function in advising *Shari'ah* matters, to ensure that the operations comply with *Shari'ah* principles, endorsing and validating relevant documentations pertaining to the products and services, as well as the internal policies, manuals, and marketing advertisements, and ensuring all its decisions are properly implemented. The *Shari'ah* board at the national level acts as the highest

Shari'ah authority and has the ability to establish a *Shari'ah* governance framework and to formulate national policy and rulings for the industry. Meanwhile, a *Shari'ah* board at the international level, such as the AAOIFI, is engaged mostly in the aspects of harmonisation and development of *Shari'ah* standards.

3.6 International standard-setting agencies

The existing standard-setting agencies, such as the OECD, the International Organization of Securities Commission (IOSCO) and the BCBS, have issued numerous guidelines on governance and risk management for financial institutions. The OECD has issued guidelines on corporate governance, the IOSCO on capital markets and the BCBS on Basel Committee I, II and III. Nevertheless, these standard guidelines have failed to address specific issues of Islamic finance. As the nature and financing model of Islamic finance are different to those in its conventional counterparts, the need for an independent standard-setting agency specifically for Islamic finance is really crucial. Hence, with the initiative of several IFIs and regulatory authorities, the AAOIFI and the IFSB were established in 2002 and 2004 respectively. The difference between the two is that the IFSB is more concerned with regulators while the AAOIFI focuses on the individual IFI level. Although the guidelines and governance standards of the AAOIFI and the IFSB are not officially binding, the principles embedded in those documents are certainly taken into consideration by policymakers and practitioners.

3.6.1 The AAOIFI governance standards
The AAOIFI has issued eighty-one standards and guidelines, including twenty-five accounting standards, six

auditing standards, sevengovernance standards, forty-one *Shari'ah* standards and two codes of ethics (IFSB 2010). In the absence of any corporate governance framework for IFIs in the late 1990s, the AAOIFI took the initiative to provide basic guidelines for *Shari'ah* governance in its governance standards, numbers 1–5. It is important to note that these five standards must not be read in isolation as they complement each other.

(a) Governance Standard for IFIs No. 1: *Shari'ah* supervisory board: appointment, composition and report

Governance Standard No.1 was adopted by the Accounting and Auditing Standard Board (AASB) in its meeting No. 13 held on 15–16 June 1997 (AAOIFI 2005a). It consists of eight parts, namely introduction, definition, appointment, composition, selection and dismissal, basic elements of report, publication of the report, publication of *Shari'ah* rulings and guidelines, and the effective date. Section 2 represents the most important provision in Governance Standard No.1. It has three elements which define the term '*Shari'ah* board'. Firstly, a *Shari'ah* board is an independent body of specialised jurists in *fiqh al muāmalāt*. This section allows the appointment of *Shari'ah* board members who are not specialised in *fiqh al muāmalāt* but who are expert in the field of Islamic finance. Secondly, it elaborates the role of the *Shari'ah* board to ensure compliance with *Shari'ah* principles by having the authority to direct, review and supervise the activities of IFIs. Thirdly, it indicates the binding authority of the *Shari'ah* board upon the IFIs.

Sections 3–6 mention the process of appointment and remuneration of the *Shari'ah* board. With the motive of ensuring the independence of the *Shari'ah* board, the AAOIFI prefers appointments as well as dismissals to be

made by the shareholders in the AGM upon recommendation of the BOD. In view of the practicalities in actual market
practice, the appointment of the *Shari'ah* board as recommended by the AAOIFI may not always be appropriate. The
author considers that the appointment of board members
may also be made by the BOD with the consideration that
there are other mechanisms to ensure independence and to
manage any potential conflict of interest, such as appointment and termination being subject to the approval of the
regulatory authorities. The terms of the appointment must
be agreed by the *Shari'ah* board and need to be recorded. In
terms of remuneration, the BOD, with the authorisation of
the shareholders, has the authority to fix appropriate remuneration for the *Shari'ah* board. The AAOIFI requires the
composition of a *Shari'ah* board to be a minimum of three
members. The directors or significant shareholders of the
IFIs cannot be appointed as *Shari'ah* board members, even
if they are qualified. Sections 9–26 specify the format of
the *Shari'ah* report, which must be published in the annual
report of the IFI.

(b) Governance Standard for IFIs No. 2: *Shari'ah* review
Governance Standard No. 2 was adopted by the AASB in its
meeting No. 15 held on 21–22 June 1998 (AAOIFI 2005b).
It consists of eight parts with eighteen sections. Section 3
explains the *Shari'ah* review as an examination of the extent
of the IFIs' *Shari'ah* compliance. While this section further
confirms the *Shari'ah* board's authority to access all necessary information for the *Shari'ah* review, section 5 on the
other hand puts the responsibility for compliance upon the
management. The *Shari'ah* board is only responsible for
forming and expressing opinions on the extent of *Shari'ah*
compliance. Sections 7–13 detail the *Shari'ah* review procedures, which involve planning, designing, executing,

preparing and reviewing. The *Shari'ah* review report should be submitted to the AGM.

(c) Governance Standard for IFIs No. 3: internal *Shari'ah* review

Governance Standard No. 3 was adopted by the AASB in its meeting No. 17 held on 13–14 June 1999 (AAOIFI 2005c). It consists of eleven parts and thirty sections which complement Governance Standard No. 2. Standard No. 3 aims at establishing standards and guidance on the internal *Shari'ah* review. As the management of IFIs is responsible for the extent of *Shari'ah* compliance, it is incumbent upon them to have a proper mechanism of internal *Shari'ah* review. While the AAOIFI requires IFIs to carry out an internal *Shari'ah* review, it does not specify the requirement of establishing a separate internal *Shari'ah* audit department. The internal *Shari'ah* review can be carried out by either an independent department or part of the internal audit division.

The AAOIFI insists that the internal *Shari'ah* review must be conducted independently and comply with the Code of Ethics for Accountants and Auditors of IFIs. The management and the BOD must give full and continuous support to the internal *Shari'ah* reviewers. In this aspect, the head of the internal *Shari'ah* reviewers is accountable to the BOD. Since the nature of the internal *Shari'ah* review is different to the normal auditing process, the internal *Shari'ah* reviewer must be proficient and have the appropriate academic background and necessary training relevant to *Shari'ah* review, particularly proficiency in *Shari'ah* and *fiqh al muāmalāt*. The reporting structure requires the head of the internal *Shari'ah* review to discuss the findings with the management, and the final report must be addressed to the BOD and copied to the *Shari'ah* board and management.

Any disputes between management and internal *Shari'ah* reviewers should be referred to the *Shari'ah* board for determination.

(d) Governance Standard for IFIs No. 4: audit and governance committee

Governance Standard No. 4 was adopted by the AASB in its meeting No. 21 held in May 2001 (AAOIFI 2005d). To complement the corporate governance framework for IFIs, the AAOIFI strongly recommends the establishment of an Audit and Governance Committee (AGC) at the board level. The AGC should consist of a minimum of three members, appointed by the BOD from its non-executive and independent board members, who are knowledgeable about the affairs of the institution and applicable regulations and laws, including *Shari'ah* rules and principles.

On top of the *Shari'ah* board and the BOD, the AGC has the specific function of preserving the integrity of financial reporting and processes, safeguarding the interest of stakeholders, providing additional assurance on the reliability of information and acting as an independent link between the management and other stakeholders. It is incumbent upon the AGC to conduct reviews of internal controls, accounting practices and audit plans, interim and annual accounts, financial reports, compliance with *Shari'ah* principles, and the use of restricted investment accounts' funds in accordance with the AAOIFI's Code of Ethics for Accountants and Auditors of IFIs. The AGC report should then be submitted to the BOD and copied to the CEO.

(e) Governance Standard for IFIs No. 5: independence of *Shari'ah* board

Governance Standard No. 5 was adopted by the AASB in its meeting No. 29 held on 7–8 June 2005 and is aimed at providing guidelines for its independence and mechanisms to resolve issues of independence (AAOIFI 2005e). There are nine sections with an appendix of an example of a possible issue of independence impairment. The state of independence of the *Shari'ah* board is of the essence in enhancing public confidence on the aspect of *Shari'ah* compliance. Section 3 restricts the *Shari'ah* board to subordinating their judgment on *Shari'ah* supervision to third parties. The *Shari'ah* board is not recommended to consist of employees of the same IFIs or be involved in managerial decisions and operational responsibilities. The *Shari'ah* board is required to conduct continuous assessment of the IFIs and do anything necessary to resolve any issues of independence impairment.[14]

3.6.2 *The IFSB guiding principles*

The IFSB is another standard-setting agency with the exclusive aim of supporting the Islamic finance industry in terms of regulations, guidelines, training, research, databases and standard practices, and promoting greater uniformity. The IFSB does not have its own *Shari'ah* board as it plays a different role to internal and external *Shari'ah* boards and it does not issue any *fatwa* or rulings pertaining to Islamic banking and finance. The objectives of the IFSB include establishing various standards and recommending them for adoption, providing supervisory and regulatory guidelines, encouraging cooperation among its members, facilitating training and development, undertaking research, and establishing databases of participants in the Islamic finance industry (IFSB 2008c).

The IFSB has issued ten guiding principles for IFIs: two for capital adequacy requirements,[15] one for risk management,[16] and seven for governance, disclosure and supervisory review processes.[17] The need for a *Shari'ah* governance mechanism has already been addressed in IFSB-1 and IFSB-5, which both insist IFIs establish appropriate policies and institutional arrangements to manage operational risks, specifically *Shari'ah*-compliance risks, as well as specifying the mechanism of the supervisory review process. In addition, IFSB-3, IFSB-6 and IFSB-8 specify the governance standards for IFIs, Islamic Collective Investment Schemes and *Takāful* respectively. All of these earlier guidelines only address the general framework of corporate governance without specifying its relevance to the *Shari'ah* governance matter exclusively. The IFSB then initiated IFSB-10, which specifically addresses the issue of the *Shari'ah* governance system in IFIs. The basic premise of IFSB-10 is to promote best practice of *Shari'ah* governance by emphasising four key elements, which are summarised in Table 3.2.

The *Shari'ah* governance framework of IFSB-10 tends to cover the overall aspects of *Shari'ah* compliance processes by invoking the most important elements necessary for an effective *Shari'ah* governance system. It is the duty of regulatory authorities to determine the adoption of IFSB-10, as this guiding principle on the *Shari'ah* governance system is strongly commendable. Nevertheless, there is some inconsistency between IFSB-10 and the AAOIFI governance standards which needs to be resolved. Since some jurisdictions, such as Bahrain, the UAE and Qatar, have already adopted the AAOIFI governance standards while others have remained silent, IFSB-10 may be irrelevant to these jurisdictions. In addition, IFSB-10 seems to fail to provide an adequate framework for a *Shari'ah* advisory firm. With the trend for *Shari'ah* advisory firms being likely to increase in time, it is of the utmost importance to have adequate guidelines and guiding principles for such a practice.

Table 3.2 *Key elements of* Shari'ah *governance in IFSB-10*

Key element	Principle	Operational framework
Competence	Fit and proper criteria Professional training Formal assessment	*Ex ante*: Screening process *Ex post*: Review and assessment
Independence	Adequate capability to exercise objective judgment Complete, adequate and timely information	*Ex ante*: Appointment, disclosure and full mandate *Ex post*: Review and assessment
Confidentiality	Strictly observe the confidentiality	*Ex ante*: Undertaking secrecy *Ex post*: Review and assessment
Consistency	Fully understand the legal and regulatory framework; strictly observe the said framework	There must be consistency in all *ex ante* and *ex post* Shari'ah governance processes

Source: modified from IFSB (2009d).

3.7 *Shari'ah* governance process

The most important element of *Shari'ah* governance refers to its process. The *Shari'ah* governance process represents the instrumental functions of the *Shari'ah* board as part of the internal governance structure of corporate governance in IFIs. This section provides a brief explanation of the *Shari'ah* governance process and this includes the appointment, composition and qualification of the *Shari'ah* board, the *Shari'ah* compliance process, *Shari'ah* coordination, the *Shari'ah* compliance review and the *Shari'ah* report.

3.7.1 *Appointment*

In contemporary practice, the members of the *Shari'ah* board are appointed by the shareholders in the annual general meeting (AGM) or by the BOD. The IAIB document mentions that, in order to ensure freedom and independence, the *Shari'ah* board members must not be working as personnel in the bank and must not be subject to the authority of the BOD (Rammal 2006: 205). In addition, the AAOIFI governance standard provides that the shareholders have the authority to appoint members of the *Shari'ah* board during the AGM but the BOD does not have this authority.[18] This is to ensure the independence of the *Shari'ah* board because the management board does not have power to appoint or to dismiss any members of the board as the authority is vested in the shareholders. In the case of appointment made by the shareholders during the AGM with recommendation by the BOD, the *Shari'ah* board is allowed to attend the BOD meetings to discuss the religious aspects of their decisions (Nathan and Ribiere 2007: 472).

In actual practice, numerous IFIs appoint members of their *Shari'ah* board through their BOD, as in the case of Malaysia and Pakistan. Section 27(a) of the Jordanian Islamic Banking Law provides that the BOD will appoint a *Shari'ah* advisor amongst the experts on *Shari'ah* for a maximum period of five years (Bakar 2002: 78).[19] In Pakistan, the appointment of the *Shari'ah* board should be approved by the BOD in the case of domestic IFIs and, in the case of foreign banks having Islamic banking subsidiaries, the appointment should be made by the management (SBP 2008: 1). The practice is different in the case of the appointment of *Shari'ah* board members at the national level where the power is vested in the government, as in the case of the *Shari'ah* board of the Central Bank of Sudan and Malaysia. In Malaysia, the *Shari'ah* board of the BNM is appointed by the Yang di-Pertuan Agong on the recommendation of the finance minister pursuant to the Central Bank of Malaysia Act 2009 (CBA). Therefore, it can be concluded that there are various methods of appointment of the *Shari'ah* board across jurisdictions.

3.7.2 *Composition*

At present, a *Shari'ah* board is normally comprised of *Shari'ah* scholars who are experts in *fiqh al muāmalāt* and *usul al fiqh*. The composition of the *Shari'ah* board varies from one IFI to another. The *Shari'ah* board of international institutions and at the national level is usually comprised of leading internationalist and regional scholars, whereas *Shari'ah* boards of individual IFIs consist of regional and local scholars, with some of them also having so-called internationalist scholars sitting on their *Shari'ah* board.[20]

By and large, most IFIs appoint three to six members to their *Shari'ah* board. The AAOIFI *Shari'ah* board is composed of not more than twenty members who are appointed by the Board of Trustees for a four-year term from among *Shari'ah* scholars. The AAOIFI governance standard requires at least three members at IFI level and this is followed by a few countries such as Bahrain, Dubai, Jordan (Article 58 of Law 28 of 2000 as amended by Law No. 46 of 2003), Lebanon (Law No. 575 of 2004 on the Establishment of Islamic Banks in Lebanon), the UAE and Malaysia. For instance, *Shari'ah* governance in Indonesia puts a requirement of a minimum of two persons and maximum of not more than half the number of members of the BOD of the IFI (Ilyas 2008). The *Shari'ah* board of the SBP comprises two *Shari'ah* scholars and three experts in the areas of banking, accounting and law and at each individual IFI there must be at least one *Shari'ah* advisor and the *Shari'ah* board may be set up at the bank's discretion (Ayub 2007: 473).

3.7.3 *Qualifications*

It is contended that the ideal *Shari'ah* board members are those who are experts in *Shari'ah* and law, specifically in the area of *fiqh al muāmalāt* and *usul al fiqh*. The reason behind this is that the *Shari'ah* board mostly deals with issues related to commercial transactions (Bakar 2002: 74–89). The AAOIFI governance standards and IFSB-10 allow the appointment of an inexpert person in *fiqh al muāmalāt* to be a *Shari'ah* board member[21] with the purpose of strengthening the ability of the *Shari'ah* board to scrutinise and understand banking business and its operations, as in the case of the SBP and BNM.

The *Shari'ah* boards of the SBP and the BNM consist of experts from various fields, including *Shari'ah* scholars, chartered accountants, lawyers, judges and central bankers. The SBP has gone even further by putting very strict conditions on its *Shari'ah* board members. In terms of educational qualification, any board member must have a minimum of a second-class Bachelor Degree in Economics or a degree with *Takhassus Fil Fiqh* and sufficient understanding of banking and finance or a postgraduate degree in Islamic jurisprudence or *Usuluddin* or LL.M (*Shari'ah*) from any recognised university with exposure to banking and finance (SBP 2007: 1). In the case of experience and exposure, any members must have at least three years' experience of giving *Shari'ah* rulings or at least five years' experience in research and development in Islamic banking and finance (SBP 2007: 1). The SBP also insists on the capability of mastering or having reasonable knowledge of Arabic and English languages (SBP 2007: 1). All of these requirements will enable the board to establish a higher standard of practice of *Shari'ah* governance in IFIs, which is extremely important.

3.7.4 *The* Shari'ah *compliance process*

Every IFI has its own procedures for its *Shari'ah* governance system. There is currently no specific standard guideline for *Shari'ah* governance as to the aspects of management, products approval, and *ex ante* and *post ante* auditing. The practice is that there is a *Shari'ah* secretariat or department to coordinate and handle *Shari'ah* matters. The officer in the *Shari'ah* department mostly handles clerical and office works pertaining to *Shari'ah* board matters, such as compiling and handling documents that need to be presented during the *Shari'ah* board meeting.

In terms of meeting, the *Shari'ah* board normally has a weekly or monthly meeting depending on the needs of the individual IFI. Research conducted by Aboumouamer (1989: 188) reveals that of forty-one *Shari'ah* boards, ten or 24.4 per cent have a weekly meeting, three or 7.3 per cent have a monthly meeting, twenty or 48.8 per cent have a quarterly meeting and one or 2.4 per cent has a biannual meeting. The meeting varies from one *Shari'ah* board to another and it may be attended by the CEO, management, bank officers, legal officers, lawyers and representatives from the IFI's branches. The range of attendees depends on the *Shari'ah* issues involved, whether they relate to operational, product, legal documentation or any other matters.

A *Shari'ah* board meeting involves discussion of various *Shari'ah* issues including the concept and structure of new and existing products, documentations, operations and investment portfolios. *Shari'ah* board members will receive all relevant documents from the IFI at least a week before the date of the meeting to give them sufficient time to read and study the documents. The meeting will be chaired by the chairman of the *Shari'ah* board and the decisions are usually made unanimously. Some *Shari'ah* boards allow decisions to be made by a simple majority and this happens mostly in the case of *sukuk* issuance by an international IFI (Ayub 2007: 472). A certain *Shari'ah* board practice requires one of its members to be the administrative member. The administrative board member acts as a selection committee who has the authority to exercise discretion over whether to convene discussion on specific issue or not (McMillen 2006: 141). Another practice grants power to the *Shari'ah* officer to decide the matter. The determination of the *Shari'ah* board in the meeting will then be distributed to the relevant parties in the IFI for reference and they are bound to follow all of its decisions.

3.7.5 Shari'ah *coordination*

Shari'ah coordination is vital to the *Shari'ah* governance system and is as important as the company secretary is to the BOD. The *Shari'ah* coordinator acts as a secretary or liaison officer that coordinates the *Shari'ah* governance process, including the interaction with the *Shari'ah* board, internal or external review, and other organs of governance. This book identifies several models of *Shari'ah* coordination which can be classified into the following: secretary of the *Shari'ah* board serving as the *Shari''ah* coordinator, internal *Shari'ah* coordinator, *Shari'ah* compliance officer, *Shari'ah* coordination department, external *Shari'ah* coordination, *Shari'ah* advisory firm as external *Shari'ah* coordinator and internal *Shari'ah* liaison officer (Dar 2009a). The most prevalent practice of *Shari'ah* coordination is having a secretary of the *Shari'ah* board or a *Shari'ah* compliance officer serving as the *Shari'ah* coordinator. In fact, some *Shari'ah* compliance officers in IFIs play many roles and not only act as *Shari‘ah* coordinators but also have the responsibility of handling the *Shari‘ah* review process.

3.7.6 Shari‘ah *compliance review*

Unlike conventional banks, IFIs are required to undertake a *Shari‘ah* review and internal *Shari‘ah* review process for the purpose of ensuring that all transactions are in conformity with *Shari‘ah* principles. In the former, the *Shari‘ah* board examines the extent of *Shari‘ah* compliance of the IFIs' products, activities and business transactions, whereas the latter refers to the examination of the extent of *Shari‘ah* compliance by an independent internal *Shari‘ah* audit or as part of the internal audit based on the *Shari‘ah* rulings, guidelines and instructions issued by the *Shari‘ah* board. The *Shari‘ah* board is normally assisted by this internal audit unit to review the *Shari‘ah* compliance aspects in IFIs.

The chief purpose of the *Shari‘ah* review exercise is to ensure compliance with the *Shari‘ah* rules and principles as reflected in the rulings and instructions issued by the *Shari‘ah* board. In this regard, the AAOIFI governance standards lay down several procedures for *Shari‘ah* reviews and these include planning review procedures, executing review procedures, preparing and reviewing working papers, as well as procedures in documenting conclusions and preparing the *Shari‘ah* review report (AAOIFI 2005b). In actual practice, there is no standard format for *Shari‘ah* review procedures or the *Shari‘ah* compliance report. The IFSB survey shows that more than 90 per cent of sixty-nine IFIs undertake a *Shari‘ah* compliance review (IFSB 2008b: 27). As the main objective of the *Shari‘ah* review is to ensure that the management of the IFI is discharging its responsibilities in compliance with *Shari‘ah* rules and principles, the scope of a *Shari‘ah* review is different from a normal auditing task as it specifically concerns the *Shari'ah* aspects and the process is guided by Islamic principles.

The *Shari'ah* review addresses the *Shari'ah* compliance matters of products offered and this process needs a sound *Shari'ah* internal control system. The *Shari'ah* review process requires an internal auditor to review every stage of the *Shari'ah* governance process and this includes the conception of a product, product design, product documentation, product testing, product implementation and product review. The *Shari'ah* review practice nevertheless indicates that the majority of IFIs are not involved in a review of their products (IFSB 2008b: 29). In most IFIs, the *Shari'ah* review is carried out by the internal auditors either as part of the regular internal audit or as a separate part of the *Shari'ah* audit. Some IFIs prefer to use the external auditor for its *Shari'ah* review requirements.[22] The IFSB demonstrates that 41 per cent of IFIs adopt an external review and 89 per cent an internal review (IFSB 2008b: 34). The *Shari'ah* compliance framework in Pakistan puts a mandatory requirement for an annual *Shari'ah* review and auditors of the SBP conduct periodical *Shari'ah* compliance inspections in every individual IFI. On top of that, the SBP has issued a manual for *Shari'ah* reviews for IFIs to ensure a uniform review process, *Shari'ah* compliance and to enhance the credibility of the Islamic finance system (Ayub 2007: 474).

Basically, the *Shari'ah* board has a responsibility to perform pre-audit, audit and post-audit functions. This is evident in Aboumouamer's (1989: 285–8) findings, which show that 78 per cent of the *Shari'ah* board members perform pre-audit work, 80.5 per cent during the audit work and 61 per cent post-audit work. Some *Shari'ah* boards do not engage directly in the *Shari'ah* auditing process due to their small size and most of them are not employees of the respective IFIs and have limited time and material resources to do the job. Moreover, they are also not qualified to perform the auditing task because of lack of audit skills and required knowledge on the operational side of IFIs' activities (Banaga *et al.* 1994: 65). Typically, the *Shari'ah* board will only be involved in the *Shari'ah* auditing process when there is dispute or issue over *Shari'ah* matters which need its deliberation. This requires that the auditor who is responsible for undertaking the *Shari'ah* auditing process possesses adequate religious knowledge to be able to identify *Shari'ah* issues and give opinions on compliance with *Shari'ah* rules.

Khan (1985: 36–8) suggests that the specific areas in which the *Shari'ah* auditor would report include *bakhs* (decrease in the quality of the product), *tatfīf* (causing damage to the other party in weights and measures), *uqūd* (contract), *ihtikār* (hoarding), *khiyānah* (embezzlements), *isrāf* (extravagance), *tanājush* (bidding up prices in auction by planting a fake bidder) and speculation. The scope of the *Shari'ah* review proposed by Khan seems to cover a very wide area of audit which is ambiguous and complex. In actual practice, the *Shari'ah* review contains observations and assessments of systems and controls for *Shari'ah* compliance, recommendations for potential improvements, corrective actions needing to be taken (SBP 2008: 2) and the audit of *zakah* funds (Aboumouamer 1989: 79–80). In the event of disputes or conflict of opinion between management and *Shari'ah* auditors, the matters may be referred to individual *Shari'ah* boards. Similar to the normal review process, the *Shari'ah* review report should be presented before the *Shari'ah* board, the audit committee, the BOD and the shareholders of the IFIs.

3.7.7 Shari'ah *report*

Shari'ah governance favours fair and true disclosure and transparency. The fundamental concept of governance in

Shari'ah is accountability and hence requires IFIs to make true disclosure and to provide accurate necessary information. This is in line with the spirit of *al-Qur'an* where Allah says 'O ye who believe! When ye deal with each other in transactions involving future obligations in a fixed period of time, reduce them to writing and let a scribe write down faithfully as between the parties' (*al-Qur'an* 2: 282). This verse mandates and strongly encourages that any business dealing or transaction should be recorded and written down in a proper way. In the context of *Shari'ah* governance, it refers to the duty of the *Shari'ah* board to produce a *Shari'ah* report either periodically or annually.[23]

The *Shari'ah* board is expected to prepare and issue a report on its activities, information on duties and services, *Shari'ah* pronouncements and declaration of *Shari'ah* compliance. As a general practice, the *Shari'ah* report will be submitted to the BOD. Some IFIs submit the *Shari'ah* report to the BOD and also seek the endorsement of the shareholders.[24] Current practice shows that only 49 per cent of IFIs present the *Shari'ah* report to the shareholders for approval and 48 per cent to the audit committee (IFSB 2008b: 35). This position perhaps reflects the mode of appointment of the *Shari'ah* board and whether it was made through the BOD or the shareholders.

The content of the annual *Shari'ah* report is generally information as to the duties and services of the IFI, *fatwa* issuance, the *Shari'ah* board's activities, and a declaration on *Shari'ah* compliance (Banaga *et al.* 1994: 11–13). Haniffa and Hudaib (2007: 102–3) take the view that the *Shari'ah* report should contain more information, including names, pictures and remuneration of the *Shari'ah* board, number of meetings held, disclosure as to the defects in the products offered and recommendations to rectify the defects including actions taken by management, basis of examination of the documents, declaration of *Shari'ah* compliance, and signatures of all *Shari'ah* board members.

Practice indicates that most *Shari'ah* reports are concerned with product compliance rather than emphasising the efficiency of the internal *Shari'ah* control system (IFSB 2008b: 48). The instructions for *Shari'ah* compliance in Islamic banking institutions of Pakistan state specific requirements for the *Shari'ah* report and these include examining all transactions, relevant documentation and procedures, observing whether the IFI has complied with *Shari'ah* rules and principles, scrutinising whether the allocation of funds, profit-sharing ratios, profits and charging of losses are in accordance with *Shari'ah*, and ensuring that any earnings that have been realised from illegitimate sources have been credited to the charity account (SBP 2008: 4–5).

In terms of the format of the *Shari'ah* report, the AAOIFI governance standards provide specific guidelines. In actual practice, the format and content of the *Shari'ah* report are nevertheless different and even some of the *Shari'ah* boards do not issue an annual report. A survey conducted by Grais and Pellegrini (2006a: 8) found that four out of thirteen IFIs failed to issue a *Shari'ah* report. Other research carried out by Maali *et al.* (2006: 285) discovered that, from a sample of twenty-nine banks, only 72 per cent or twenty-one banks issued a *Shari'ah* report. The *Shari'ah* report is very important as an endorsement of the compliance of an IFI with *Shari'ah* principles and it is considered a crucial means by which the general public and interested parties can find information about to what extent services and products of the IFI meet *Shari'ah* requirements. For this reason, due to the very essence of the *Shari'ah* report, the *Shari'ah* board should issue an annual *Shari'ah* report in accordance with the specific format laid down by the AAOIFI governance standards.

3.8 Issues and challenges

The cross-border practice of Islamic finance raises significant issues and poses great challenges to the Islamic finance industry, in particular to its *Shari'ah* governance system. Since *Shari'ah* compliance aspects cannot be compromised at any time, these unresolved issues and challenges must be properly addressed. This book identifies six main issues and challenges pertaining to the *Shari'ah* governance system which are of the essence to the Islamic finance industry.

3.8.1 *Independence of* Shari'ah *board*

IFSB-10 explains the independence of the *Shari'ah* board as the ability to exercise sound judgment after fair consideration of all relevant information and views, without influence from management or inappropriate outside interests. Section 2 of the AAOIFI Governance Standard No. 5 defines independence as 'an attitude of mind which does not allow the view points and conclusions of its possessor to become reliant on or subordinate to the influences and pressures of conflicting interests. It is achieved through organizational status and objectivity' (AAOIFI 2005e). There are two types of independence: practitioner independence and professional independence; the former is important to maintain a proper attitude toward planning, performing and reporting on an audit and the latter to avoid any appearance which may reduce the perceived independence of the auditors (Mautz and Sharaf 1961). The *Shari'ah* governance system is more concerned with professional independence as it involves public perception and stakeholders' confidence in the IFIs.

There has long been debate on the issue of the independence of the *Shari'ah* board. One of the reasons is that *Shari'ah* board members receive remuneration from the IFIs and there exists a potential for conflict of interest by which members could legitimise unlawful or dubious operations to ensure they remain on the *Shari'ah* board (Rammal 2006: 207). Even though such an assumption is not truly accurate, as the *Shari'ah* board members are expected to be guided by moral beliefs and religious values, it still needs a proper framework in the form of policy or regulation because the credibility of IFIs depends on the perceived independence of the *Shari'ah* board. In fact, with the tremendous growth of the Islamic finance industry, it is expected that the number of conflicting *fatwa* is likely to increase. With this in mind, it is imperative to examine the method of appointment of the *Shari'ah* board.

According to a survey by Aboumouamer (1989: 185), it is found that most *Shari'ah* board members, out of forty-one surveyed, felt that the *Shari'ah* board's authority is derived from the shareholders (75%) and their relationships with the management and directors only related to coordination and advisory roles. This book finding, however, only illustrates the perception of the BOD upon the appointment of the *Shari'ah* board and cannot be regarded as conclusive. Despite the above finding, other research carried out by the International Institute of Islamic Thought in 1996 seems to demonstrate a different scenario as it found that almost 80 per cent of appointments to the *Shari'ah* board were done by the BOD and only 39 per cent were made by the shareholders (Bakar 2002: 78). These two surveys establish that the practice of the appointment of the *Shari'ah* board in actual fact differs amongst the IFIs and is contrary to the assumption that the board's independence can only be guaranteed if the appointment is made by the shareholders.

The notion of assuming that the independence of the *Shari'ah* board can be assured with appointment by the shareholders is not truly convincing per se. Even if the appointment is made by the shareholders, the BOD may still influence the shareholders in the process of selecting the *Shari'ah* board members. In view of this, it is worth mentioning the work of Grais and Pellegrini (2006a: 11), in which they discuss three possible approaches to resolving the issue of the independence of the *Shari'ah* board. The approaches seem to focus on the issues of power and authority and they are: to define clearly the responsibilities and powers of the *Shari'ah* board in the articles of association; to grant the board sufficient powers, proper organisational status and audit responsibilities; and to provide adequate authority as enjoyed by independent directors in the audit committee.

3.8.2 *Competence, conflict of interest and confidentiality*

In terms of the qualifications of *Shari'ah* board members, a survey on Islamic banking practices shows that 76.6 per cent of the members have training and qualifications, 8.6 per cent are well versed in *Shari'ah* and commercial law, and only 11.4 per cent have expertise in *Shari'ah*, law and economics (Bakar 2002: 78). Another study found that from the members of forty-one *Shari'ah* boards, only ninety-two people have Islamic law training and 60 per cent had studied non-religious subjects (Aboumouamer 1989: 226). This result indicates that there are issues about the different criteria and qualifications of the *Shari'ah* board.[25] Moreover, the education of *Shari'ah* board members is not properly coordinated and there are no established specific curricula for them (McMillen 2006: 139).[26] This position may affect the effectiveness of the *Shari'ah* board, particularly in providing solid and concrete *Shari'ah* rulings, as they must have the necessary professional knowledge and training as well as expertise in *Shari'ah*.

For many years, numerous *Shari'ah* scholars have enjoyed the right to sit on different *Shari'ah* boards without any sort of restriction, such as those in Saudi Arabia, Kuwait, Bahrain, the UAE and Qatar. In fact, the existing practices in many countries show that there is no restriction on the members of a *Shari'ah* board to stop them serving in any other IFI boards. This situation denotes a negative perception of the *Shari'ah* board as it raises the issue of conflict of interest as well as confidentiality. As an illustration, we may refer to the possible situation of conflict of interest and breach of confidentiality in the case of a new Islamic banking product of an IFI being brought up for approval to the *Shari'ah* board at the central bank's level, where the same advisors that are sitting on the central bank's *Shari'ah* board at the same time also serve that particular IFI. In this case, the *Shari'ah* advisors who have access to proprietary information about different features of financial products in various IFIs are not supposed to represent either both or one of the *Shari'ah* boards since they have a common interest and redundant contractual duties.

The absence of restrictions on the multiple appointments of *Shari'ah* board members may also contribute to the issue of the shortage of *Shari'ah* scholars. According to a survey of the *Shari'ah* Network in GCC – A Network Analytic Perspective conducted by Funds@Work – of ninety-four scholars sat on the boards of 467 IFIs, only twenty of them are heavily utilised; they represent 339 board positions equalling a total of seventeen board positions per scholar. This position may seriously negate public confidence in the *Shari'ah* board's credibility and there are even allegations of *Shari'ah* arbitrage being practised by some *Shari'ah* scholars.[27] The fact that there is a lack of a pool of expert, experienced and competent *Shari'ah* scholars should not be an everlasting justification for employing the same scholars on numerous *Shari'ah* boards.

In order to avoid any issues or a perception of conflict of interest, it is necessary to have a legal provision that states clearly a restriction on sitting on more than one *Shari'ah* board at one particular time. For instance, section 5.4 of the *Shari'ah* governance framework for IFIs (SGF) issued by the BNM provides that IFIs are not allowed to appoint any member of a *Shari'ah* board in another IFI in the same industry. Besides avoiding any element of conflict of interest, this requirement is also important in guaranteeing secrecy in confidential matters and stimulating further *Shari'ah* research by allowing more potential *Shari'ah* scholars to be involved directly in the Islamic financial sector. This policy also ensures the full-time availability of the *Shari'ah* board to guide and monitor IFIs more effectively. In parallel with the rapid expansion of the Islamic finance industry and the increasing numbers of *Shari'ah* boards, the issues of competence of *Shari'ah* advisors and conflict of interest may be solved by having a legal framework pertaining to their qualifications and certain limitations on their practice.

3.8.3 Disclosure and transparency

The crucial element of the *Shari'ah* governance system is disclosure and transparency. IFSB-4 defines transparency in IFIs 'an environment where material and reliable information is made available in a timely and accessible manner to the market at large and to all stakeholders. Such transparency can reduce asymmetric information and uncertainty in financial markets' (IFSB 2007b: 30). Iqbal and Mirakhor (2007: 291) refer to disclosure as 'the process and methodology of providing information and making policy decisions known through timely dissemination and openness' and transparency as 'the principle of creating an environment where information on existing conditions, decisions and actions is made accessible, visible and understandable by all market participants'.

Transparency is of the utmost importance for IFIs so that they comply with *Shari'ah*, as *al-Qur'an* specifically forbids concealing of evidence. As Allah says,

> If ye are on a journey, and cannot find a scribe, a pledge with possession (may serve the purpose) and if one of you deposits a thing on trust with another, let the trustee (faithfully) discharge his trust and let him fear his Lord. Conceal not evidence for whoever conceals it, his heart is tainted with sin and Allah is knoweth all that ye do. (*Al-Qur'an* 2: 283)

According to the IFSB, IFIs must ensure that their financial and non-financial reports meet the requirements of the internationally recognised accounting codes and comply with *Shari'ah* principles (IFSB 2006a: 5). The various *Shari'ah* governance practices demonstrate that disclosure of information is currently minimal and even information on the *Shari'ah* resolutions are hardly available for public viewing.

In addition, surveys conducted by Grais and Pellegrini (2006a: 34) and Maali *et al.* (2006: 285) indicate the shortcomings and weaknesses of the current disclosure of information practice, in particular the *Shari'ah* report. Numerous IFIs are still neglecting the requirement of a *Shari'ah* report, even though it is very important as an endorsement of their compliance with *Shari'ah* principles and it is considered a crucial means by which the general public and interested parties can find information as to what extent the services and products of the IFI meet *Shari'ah* requirements. The ideal *Shari'ah* governance system, then, must be able to address the issues of disclosure and transparency.

3.8.4 Shari'ah *compliant versus* Shari'ah *based*

Numerous criticisms of the current practices of Islamic finance have led to intensive debate, particularly on the issue of whether something is Shari'ah compliant or Shari'ah based, where the latter can be defined as adhering to the Shari'ah objectives and spirit, while the former is comply-ing with the legal aspects of Shari'ah law but not necessarily the spirit of Shari'ah.[28] Although there is no exact definition of Shari'ah compliant and Shari'ah based, the proponents of the Shari'ah-based approach insist that Islamic financial products and services must not only be concerned about compliance with Islamic law but they should go beyond that, that is, fulfil the maqāsid Shari'ah (Dar 2009b: 11). Another contention refers to Shari'ah-based products as Islamic financial instruments which have no origin in the conventional market (ISRA 2009: 2). In this regard, Siddiqi (2008: 76) insists that product innovation is really crucial, especially in designing financial ways that would serve the maqāsid Shari'ah.[29]

Some scholars indicate that there is no difference between a product being Shari'ah compliant and Shari'ah based. As long as a financial product is deemed Shari'ah compliant, in that it is free from interest, uncertainty, gambling and prohibited things and it fulfils the requirement of contracts, the product is said to be Shari'ah compliant, Shari'ah based or Shari'ah tolerant (ISRA 2009: 2). Dar (2009b: 10–12), on the other hand, refers to the Shari'ah-based approach as a combination of two dimensions, namely compliance with Shari'ah principles and fulfilling social responsibilities. He further characterises Islamic financial products as Shari'ah tolerant, such as tawarruq and bay' al inah, Shari'ah com-pliant, like murābahah-based short selling and arbun-based short selling, and Shari'ah based, such as zakah, waqf-based financial products, Islamic private equity and Islamic venture capital. This general classification of Islamic financial products is based on the degree of *Shari'ah* compliance.

The diverse understanding of *Shari'ah*-compliant and *Shari'ah*-based products may affect the framework of the *Shari'ah* governance system. If it is only a matter of *Shari'ah* compliance, the scope of *Shari'ah* governance will be the legal technicalities of Islamic financial products and IFIs' operations, whereas if it goes beyond that, to social responsibility, public interest and *maṣlahah*, the framework of the *Shari'ah* governance system will be wider and more complicated. In this case the *Shari'ah*-based approach requires IFIs to not only be concerned about the *Shari'ah* compliance aspect but also to fulfil their social responsibilities.[30] This may have certain implications for IFIs as it widens the scope and objective of the *Shari'ah* governance system.

3.8.5 *Consistency*

The CIBAFI reported that, out of 6,000 *fatwa* issued by different IFIs with over 100 *Shari'ah* scholars, only 10 per cent were not consistent across IFIs (Iqbal and Mirakhor 2007: 290). Although this figure tends to show that consistency is at an acceptable level, it is expected that greater inconsistencies are likely to happen in the future when the Islamic finance industry expands further. In view of the diversity of Islamic finance practices in different jurisdictions, the likelihood of conflicting *fatwa* or *Shari'ah* pronouncements is relatively high, which may undermine the stakeholders' confidence in the industry. Therefore, there must be continuous efforts to harmonise the *Shari'ah* standards for the purpose of consistency.

The idea of *Shari'ah* harmonisation, despite its pros and cons,[31] would be a good approach to achieve a certain level of consistency that is crucial to the Islamic finance industry. Besides, the adoption of the AAOIFI *Shari'ah* standards would help to promote consistency in Islamic finance practices across jurisdictions as well as ensuring the enforceability of transactions. The IFSB survey demonstrates different countries' perspectives on the adoption of the *Shari'ah* standards, where IFIs from Brunei, Jordan and Qatar fully supported its adoption, Sudan and Indonesia viewed it as favourable and Pakistan, Malaysia and the UAE only indicated their fair support (IFSB 2008b: 26). The survey further shows that 65 per cent of IFIs (out of sixty-nine) do not recognise the importance of the AAOIFI *Shari'ah* standards.

Although, the idea of *Shari'ah* harmonisation is commendable, it is also important to look at another dimension of its implementation. To this end, Peters (2003: 92–3) critically analysed the effect of *Shari'ah* codification. He mentions that the codification of *Shari'ah* has actually transferred the authority to determine the *Shari'ah* norms to the state and it has finally become a part of national politics. Vikor (1998) makes a similar observation where he states that *Shari'ah* codification is actually against theological reason. In addition, he mentions that, historically, *Shari'ah* has developed independently and always in opposition to the power of state. In view of these arguments, any element of political interference in the process of *Shari'ah* harmonisation in Islamic finance must be avoided with appropriate measures.

3.8.6 *The remit of various institutions of* Shari'ah *boards*

The establishment of *Shari'ah* boards in numerous IFIs and at the national level may raise an issue of lack of coordination and overlapping jurisdiction. IFIs may need to get products approved by different levels of *Shari'ah* boards. As an illustration, we refer to the Malaysian *Shari'ah* governance approach. As a general requirement, IFIs are expected to refer to their internal *Shari'ah* board as well as to the national *Shari'ah* advisory council for approval of any Islamic financial products. If it involves Islamic capital market products, IFIs are additionally required to get the approval of the *Shari'ah* board of the Securities Commission (SC). This long process may have certain implications to IFIs in terms of cost, time and effort, as well as potential conflicting *fatwa*.

The IFSB survey discloses that there is a lack of communication amongst the *Shari'ah* boards that facilitate the harmonisation of *Shari'ah* matters and practices. Only 65 per cent of *Shari'ah* boards communicate with the *Shari'ah* boards of other IFIs and only 45 per cent of *Shari'ah* boards at individual IFI level communicate with the national *Shari'ah* board (IFSB 2008b: 40). With this shortcoming, the *Shari'ah* governance system must then be able to address the issue of the remit of *Shari'ah* boards by having effective *Shari'ah* coordination at 'micro' and 'macro' levels.

3.9 Conclusion

Shari'ah governance adds additional values to the existing corporate governance framework. It inculcates transparency, trust, credibility, philosophy, values, beliefs (*aqīdah*), *Shari'ah* and ethics (*akhlāq*; Nathan and Ribieri 2007: 477). While *Shari'ah* governance is expected to add Islamic values, there are also criticisms of its current practice, particularly in relation to the affairs of the *Shari'ah* board. Kahf (2004: 26) mentions that many *Shari'ah* advisors of the IFIs are now being alleged to be 'bankers' window-dressers and overstretching the rules of *Shari'ah* to provide easy *fatwa* for the new breed of bankers'. El-Gamal (2006: 26–45) heavily criticises the practice of *Shari'ah* arbitrage and the failure of Islamic finance to serve *maqāsid Shari'ah*. Although this allegation has not been proven by any empirical research, this negative perception of the *Shari'ah* board should be obliterated with the implementation of strong and good *Shari'ah* governance.

The need to have effective *Shari'ah* governance is crucial as it would strengthen the credibility of IFIs. The AAOIFI governance standards and the IFSB guiding principles are very important for the purpose of improving and bringing harmonisation to *Shari'ah* governance practices. The standards are expected to effectively resolve numerous issues with respect to *Shari'ah* governance. In conclusion, therefore, the foregoing discussion seems to suggest that the existing *Shari'ah* governance framework needs further enhancement and improvement in order to reinforce the development and growth of the Islamic finance industry.

Notes

1. Sheikh Mohammad Ali El Gari, a prominent Saudi *Shari'ah* scholar, defines *Shari'ah* governance as 'the set of procedures, institutions and organizational arrangements through which the *Shari'ah* position on contemporary issues is revealed and *Shari'ah* compliance ensured' (Parker 2010). This definition nevertheless provides a narrow interpretation of the concept of *Shari'ah* governance as it mainly refers to *fatwa* issuing and the process of *Shari'ah* compliance.

2. Bearing in mind that there are other *fatwa* institutions which issue rulings pertaining to Islamic banking and finance, such as the Council of Islamic *Fiqh* Academy, the Egyptian Office of the *Mufti*, the Council of Islamic Studies, Al-Azhar, Cairo, Egypt, the Council of Islamic *Fiqh*, Muslim World League, the General's Presidency of *Ifta'* in Saudi Arabia and others, the scope of this book nevertheless is confined to the *Shari'ah* governance system in IFIs. In this regard, it is important to note

that such *fatwa* institutions are excluded from the definition of *Shari'ah* governance in this book. Meanwhile, although the term *Shari'ah* board has been used interchangeably with other names, such as *Shari'ah* committee, *Shari'ah* advisory body, *Shari'ah* advisory council, *Shari'ah* control board, *Shari'ah* advisor, *Shari'ah* control committee, *Shari'ah* controller, *Shari'ah* council and religious committee, this book prefers to use the term *Shari'ah* board.

3. It is reported that 81.4 per cent of the total number of 468 depositors from Bahrain, Bangladesh and Sudan will transfer their funds to other banks due to non-compliance to *Shari'ah* principles and 70 per cent of depositors will also move their funds if they know that the bank's income is derived from interest-based earnings (Chapra and Ahmed 2002: 118–20).

4. The Islamic *Fiqh* Academy of the OIC issued the final resolution on *tawarruq* at the nineteenth meeting in Sharjah, United Arab Emirates on 26–30 April 2009, which confirmed its impermissibility.

5. Sales of *sukuk* dropped 50 per cent in 2008 and prices fell at an average of 1.51 per cent (Kettell 2008: 38). According to Bloomberg, sales of global *sukuk* had dropped to USD 856 million in 2008 (Sobri 2008: 16).

6. The literature on *hisbah* can be divided into theoretical, such as *Public Duties in Islam: the Institutions of the hisbah* by Ibnu Taymiya and *Al Ahkam Al Sultaniya* by Al Mawardı, and prescriptive-legal literature (*hisbah* manuals), such as the manuals of Ibnu Bassam and Ibnu Ukhuwa (Klein 2006: 42–3). Ibnu Taymiya discusses in great detail the institution of *hisbah*, pertaining to its duties, rights and obligations upon specific socio-economic activities as well as market regulation (see Ibnu Taymiya 1985).

7. The *muhtasib* is the executor who discharged the principles of religious obligation of the individual believer 'to command

right, when its omission becomes apparent and to forbid wrong, when its realization becomes imminent' (Wittmann 2006: 109).

8. Some of IFIs do not have a *Shari'ah* board, such as Iskan Finance of Australia, but refer to the existing various *fatwa* issued by leading Islamic scholars and seek the opinion of Al-Azhar University, Egypt. The establishment of a *Shari'ah* board in Islamic banks, however, was determined as a prerequisite for admission into the IAIB (Rammal 2006: 205).

9. HSBC Amanah has established a Global *Shari'ah* Advisory Board, with the purpose of promoting the harmonisation of *Shari'ah* standards and practices of the Islamic finance industry, a Central *Shari'ah* Committee to supervise businesses and operations in seven regions (UAE, Qatar, Bahrain, Bangladesh, Mauritius, the United States and the UK) and a Regional *Shari'ah* Committee to oversee *Shari'ah* compliance matters in respective markets (HSBC 2009).

10. Iqbal (2002: 47) mentions that one of the factors of the failure of Kleinwort Benson, the first investment bank to introduce an Islamic unit trust in 1986, was due to investors' reservations about the absence of a *Shari'ah* board. This indicates how important the establishment of *Shari'ah* boards in IFIs is for the sake of gaining the confidence of investors and the general public as well as to ensure *Shari'ah* compliance.

11. The concept of a group *ijtihād* in the form of a *Shari'ah* board is important, especially within the individual IFIs, and its establishment is really necessary to facilitate research, enhance credibility and to promote standard practice in the industry (Vogel and Hayes 2006: 47–50).

12. The *Shari'ah* board of the IDB consists of Sheikh Mohamed Mokhtar Sellami as Chairman, Sheikh Saleh bin AbdulRahman bin Abdul Aziz Al Husayn as Deputy Chairman, and Sheikh Abdul Sattar Abu Ghodda, Sheikh

Hussein Hamed Hassan, Sheikh Mohammad Ali Taskhiri and Sheikh Mohamed Hashim Bin Yahaya as members (IFSB 2006a: ii).

13. For instance, the *Shari'ah* Advisory Council (SAC) is the highest authority for the ascertainment of Islamic law pertaining to banking and finance in Malaysia. The decision made by the SAC is binding and statutorily enforceable to all IFIs in Malaysia.

14. Appendix A of the AAOIFI Governance Standard No. 5 illustrates the example of independence impairment as financial involvement with clients, personal and family relationships, fees, contingency fees, performance-related bonuses, goods and services, threatened litigation and long association with IFIs (AAOIFI 2005e).

15. IFSB-2: *Capital Adequacy Standard for Institutions (other than Insurance Institutions) offering only Islamic Financial Services* (IFSB 2003) and IFSB-7: *Capital Adequacy Requirements for Sukuk, Securitisations and Real Estate Investment* (IFSB 2008a).

16. IFSB-1: *Guiding Principles of Risk Management for Institutions (other than Insurance Institutions) offering only Islamic Financial Services* (IFSB 2005).

17. IFSB-6: *Guiding Principles on Governance for Islamic Collective Investment Schemes, GN-1: Guidance Note In Connection with the Capital Adequacy Standard: Recognition of Ratings by External Credit Assessment Institutions (ECAIs) on Shari'ah-Compliant Financial Instruments* (IFSB, 2007a); IFSB-5: *Guidance on Key Elements in the Supervisory Review Process of Institutions offering Islamic Financial Services (excluding Islamic Insurance (*Takāful*) Institutions and Islamic Mutual Funds)* (IFSB 2006a); IFSB-4: *Disclosures to Promote Transparency and Market Discipline for Institutions offering Islamic Financial Services (excluding Islamic Insurance (*Takāful*) Institutions and Islamic Mutual Funds)*

(IFSB, 2007b); IFSB-3: *Guiding Principles on Corporate Governance for Institutions Offering Only Islamic Financial Services (Excluding Islamic Insurance (*Takāful*) Institutions and Islamic Mutual Funds* (IFSB 2006b); IFSB-8: *Guiding Principles on Governance for Takāful Operations* (IFSB 2009b); IFSB-9: *Guiding Principles on Conduct of Business for Institutions offering Islamic Financial Services* (IFSB 2009c); and IFSB-10: the *Guiding Principles on* Shari'ah *governance System for Institutions offering Islamic Financial Services* (IFSB, 2009d).

18. For instance, in the case of the *Shari'ah* board of Al Rajhi Bank in Saudi Arabia, the appointment is made by the shareholders during the AGM with the recommendation of the BOD (Al Rajhi 2008).

19. This practice has been changed with the amendment of Article 58 of Law 28 of 2000 in 2003. The appointments of *Shari'ah* board members are made by the shareholders during the AGM and members may only be dismissed by a two-thirds majority of the BOD and if endorsed by the general assembly (Grais and Pellegrini 2006a: 31).

20. The term 'internationalist scholars' refers to *Shari'ah* board members who most often sit on the *Shari'ah* boards of the investment funds and international organisations such as the AAOIFI and the IDB and have expertise and experience in sophisticated financial transactions in various jurisdictions around the world (McMillen 2006: 140).

21. Those *Shari'ah* board members, however, need to have a certain degree of knowledge of Islamic commercial law. In this regard, the majority of the *Shari'ah* board members must be *Shari'ah* scholars in order to avoid the dominance of inexpert *Shari'ah* advisors in the decision-making process (Bakar 2002:77–8).

22. The current practice indicates that the external review panel consists of 19 per cent auditors, 13 per cent *Shari'ah* board and

21 per cent supervisory authority, while the internal review comprises of 73 per cent *Shari'ah* board, 37 per cent internal auditors and and 17 per cent audit committee (IFSB 2008b: 35).

23. A survey conducted by Al Hajj on fourteen institutional investors, thirty-three IFIs and thirty IFI customers revealed that the customers and the IFIs were very concerned about the *Shari'ah* report and ranked it as very important compared to the institutional investors (Al Hajj 2003: 228–9). Another study carried out by Sulaiman Al Mehmadi (2004: 228) revealed that 57 to 86 per cent of 117 investors in IFIs in Saudi Arabia considered the *Shari'ah* report an important componet for making investment decisions. These findings indicate that the IFIs as well as investors generally understand the importance of the *Shari'ah* report. Therefore, IFIs are expected to be more transparent in providing adequate and reliable information in the *Shari'ah* report.

24. In the case of IFIs in Pakistan, the *Shari'ah* boards of Islamic banks should report to their BOD while the *Shari'ah* boards of foreign banks that have Islamic banking branches should report to the CEO or country head of the bank (SBP 2008).

25. Sheikh Mohamad El Gari, one of the prominent *Shari'ah* scholars, pointed out his concern on the issue of the competence of the *Shari'ah* board. He admitted that there were many mistakes in *Shari'ah* rulings issued by *Shari'ah* boards (Parker 2009).

26. The AAOIFI has initiated a four-month training programme for *Shari'ah* scholars known as the Certified *Shari'ah* Adviser and Auditor (CSAA) qualification, which is specifically designed to equip *Shari'ah* scholars with the requisite technical understanding of and professional skills for *Shari'ah* compliance and review processes (AAOIFI 2008). The IBFIM also offers a *Shari'ah* Scholars' Introduction Program that has been endorsed by the BNM, which is specifically designed for

Shariʿah officers and advisors (MIFC 2008: 21). Another programme available is the Scholar Development Program initiated by the Islamic Finance Council and the Securities and Investment Institute, which provides *Shariʿah* scholars with knowledge of the conventional system (HM Treasury 2008a: 26).

27. El Gamal (2006: 175) explains *Shariʿah* arbitrage as an act of 'identifying a captive market, with religious injunctions that forbid a given set of financial products and services, and synthesizing those products and services from variations on those pre-modern nominate contract'. The *Shariʿah* arbitrage increases transaction costs, which justify the high related fees and excessive profit rate charged by IFIs.

28. Sheikh Saleh Kamel, chairman and founder of the Dallah Al Baraka Group as well as chairman of the General Council for Islamic Banks and Financial Institutions, also states his concern about the existing practice of Islamic finance, where he personally opines that most of the Islamic financial products and services that are available in the market are not Islamic (Mahdi 2008).

29. With the existing mode of financing that replicates conventional banking, Islamic finance has failed to serve the objectives of Islamic law (El-Gamal 2006: xiii). Asutay (2007) posits that the Islamic finance industry has failed to realise the very reason for its existence: providing socio-economic development for the larger parts of the Muslim world and communities.

30. Haniffa and Hudaib (2007: 97–116) attempted to assess the strength and degree of ethical identity by analysing annual reports of seven IFIs in the Gulf region in four different dimensions: commitment to society, vision and mission; contribution and management of *zakah*; charity and benevolent loans; and information about top management. The survey results indicate that there was a serious lack of communication in

IFIs on the socio-economic dimensions, which significantly failed to reflect their accountability and duty towards social justice (Haniffa and Hudaib 2007: 111).

31. It is contended that *Shari'ah* harmonisation may create rigidity and impede the development of Islamic finance particularly in the aspect of product innovation.

CHAPTER 4

REGULATORY FRAMEWORK OF THE *SHARI'AH* GOVERNANCE SYSTEM IN MALAYSIA, GCC COUNTRIES AND THE UK

4.0 Introduction

The *Shari'ah* governance system as defined by IFSB-10 refers to a set of institutional and organisational arrangements to oversee *Shari'ah* compliance aspects in IFIs. In this regard, the majority of IFIs have established their own *Shari'ah* boards and some of them have even set up a dedicated internal *Shari'ah* review unit or department to support the *Shari'ah* board in performing its function. This indicates a positive development in the *Shari'ah* governance systems of IFIs. Looking at the different frameworks and styles of *Shari'ah* governance in various legal environments and diverse banking models, it is worth examining the regulatory framework of the *Shari'ah* governance system in different jurisdictions.

This chapter focuses on the regulatory framework of the *Shari'ah* governance system in Malaysia, GCC countries and the UK as the case studies. Uniquely, significant differences are a prerequisite of the *Shari'ah* governance system, in particular from the regulatory overview, as Malaysia represents a model in a mixed legal jurisdiction, GCC in an Islamic and mixed legal environment and the UK in a non-Islamic legal environment. This chapter concludes with a brief review of the legal backgrounds and some observations on the *Shari'ah* governance framework of the case countries.

4.1 The *Shari'ah* governance model from a regulatory perspective

The existing framework of Islamic finance in various jurisdictions demonstrates the diverse practices and models of the *Shari'ah* governance system. Some jurisdictions prefer greater involvement of regulatory authorities and some countries favour otherwise. To date, it is still debatable whether the former or the latter is more prevalent and appropriate for possible adoption. To illustrate these diverse approaches, this book identifies five *Shari'ah* governance models in the context of their regulatory perspective.

4.1.1 Reactive approach

This model is more prevalent in non-Islamic legal environment countries such as the UK and Turkey. Although several Islamic banking licences have been issued to IFIs, the regulatory authority is silent on the *Shari'ah* governance framework. Like conventional banks, IFIs are required to comply with the existing legislation and regulations. On top of that, IFIs have a duty to make sure that all their business operations and products are *Shari'ah* compliant. There is no specific legislation governing IFIs or any directive from the regulatory authorities specifying *Shari'ah* governance requirements. At the moment, the regulators will only react and intervene in *Shari'ah* governance matters if there is any significant issue involved which may affect the finance sector. For instance, the UK Financial Services Authority only sees the role played by the *Shari'ah* boards of IFIs as being advisory and supervisory, not as having executive authority as in the case of the BOD.

4.1.2 *Passive approach*

This approach is exclusive to the *Shari'ah* governance model in Saudi Arabia. The Saudi Authority Monetary Agency (SAMA) treats IFIs as equal to their conventional counterparts. SAMA has yet to issue legislation pertaining to Islamic finance and guidelines on a *Shari'ah* governance system. There is no national *Shari'ah* advisory board, nor are any institutions the sole authoritative body in Islamic finance. The existing *Shari'ah* governance system, as practised by IFIs in the kingdom, is a product of self-initiative rather than a regulatory requirement or at a regulator's direction.

4.1.3 *Minimalist approach*

This model is mainly practised by GCC countries, with the exceptions of Oman and Saudi Arabia. Unlike the reactive approach, the minimalist model allows slight intervention on the part of regulatory authorities. The regulatory authorities expect IFIs to have a proper *Shari'ah* governance system without specifying the requirements in detail. There is no restriction on multiple appointments of the *Shari'ah* board to sit for various institutions at one particular time. Some jurisdictions in GCC countries, such as Bahrain, the UAE and Qatar, favour the adoption of the AAOIFI governance standards. The minimalist approach prefers the market to develop its own *Shari'ah* governance system rather than have greater intervention on the part of regulators.

4.1.4 *Proactive approach*

This model is favoured by the Malaysian regulatory authority. The proponents of this model have strong faith in the regulatory-based approach to strengthen the *Shari'ah* governance framework. With this motivation, the Malaysian regulator initiates a comprehensive *Shari'ah* governance framework from regulatory and non-regulatory aspects. There were several laws passed and amended by the parliament such as the Islamic Banking Act 1983 (IBA), the Banking and Financial Istitutions Act 1989 (BAFIA), the *Takāful* Act 1984 (TA) and the Securities Commission Act 1993. The CBA confirms the status of the SAC as the sole authoritative body in Islamic finance. To complement this, the BNM issued the BNM/GPS1 in 2004 as well as a *Shari'ah* governance framework for IFIs in 2010, and the SC issued the Registration of *Shari'ah* Advisers Guidelines in 2009, which set the criteria for the registration of a *Shari'ah* advisor in the capital-market sector.

4.1.5 *Interventionist approach*

While the passive approach is exclusive to Saudi Arabia, the interventionist model is unique to the *Shari'ah* governance model of Pakistan. The interventionist model allows third-party institutions to make decisions on *Shari'ah* matters pertaining to Islamic finance. In the case of Pakistan, the *Shari'ah* Federal Court is the highest authority in matters involving Islamic finance, despite the establishment of a *Shari'ah* board at the State Bank of Pakistan level.

4.2 *Shari'ah* governance systems in Malaysia, GCC countries and the UK

4.2.1 *Malaysia*

(a) Regulatory overview

Malaysia has a unique legislative framework consisting of mixed legal systems, namely common law and *Shari'ah*. The common law principles are applied in the civil court in almost all matters of jurisdiction. Islamic law, in contrast, is practised in the *Shari'ah* court and only pertaining to family matters and laws of inheritance. The Federal Constitution of Malaysia puts Islamic banking matters under the jurisdiction of the civil court. This is due to the fact that Islamic banking is considered as being under the item 'finance' in the Federal Constitution. As a matter of fact, the BNM, with the cooperation of the judicial body, has agreed to set up a special high court in the Commercial Division known as the *muāmalāt* bench. According to Practice Direction No.1/2003, paragraph 2, all cases under the code 22A filed in the High Court of Malaya will be registered and heard in the High Court Commercial Division 4 and this special high court will only hear cases on Islamic banking.

The development of the Islamic banking industry in Malaysia involved two phases: the first phase was from 1983 until 1993 and the second phase began in 1994. Malaysia has liberalised its policy on the implementation of Islamic finance by allowing foreign entities to set up Islamic banks in the local market. These staggered developments are facilitated and supported by legal infrastructure through several legislations and directives.

The first *Shari'ah* board was set up in 1983 by Bank Islam Malaysia Berhad. After ten years, on 4 March 1993, the BNM introduced an interest-free banking scheme, in which conventional banks could offer Islamic banking products through its windows. With that policy, many conventional banks set up Islamic windows and at the same time appointed selected Muslim scholars to be members of the *Shari'ah* board. As part of the effort to streamline and harmonise the *Shari'ah* interpretations, the SAC was established on 1 May 1997 under the BAFIA and is considered the highest *Shari'ah* authority pertaining to Islamic banking, finance and *takāful* in Malaysia.

The terms *Shari'ah* committee, *Shari'ah* supervisory council or *Shari'ah* advisory council are used interchangeably in Malaysia. The IBA refers to the *Shari'ah* board as the *Shari'ah* supervisory council and the BAFIA as the *Shari'ah* advisory council. With the issuance of the BNM/GPS1, all *Shari'ah* boards of IFIs and *takāful* operators are recognised as *Shari'ah* Committees (SHCs) and the SAC is used as a reference to the *Shari'ah* board of the BNM. The establishment of an SHC is a statutory requirement of all banks offering Islamic banking products pursuant to section 3 (5) (b) of the IBA for Islamic banks and section 124 (7) of the BAFIA for Islamic banking scheme banks. The main objective of the establishment of an SHC is to advise IFIs on any *Shari'ah* matter and to ensure compliance with the *Shari'ah* tenets and requirements. Section 3 (5) (b) of the IBA makes the establishment of a *Shari'ah* board a mandatory requirement, which must be clearly stipulated in the articles of association of the bank.

As a response to the positive demands of the conventional banks to open Islamic counters, section 124 (7) of the BAFIA was then introduced which regulated the establishment of SHCs for Islamic windows. Similar to the IBA and the BAFIA, section 8 of the TA puts two conditions on the *takāful* licence, namely that the aims and operations of the *takāful* business are in line with *Shari'ah* principles and there is a clear statement for the establishment of a *Shari'ah* board in the articles of association. Apart from institutions under the IBA, the BAFIA and the TA, SHCs also exist in institutions under the Development Financial Institutions Act 2002 (DFIA).

(b) *Shari'ah* governance

The BNM issued the BNM/GPS 1 that provides an appropriate governance framework for *Shari'ah* boards. The amendment to the Central Bank of Malaysia Act 1958 enhances the functions and jurisdiction of the SAC, where it will be the sole *Shari'ah* authority in Islamic finance and will be referred to by the court or arbitrator in disputes involving *Shari'ah* issues. The BNM has also issued guidelines on the disclosure of reports and financial statements of Islamic banks known as BNM/GPS8-i. In April 2010, the BNM issued another guideline, namely the Shari'ah *governance Framework for IFIs* (SGF) which will replace the BNM/GPS1 and become officially effective in 2011.

The SGF consists of two parts and one appendix, with part I comprising five sections and part II, six sections. Part I provides an overview of *Shari'ah* governance consisting of objectives, scope of application, legal provision, effective date and compliance deadline and approach. Part II details the *Shari'ah* governance arrangements and these include general requirements of the *Shari'ah* governance framework, oversight, accountability and responsibility, independence, competence, confidentiality and consistency, and *Shari'ah* compliance and research functions. All IFIs licensed under the IBA, the BAFIA, the DFIA and the TA are required to comply with the SGF.

In terms of appointment of the *Shari'ah* board, section 3.8 mentions that the BOD of IFIs upon recommendation of its Nomination Committee should appoint the members of the SHC, subject to the approval of the BNM and the SAC. Appendix 2 on qualification requires the *Shari'ah* board members to at least either have qualifications or possess the necessary knowledge, expertise or experience in Islamic jurisprudence or Islamic commercial law.[1] To ensure that the SHC is able to function effectively, it should consist of a minimum of five members and its activities and functions will be coordinated by the *Shari'ah* secretariat of the respective IFIs (section 2.3).

There are certain restrictions with regard to *Shari'ah* governance practice. With the purpose of mitigating the risk of potential conflict of interest and confidentiality issues, IFIs are not allowed to appoint any member of the SC in another IFI of the same industry (section 5.4). Appendix 2 on disqualification provides that an SHC member may be disqualified if he fails to satisfy that he is fit for the position; fails to attend 75 per cent of meetings in a year without reasonable excuse; has been declared bankrupt, or a petition under bankruptcy laws is filed against him; was found guilty of any serious criminal offence or any other offence punishable with imprisonment of one year or more; or is subject to any order of detention, supervision, restricted residence or banishment.

With regard to functions of the *Shari'ah* board, Appendix 4 of the SGF provides the clear duties and responsibilities of the SHC and these include: to advise the BOD on *Shari'ah* matters in its business operations; to endorse *Shari'ah* compliance manuals; to endorse and validate relevant documentations; to assist related parties with advice on *Shari'ah* matters upon request; to advise on matters to be referred to the SAC; to provide written *Shari'ah* opinions; and to assist the SAC with referals for advice.

The SHC is legally required to produce a *Shari'ah* report expressing their observations on IFIs' compliance with

Shari'ah principles as illustrated in Appendix 3 of the SGF. To this end, the BNM/GP8-i specifies the minimum requirements of the *Shari'ah* report. The BNM/GP8-i requires the *Shari'ah* report to be, at least, a declaration of *Shari'ah* compliance endorsed by the *Shari'ah* committee members.[2] In terms of reporting structure, the SHC will report functionally to the BOD as this reflects the status of the SHC as an independent body of the IFIs. The BOD is bound by any decision of the SHC and they have to consider their views on certain issues related to operational matters, policy or business transactions.

Due to the potential of significant impact on the Islamic finance industry, the Malaysian government took a further step in enhancing the legal framework by passing the Central Bank of Malaysia Act 2009 (CBA). The CBA was passed by parliament in July 2009, received royal assent on 19 August 2009 and was gazetted on 3 September 2009. Unlike the earlier act, the CBA inserts a new provision in Part VII which covers matters pertaining to Islamic finance. Chapter 1 of Part VII aims at resolving issues pertinent to *Shari'ah* matters. Sections 51–8 of the CBA clarify and enhance the *Shari'ah* governance framework for IFIs in Malaysia in a number of ways (Hasan 2010: 105–8). Table 4.1 summarises the differences between the CBA and the retired section 16B.

The CBA provides a clear and precise legal framework for Islamic finance particularly about the legal status of *Shari'ah* resolutions and the SAC as the highest authority on Islamic banking and finance. In the same year of its enforcement, in the case of *Tan Sri Khalid Ibrahim* v. *Bank Islam Malaysia Berhad* [2009] 6 MLJ 416, for the first time in the history of the Malaysian court, the High Court judge made reference to the SAC for confirmation of the *Shari'ah* status of the agreement.

Table 4.1 *The differences between Part VII, Chapter 1 of the CBA and Section 16B of the Central Bank of Malaysia (Amendment) Act 2003*

Part VII, Chapter 1 of the CBA	Section 16B
It should be read together with the *Shari'ah* Governance Framework for IFIs 2010.	It should be read together with the *Guidelines on the Governance of Shari'ah Committee for the Islamic Banks 2004* (BNM/GPS 1).
It grants authority to the BNM to establish the *Shari'ah* Advisory Council (SAC) and to specify its functions as well as the secretariat to assist the SAC in carrying out its definitive roles. This vividly clarifies the role and responsibilities of the SAC as the highest and sole authority in Islamic financial matters.	It provides the establishment of the SAC but does not clearly clarify the role and responsibilities of the SAC. No provision mentioning the setting up of the SAC's secretariat.
In parallel with the status of the SAC as the highest authority, the appointment of the SAC members shall be made by the Yang di-Pertuan Agong. The SAC's remuneration and the terms of reference shall then be determined by the BNM.	The appointment shall be made by the Minister on the recommendation of the BNM.
It sets the minimum fit and proper criteria of the SAC members. The candidate must be at least knowledgeable and qualified in *Shari'ah* or have appropriate knowledge and experience in banking, finance and law. Section 53 of the CBA also allows experts in other related disciplines, as well as judges of the civil and *Shari'ah* courts, to be SAC members.	It has similar provision.

Table 4.1 (cont.)

Part VII, Chapter 1 of the CBA	Section 16B
No similar provision with the retired section 16B (6).	No member of the SAC shall become a member of any *Shari'ah* advisory body with any IFI.
It affirms the legal status of the *Shari'ah* pronouncement issued by the SAC to be binding upon both the court as well as arbitration.	It merely provides that *Shari'ah* rulings issued by the SAC are binding upon the arbitration.
It is mandatory for the court or arbitrator to refer to the SAC for deliberation on any *Shari'ah* issue, as well as taking into account its existing *Shari'ah* rulings	The court or arbitrator is not obligated to refer to the SAC to resolve any *Shari'ah* issue
It clarifies the status of the *Shari'ah* rulings issued by the SAC in the event that they contradict the *Shari'ah* pronouncement of a *Shari'ah* committee at an individual IFI. The *Shari'ah* rulings of the SAC shall prevail and have binding force over the *Shari'ah* resolutions of the *Shari'ah* committees of IFIs.	It does not clearly stipulate the position of *Shari'ah* rulings in the case of conflict with any other *Shari'ah* resolutions.

Despite the recent legal development, it is worth noting that the CBA has jurisdiction only in matters that fall under the auspices of the BNM, which therefore excludes the *Shari'ah* board in the SC. The SC has its own *Shari'ah* board and, in August 2009, it issued the Registration of *Shari'ah* Adviser's Guidelines under section 377 of the Capital Markets and Services Act 2007. This guideline specifically provides rules and procedures for registration of *Shari'ah* advisors in matters regulated and supervised by the SC (SC 2009).

4.2.2 *GCC countries*

The GCC was established on 26 May 1981 in Abu Dhabi, with the aim of fostering and furthering cooperation amongst the member states (Anon. 1987). The IFIs in the GCC region have their own framework of *Shari'ah* governance. The monetary agencies or financial authorities are responsible for the regulation and supervision of the IFIs, including matters of *Shari'ah* governance.

It is imperative to understand the legal background of GCC countries, particularly the application of Islamic law in their judicial system, before discussing their *Shari'ah* governance framework. With the fact that not all GCC countries' constitutions prescribe *Shari'ah* as a source of legislation, there is an issue around to what extent *Shari'ah* applies or could apply, in particular in relation to Islamic finance. Therefore, this subsection not only discusses laws and regulations pertaining to *Shari'ah* governance in GCC countries, but also provides some basic information on their legal backgrounds. This book explores the application of *Shari'ah* and tries to relate it to the implementation of Islamic finance in GCC countries.

Generally, the *Shari'ah* governance approach in GCC countries can be classified into two types: either it is regulated via legal and supervisory requirements, as in the cases of Bahrain, Kuwait, the UAE and Qatar, or through self-regulation as in the case of Saudi Arabia. This section presents the diverse *Shari'ah* governance systems within GCC countries and therefore enables this book to highlight and identify essential issues that would benefit from further analysis.

4.2.2.1 Bahrain

(a) Regulatory overview

Bahrain was exposed to the English system more than other GCC countries (Al-Suwaidi 1993: 292–3). However, after independence in 1971, Bahrain developed several substantive and procedural laws and at the same time put *Shari'ah* as a main source of legislation, as stated in Article 2 of the Constitution of Bahrain. This position created difficulties for commercial sectors, particularly financial institutions, because interest-based transactions would have been declared illegal. In view of this, Bahrain developed its own laws, such as the Law of Civil and Commercial Procedure of 1971, the Law on the Establishment of the Bahrain Monetary Agency of 1973, the Companies Registration Act of 1983, and the Commercial Law of 1987, which are based mainly on the Egyptian code. Article 76 of the Commercial Law of 1987 clearly allows interest charges in commercial loans but subject to the rate determined by the Bahrain Monetary Agency (Al-Suwaidi 1993: 292). As such, the Civil Court of Bahrain has comprehensive jurisdiction over civil and commercial matters, except those relating to *Shari'ah* disputes.

With reference to the Islamic finance industry, Bahrain is known as one of the leading players in Islamic finance. Besides initiating the establishment of the Bahrain-based Liquidity Management Centre, Bahrain also hosts two international institutions for Islamic finance, namely the AAOIFI and the International Islamic Financial Market (IIFM). The Central Bank of Bahrain (CBB) is the sole regulator of the financial sector. It is responsible for regulating and supervising all financial institutions, the insurance sector and capital markets. There are five main pieces of legislation that govern the financial system of Bahrain: the Central Bank of

Bahrain and Financial Institutions Law 2006, the Bahrain Stock Exchange Law 1987, the Commercial Companies Law 2001, the Anti-Money-Laundering Law 2001, and the Financial Trust Law 2006. The legal provision for the implementation of Islamic finance in Bahrain is provided in the CBB Rule Book Volume 2, Islamic Banks.

(b) Shari'ah *governance*
The CBB Rule Book Volume 2, Islamic Banks, Part A, High Level Control, section 1.3.15 provides that the CBB requires all banks to establish an independent *Shari'ah* board complying with the AAOIFI governance standards for IFIs No. 1 and No. 2. This section provides a clear legal requirement for the establishment of a *Shari'ah* board in IFIs in Bahrain and failure to do so will constitute non-compliance with the CBB's directive.

Unlike the other GCC countries, Bahrain has established a National *Shari'ah* Advisory Board of the CBB with the purpose of serving and verifying *Shari'ah* compliance (Hasan 2007). The *Shari'ah* board of the CBB is nevertheless different to the other national *Shari'ah* boards of Malaysia, Sudan, Indonesia, Pakistan and Brunei, as it does not have authority at institutional level. With regard to the *Shari'ah* governance system, Bahrain follows the AAOIFI governance standards, where it requires all IFIs to establish a *Shari'ah* board. Section 1.3.16 of the CBB Rule Book requires IFIs to adopt the AAOIFI governance standards as well as having a separate function of *Shari'ah* review for the purpose of ensuring *Shari'ah* compliance as stipulated in the AAOIFI Governance Standard No.3. The legal requirement for the adoption of the AAOIFI governance standards reflects the role of Bahrain as the host of the AAOIFI since its establishment in 2001.[3]

4.2.2.2 United Arab Emirates

(a) Regulatory overview

On 2 December 1970, seven emirates decided to form a federal union consisting of Abu Dhabi, Dubai, Sharjah, Ajman, Umm Al-Quwain, Al Fujairah and Ras Al-Khaima, known as the United Arab Emirates or UAE (Al Muhairi 1996: 119). After independence in 1971, the government passed the UAE Provisional Constitution of 1971 with the aim of preserving the internal autonomy of the seven emirates (Al-Muhairi 1996: 118). In the meantime, Article 7 of the UAE Constitution recognised *Shari'ah* as a main source of legislation and the religion of the state as Islam. In addition, Article 75 of Federal Law No. 10/1973 provides that

> the Supreme Court shall apply the provisions of the *Sharī'ah*, Federal Laws and other laws in force in the member Emirates of the Union, conforming to the Islamic *Sharī'ah*. Likewise it shall apply those rules of custom and those principles of natural and comparative laws which do not conflict with the principle of the *Sharī'ah*.

In terms of the banking and finance sectors, the Union Law No. 10 of 1980 Concerning the Central Bank, the Monetary System and Organization of Banking is the main governing law for the financial sector in the UAE. This legislation grants power to the UAE Central Bank to regulate and supervise the financial institutions.

At the beginning of the financial-regulation development of the UAE, any kind of interest in respect of civil transactions was prohibited by virtue of Article 714 of Federal Law No. 5 of 1985. This provision implicates that interest-based transactions are void and unenforceable. In 1987, the Civil Transactions Law was amended by Federal Law No. 1, which excluded commercial transactions from being governed by the civil transactions law and, finally, Federal Law No. 11 of 1992 invalidated all previous laws with respect to the interest prohibition. As a result, the charging of interest in commercial transactions is now permissible in the UAE.[4] Federal Law No. 18 of 1993 grants the bank's right to charge interest in respect of a commercial loan as per the agreed rate in the contract (Tamimi 2002: 51). This position was taken in view of the necessity, or *dharuriyah*, for economic stability and the needs of the people. Moreover, during this time, the implementation of Islamic finance in the UAE was still in its infancy and could not cater for the market needs. The civil court has jurisdictions in banking matters and any financial transactions that involve issues pertaining to the legality of interest fall under its jurisdiction (Ballantyne 1985: 14).

Despite the above, the UAE at the same time makes numerous efforts to promote Islamic finance and Dubai is leading the way as a centre for Islamic finance. In 1985, the UAE government passed a specific law in relation to Islamic finance – Federal Law No. 6 of 1985 Regarding Islamic Banks, Financial Institutions and Investment Companies. Article 1 of this Federal Law requires the IFIs to conduct business in accordance with *Shari'ah*, which should be stated in the articles and memorandum of associations.

Dubai presents a unique position in comparison with other parts of the UAE. The UAE authority passed a separate law with Federal Law No. 6 of 1985, known as the Dubai International Financial Centre (DIFC) Law No. 13 of 2004, and the Islamic Financial Business Module of the Dubai Financial Services Authority provides a legal framework for regulating Islamic financial business as well as regulation of the *Shari'ah* board. The DIFC Law No. 13 led to the establishment of the DIFC which enjoys certain privileges and economic incentives from the government. All institutions and corporate entities under the jurisdiction of the DIFC are governed by the DIFC Law and are subject to the DIFC Court and the DIFC Arbitration Centre.

(b) Shariʿah *governance*

The *Shariʿah* governance system in the UAE, except in Dubai, is governed by Federal Law No. 6 of 1985. Article 5 of Federal Law No. 6 of 1985 requires the establishment of a 'Higher *Shariʿah* Authority' under the Ministry of Justice and Islamic Affairs to supervise Islamic banks, financial institutions and investment companies and to provide *Shariʿah* opinion on matters pertaining to Islamic banking and finance. Article 5 clearly states the position of the Higher *Shariʿah* Authority as binding. Besides the Higher *Shariʿah* Authority, which is a government-established body, it is worth mentioning here that *Shariʿah* scholars in the UAE have voluntarily initiated the establishment of a central committee of the *Shariʿah* board for the purpose of harmonising and standardising *Shariʿah* practice (Dar 2009c). This voluntary arrangement is at least able to assure the consistency of *Shariʿah* rulings.

In terms of composition of the *Shariʿah* board, Article 6 requires all IFIs to clearly stipulate the establishment of a *Shariʿah* board in the articles and memorandum of association. This provision further puts a condition of a minimum of three members. The articles and memorandum of association must contain the manner of governance of the *Shariʿah* board, such as its duties, responsibilities, functions and appointment. In the aspect of appointment, members of the Higher *Shariʿah* Authority are appointed by the government and, at the individual IFI level, by the BOD or the shareholders. The IFIs cannot simply appoint their *Shariʿah* board members but are required to submit the proposed names of the *Shari‘ah* advisors to the Higher *Shari‘ah* Authority for approval.

IFIs registered under the DIFC have to comply with DIFC law and regulations, particularly the Law Regulating Islamic Financial Business, DIFC Law No. 13 of 2004 and the DIFC Services Authority (DFSA) Rulebook on Islamic Financial Business Module (ISF).[5] As a general requirement, the DFSA requires IFIs to adopt the AAOIFI governance standards to ensure consistency and compliance with *Shari‘ah* (Praesidium and DIFC 2007: 40–4). With respect to *Shari‘ah* governance, section 13 of the law requires IFIs to establish a *Shari‘ah* board and the DFSA has the power to make rules prescribing its appointment, formation, conduct and operation. In this instance, the ISF specifies the requirements of the *Shari‘ah* governance system of the DIFC.

Section 5.1.1 of the ISF requires the composition of the *Shari‘ah* board to be of at least three members who are competent to perform their functions. The ISF does not specify the appropriate body for the appointment of the *Shari‘ah* board; it only states that appointments should be made by the governing body of the IFIs. The practice indicates that some of the appointments are made by the shareholders and some by the BOD. The ISF restricts the *Shari‘ah* board members from being directors or controllers of any IFIs they serve in order to avoid any conflict of interest.

While section 5.1.1 deals with the issue of appointment, composition and restrictions pertaining to the *Shari‘ah* board, section 5.1.2 addresses the issue of transparency and disclosure, in which it requires the IFIs to document their policy in relation to appointments, dismissals or changes, the process, qualification and remuneration of the members of the *Shari‘ah* board. In this respect, the IFIs are required to maintain six years' records of their assessment of the competence of *Shari'ah* board members and the agreed terms of reference for each of them. In dealing with the issue of conflict of interest, the IFIs must have a mechanism in the form of a policy and procedures to manage any potential conflict of interest of the *Shari'ah* board. The IFIs should also provide reasonable assistance to the *Shari'ah* board in terms of access to relevant records and information and should not at any time provide misleading information or interfere with the *Shari'ah* board's ability to perform its duties.

Sections 5.2 and 5.3 of the ISF clearly stipulate the requirement to adopt the AAOIFI governance standards, by which the IFIs are obligated to produce a *Shari'ah* annual report which must be submitted to the DFSA. Section 5.3 further requires that the IFIs conduct an internal *Shari'ah* review and must ensure that it is performed by the internal audit function or the compliance function, either as part of the existing internal audit or compliance department or the independent internal *Shari'ah* audit department of the IFIs. The IFIs must also ensure that the internal *Shari'ah* review is conducted by a competent and sufficiently independent body to assess compliance with *Shari'ah*.

4.2.2.3 Kuwait

(a) Regulatory overview
The legal system of Kuwait is based on French and Egyptian models, particularly its commercial codes, such as the Commercial Companies Law of 1980 and the Commercial Code of 1981 (Gerald 1991: 322).[6] Article 2 of the constitution of Kuwait vividly puts *Shari'ah* as a main source of legislation and Islam as the official religion. This can be referred from Article 547 of the Civil Code Law of Kuwait of 1980,

which prohibits the practice of charging interest on loans, and Article 305, which declares such transactions to be void. Nevertheless, within the same year, the Kuwait Authority issued specific legislation to exclude commercial transactions from the application of the code (Ballantyne 1985: 5). As a result of the issuance of the Commercial Code of 1981, interest charges on loans by financial institutions are expressly permissible (Ballantyne 1987: 12–28).[7]

The principal ministerial authority for enforcement of commercial laws is the Ministry of Commerce and Industry and the Central Bank is the sole regulator for monetary financial system in the State of Kuwait. The Central Bank of Kuwait Law No. 32 of 1968 (CBK Law), amended by Law 130/1977, is the governing legislation that provides the regulatory framework for currency, grant authority to the CBK to supervise the financial institutions and matters relating to the organisation of banking business (Ross 2008: 86). In spite of that, financial institutions including IFIs must also strictly comply with the Commercial Code and Commercial Companies Law of Kuwait (Al-Suwaidi 1993: 291–2). The judicial system of Kuwait places the civil court as having jurisdiction over commercial matters and this includes banking and finance disputes.

With regards to Islamic finance, section 10 of the CBK Law (Articles 86–100) addresses the legal provision pertaining to the rules and controls of IFIs. Article 86 states that the CBK is responsible for regulating and controlling the activities of IFIs. The definition of an Islamic bank in general can be found in Article 86 of the CBK Law, which considers an Islamic bank as a business entity that exercises activities pertaining to banking which should comply with *Shari'ah* principles. This general and wide provision on the activities of Islamic banks, without a definition of every single contract or transaction in Islamic law, creates flexibility for

IFIs in relation to Islamic financial services and products in Kuwait.

(b) Shari'ah *governance*

The *Shari'ah* governance practice in Kuwait is regulated by virtue of Article 93 of the CBK Law, which provides a legal basis for the regulations of the *Shari'ah* board. Article 93 requires all IFIs to establish an independent *Shari'ah* board, which shall be appointed by the bank's general assembly. Unlike the other *Shari'ah* governance approaches, which allow the appointment of the *Shari'ah* board by the BOD, Article 93 specifically requires the appointment to be made only by the general assembly. In terms of composition of the *Shari'ah* board, the CBK Law puts a condition of a minimum of three members; this requirement is similar to the AAOIFI governance standards as well as the *Shari'ah* governance requirements in Bahrain and the UAE. IFIs are also required to mention the establishment of the *Shari'ah* board in their articles and memorandum of association and both documents must specify the powers, workings and governance of the *Shari'ah* board.

There is no *Shari'ah* board in the CBK to act as the highest *Shari'ah* authority in Islamic banking and finance. This may raise an issue of dispute settlement in the case of a conflict of opinion amongst members of the *Shari'ah* board. To address this issue, the CBK Law recognises the *Fatwa* Board in the Ministry of *Awqaf* and Islamic Affairs as the final authority for any *Shari'ah* dispute involving Islamic banking and business. The BOD of an IFI has the responsibility to refer the dispute to the *Fatwa* Board. The CBK Law nevertheless is silent about the status of the decision of the *Fatwa* Board, which should be made binding to all IFIs. Interestingly, Article 100 of the CBK Law clearly provides the supremacy of Islamic law, where it states that IFIs shall be subject to the provision of the CBK Law and subject to the Islamic *Shari'ah* principles. This is a strong legal proviso which places *Shari'ah* as the supreme law in relation to Islamic banking and finance in Kuwait.

With regard to the reporting structure, the *Shari'ah* board has a duty to submit a *Shari'ah* report to the bank's general assembly since they are also appointed by the shareholders. The CBK Law specifies that the *Shari'ah* report must contain the *Shari'ah* opinion on the bank's operation in terms of *Shari'ah* compliance, including comments and views on *Shari'ah* issues. This *Shari'ah* report must be included in the IFIs' annual report.

4.2.2.4 Saudi Arabia

(a) Regulatory overview

The history of the banking system in Saudi Arabia began in the twentieth century with the first commercial bank, the Dutch Commercial Company, which was established in 1926 (Hamed 1979: 167). As a general overview, banking and finance activities in Saudi Arabia are controlled by the Saudi Arabia Monetary Agency (SAMA), established by Royal Decree M/23 of 23.05.1377 on 15 December 1957, which functions under Banking Control Law 1966 as amended by Decree 2/1391 (Pepper 1992: 34). *Shari'ah* is the main source of legislation for Saudi Arabia and the *Shari'ah* court is the highest body in the judicial system.[8] Commercial matters, however, are put under the jurisdiction of the commercial court, which is more like a commercial council, set up by Order 32/1350 1931 (Pepper 1992: 33).

The development of Islamic finance in Saudi Arabia is considered unique and distinctive.[9] The legal framework of the financial system is governed by the Banks Control

System by virtue of Royal Decree No. 5 of 12 June 1966 and this law is silent on the issue of usury or interest (Sfeir 1988: 729–59). As a result, the majority of financial institutions have been conducting business in the conventional banking manner.[10] For instance, Articles 8 and 9 consider money lending as perfectly legitimate.

Despite the Banks Control System 1966, the legal system of Saudi Arabia is actually based on Islamic law. Vogel (2000: 2) clearly mentions that the paramount legal system in Saudi Arabia is *Shari'ah*. This means the IFIs in Saudi Arabia operate under a strange legal framework since the existing law of the Banks Control System 1966 is still applicable and has not been repealed or amended to regulate the establishment or existence of IFIs. This is supported by a statement made by Al Sayari (2004), who mentions that, as of 2004, no law had been passed by the Saudi authority and not a single Islamic banking licence had been granted from the SAMA to any companies in Saudi Arabia. Despite the Capital Market Laws of 2003, fifteen *sukuk* issuances in 2000–2008 and huge Islamic mutual funds in the kingdom, there is no single legislation specifically regulating the implementation of Islamic finance (Wilson 2009a: 10). As part of the government's policy for legal reform, it is anticipated that several new and revised regulations will be promulgated to boost the economy and increase foreign investment, such as the redraft of the companies law, settlement of the jurisdictional conflict between the Capital Market Authority and Ministry of Commerce and Industry in relation to the securities in public offering and financial sector regulation (Al-Abduljabbar and Marshal 2010: 731). In fact, the SAMA has also consulted a group of consultants, legal and banking specialists, and appointed a steering committee to study the feasibility of Islamic finance in Saudi Arabia and hence to provide the required legal framework (Al Sayari 2004).

With regard to banking disputes, SAMA set up a specific institution in October 1987 to hear cases pertaining to banking matters, including Islamic finance, known as the the Committee of Settlement for Banking Disputes (CSBD; Reumann 1995: 230). The establishment of the CSBD is governed by the CSBD Regulations (Marar 2004: 114). With the purpose of giving exclusive jurisdiction to the CSBD, another Resolution of the Council of Ministers No. 732/8 of 10.07.1407 (10 March 1987) was issued via a Circular of the Minister of Justice No. 12/138T of 28.07.1407 (28 March 1987), which specifically instructs the *Shariʿah* court not to hear any more banking disputes (Reumann 1995: 230–237). To date, the banking disputes in Saudi Arabia are heard in the CSBD and not in the *Shariʿah* court as practised pre-1987 unless authorised by the Ministerial Council (Marar 2004: 114).

(b) Shariʿah *governance*
Since there is a lacuna in the regulatory framework pertaining to Islamic finance in Saudi Arabia, the nature of the *Shariʿah* governance system is different to other jurisdictions. The notion of having a *Shariʿah* governance system within the IFIs is not due to any legal and supervisory requirement but rather as a voluntary initiative and indirect influence from the market. In other words, the *Shariʿah* governance model in Saudi Arabia is much more based on a self-initiative approach. As an illustration of the *Shariʿah* governance system in Saudi Arabia, it would be beneficial to refer to the Al Rajhi model. The Eleventh General Assembly of Al Rajhi established the *Shariʿah* board and its charter (Al Rajhi 2008). The provision of the establishment of the *Shariʿah* board was clearly stipulated in the articles of association as well as Al Rajhi internal rules and guidelines. The *Shariʿah* board of Al Rajhi is deemed to be independent

of all organs of governance, such as the management and BOD, since the appointment is made by the shareholders.

The Al Rajhi *Shariʿah* board plays four major roles to ensure and promote *Shariʿah* compliance: monitoring the activities and implementation of *Shariʿah* rulings with the assistance of the *Shariʿah* department; assisting the bank to develop products and services; promoting and creating awareness about Islamic finance to all stakeholders; and finally, ensuring proper selection of employees, particularly senior management (Al Rajhi 2008). Unlike other *Shariʿah* boards, interestingly, Al Rajhi has granted additional authority to its *Shariʿah* board to assist the management in the process of selecting employees who have the capacity and are well qualified to implement Islamic banking practices.

There are three specific organs that support the function of the *Shariʿah* board, namely its secretariat, the *Shariʿah* Control Department and the Control and Information Unit.[11] The secretariat deals with the *Shariʿah* board meeting and its operational procedures. The *Shariʿah* Control Department assists the *Shariʿah* board in performing the *Shariʿah* review, while the Control and Information Unit specifically provides information and creates awareness to promote *Shariʿah* compliance (Al Rajhi 2008). Besides that, Al Rajhi has gone even further to develop its own *Shariʿah* governance arrangement by setting up an executive committee to oversee the functions of the *Shariʿah* Control Department, to appoint *Shariʿah* controllers, and to study issues submitted to the *Shariʿah* board (Al Rajhi 2008).[12]

Since there is no standard guideline for *Shariʿah* governance issued by the regulatory authority, Al Rajhi has issued its own *Shariʿah* guidelines and procedures, known as the *Shariʿah* Monitoring Guide and *Shariʿah* Control Guidelines, with the purpose of ensuring the proper monitoring and implementation system of *Shari'ah* rulings (Al Rajhi 2008). These *Shari'ah* guidelines make it very clear that the *Shari'ah* board's rulings are considered binding. Therefore, all products or services must be approved by the *Shari'ah* board before they can be offered in the market.

4.2.2.5 Qatar

(a) Regulatory overview
Qatar celebrated its independence in 1971 with its first Provisional Constitution on 2 April 1970; this was replaced by the Amended Provisional Constitution of 19 April 1972 (Hamzeh 1994: 83). Article 1 of the 1972 constitution clearly states that Islamic law is the main source of legislation and Islam is the religion of the state. Although the constitution of Qatar specifically puts *Shari'ah* as the main source of legislation, nevertheless, in the aspect of commercial transactions, *Shari'ah* is acceptable as one of the main sources of legislation but not as a primary consideration. Moreover, there is a contradiction between the Qatar Civil and Commercial Codes and its constitution. For instance, Article 4 of the Civil and Commercial Code states that *Shari'ah* shall apply in the absence of express legislation provision or custom (Ballantyne 1985: 9).

This position puts *Shari'ah* as a secondary source of legislation with respect to commercial transactions, which contradicts Article 7 of the constitution. In view of the similar situations that happened in Kuwait, the UAE and Bahrain, it is presumed that the Qatar Civil and Commercial Code is excluded from the application of Article 7 and hence permits interest-based transactions in Qatar's financial sector. In fact, Law No. 7 of 1973, amended by Law No. 7 of 1975, granted power to the Qatar Monetary Agency to determine the interest rates on deposits and loans. The government of Qatar then established the Qatar Central Bank (QCB), which inherited all functions of the Qatar Monetary Agency in 2006 by Decree Law No. 33 of the Banking Law of Qatar 2006 (Ross 2008: 134). The QCB is the regulatory body that supervises and manages the financial sector in Qatar, while the Doha Securities Market serves as the securities market regulator. The judicial system of Qatar has the civil court hearing cases pertaining to commercial, banking and finance disputes.

In early 2005, the government of Qatar established the Qatar Financial Centre (QFC), with the purpose of creating an independent regulatory body for the financial sector, and the Qatar Financial Markets Authority (QFMA) to manage the securities market (QFC 2010a). The establishment of the QFC was regulated by QFC Law (Law No. 7 of 2005) and the QFMA by Law No. 33, where both laws are regarded as the main legislation governing the basic construction of the QFC. The QFC Law establishes four different independent bodies, namely the QFC Authority, the QFC Regulatory Authority, the Appeals Body and the QFC Tribunal. The QFC has the power to regulate the financial sector, including Islamic financial business. As the QFC is inspired by the DIFC model that has separate judicial and federal systems, the QFC also has its own civil and commercial court and regulatory tribunal as part of its legal infrastructure.

In parallel with the expansion of Islamic banking in Qatar's financial market, the QFC Regulatory Authority issued the Islamic Finance Rule Book 2007 (ISFI) in July 2007 (QFC 2010b). The ISFI provides rules and regulations pertaining to Islamic financial business, such as the endorsement of IFIs and Islamic windows, disclosure requirements, constitutional documents, systems and control, conduct of business standards, and *Shari'ah* boards. With the issuance of the ISFI, all IFIs and Islamic windows must comply with the ISFI and they are subject to the supervision of the QFC Regulatory Authority.

(b) Shari'ah *governance*
There are two sets of frameworks of the *Shari'ah* governance system for IFIs in Qatar: those under the auspices of QCB and those under the QFC. The QCB issued prudential regulations for banking supervision known as the Instructions to Banks (IB) in March 2008 and Part 7 of the Banking Supervision Instructions provides the guidelines for IFIs. Meanwhile, the QFC has its own rules and regulations pertaining to the *Shari'ah* governance system, as stipulated in the ISFI.

Chapter 1 of Banking Risk, Credit and Financing Risk of the IB requires IFIs to establish a *Shari'ah* board. The *Shari'ah* board must consist of not less than two qualified Muslim members appointed by the BOD and approved by the general assembly. It further states that the *Shari'ah* board has a duty to supervise activities and to approve products and services. As such, contracts and documentations of any transactions must be ratified by the *Shari'ah* board. In carrying out this duty, the *Shari'ah* board shall be assisted by a *Shari'ah* internal auditor and the *Shari'ah* audit report shall be submitted to the *Shari'ah* board. For purpose of standardisation of practice, the IB requires the IFIs to adopt the AAOIFI governance standards.

The IB contains two unique features which differentiate its position from other *Shari'ah* governance frameworks. Firstly, the IB restricts the *Shari'ah* board members to receive credit facilities for commercial purposes (QFC 2009: 160). This position raises an issue as to the reasonability of such a restriction. If the purpose of such a restriction is to ensure the independence of the *Shari'ah* board and to avoid conflict of interest, the prohibition should include receiving credit facilities for both personal and commercial purposes. Secondly, the IFIs are required to appoint directors and senior management who are highly qualified, experienced and trained in the field of Islamic financial services (QFC 2009: 197). This is a unique provision which cannot be found in any rules and regulations of other jurisdictions.

The ISFI specifies the *Shari'ah* governance framework for IFIs registered with the QFC. Section 5 of the ISFI requires IFIs to establish and maintain systems and controls to ensure the *Shari'ah* compliance of all their Islamic financial business. Section 5.2.1 (1) details this requirement to include the *Shari'ah* compliance aspect, the *Shari'ah* board and internal *Shari'ah* review matters. With respect to *Shari'ah* governance, section 6 of the ISFI provides a comprehensive provision pertaining to the *Shari'ah* board: section 6.1.1 places a mandatory condition on IFIs to establish their own *Shari'ah* board. Although there is no *Shari'ah* board at the QCB or the QFC, the government of Qatar has established the Supreme *Shari'ah* Council attached to the Ministry of *Awqaf* as the highest *Shari'ah* authority. The Supreme *Shari'ah* Council is the final authority in cases of *Shari'ah* disputes pertaining to Islamic finance.

With regard to the composition of the *Shari'ah* board, the ISFI includes a condition of a minimum of three members who are appointed by the governing body of the institution. Section 3 of the Interpretation and Application Rulebook 2008 defines the governing body as the BOD, the management or other governing body of an authorised firm. In this context, the appointment, as well as the dismissal and changes, of the *Shari'ah* board members will be made by the BOD.

In terms of qualifications, the ISFI does not specify the exact criteria for the appointment of *Shari'ah* board members. Section 6.1.1 (B) (ii) mentions that the members appointed must be competent to perform their functions as *Shari'ah* board members by considering their qualifications and previous experience. In addition, the ISFI forbids the *Shari'ah* board members to be appointed as directors or controllers of the IFIs. This restriction is perhaps intended to clarify the role of the *Shari'ah* board members, which is supervisory and advisory in nature. Section 6.1.2 requires IFIs to have a set of policies on the *Shari'ah* board with regard to method of appointment, dismissals, changes and remuneration. The ISFI also makes it compulsory for IFIs to retain records of its assessment of the *Shari'ah* board members and the agreed terms of engagement of each member for at least six years from the date on which the individual ceased to be a member of the *Shari'ah* board.[13]

A unique position of the ISFI is that the IFIs have legal responsibilities to take reasonable steps to ensure that the members of the *Shari'ah* board are independent and not subject to any conflict of interest. This position then requires IFIs to provide the QFC Regulatory Authority with information on the qualifications, skills, experience and independence of the *Shari'ah* board. In fact, the ISFI also emphasises the IFIs' duty to take reasonable measures, to provide assistance to the *Shari'ah* board, and to ensure their right of full access to relevant records and information for the purpose of *Shari'ah* compliance.

The ISFI clearly mentions the requirement for the adoption of the AAOIFI governance standards, particularly in the aspect of the *Shari'ah* review. Section 6.2 requires IFIs to ensure that all *Shari'ah* reviews are undertaken in accordance with AAOIFI Governance Standard No. 2 and to submit a *Shari'ah* report as stipulated in AAOIFI Governance Standard No. 1. The *Shari'ah* report must be submitted within four months of the financial year end. To complement the process of the *Shari'ah* review in accordance with

AAOIFI Governance Standard No. 3, the IFIs must perform an internal *Shari'ah* review to audit the extent to which the IFIs comply with *fatwa*, rulings and guidelines issued by the *Shari'ah* board. The internal *Shari'ah* review should be conducted by the internal audit team and the individuals or departments involved in performing the review must be competent and sufficiently independent to assess compliance with *Shari'ah*.

4.2.3 United Kingdom

(a) Regulatory overview

The attempt to introduce Islamic financial services to the UK began in the 1980s when Al Barakah Bank endeavoured to form a fully fledged Islamic bank in 1982; unfortunately, it was forced to close in June 1993 by the Bank of England after failing to satisfy certain requirements of the regulators (Housby 2005: 69). In 2000, the Bank of England, with the cooperation of HM Treasury, set up a working group to study the feasibility of Islamic finance in the UK. This working group was set up by Sir Edward George, the then Governor of the Bank of England and the members comprised representatives from the Treasury, the Financial Services Authority, the Council of Mortgage Lenders, banks and Muslim organisations including the Muslim Council of Britain (Briault 2007). Since then, several legislative measures have been introduced by HM Treasury in relation to the tax and regulatory systems to enable the development of Islamic finance in the UK and, in August 2004, the first full *Shari'ah*-compliant retail Islamic bank, the Islamic Bank of Britain, was authorised.

According to a report produced by International Financial Services London, at the beginning of 2008 the UK hosted five Islamic banks, more than twenty Islamic windows, one *takāful* operator, nine fund managers and one *Shari'ah*-compliant hedge fund manager (HM Treasury 2008a). In the meantime, the UK authorities have continued to develop Islamic finance in the UK by establishing the Islamic Finance Council based in Scotland in 2005, and a special subgroup in early 2007 to study and produce a strategy for the promotion of the UK as a centre for Islamic financial services.[14] In April 2007, HM Treasury and the UK Debt Management Office also undertook a feasibility study for sovereign *sukuk* issuance. This positive development further enhances the growth of the Islamic finance industry in the UK and may stimulate its expansion into other European countries.

(b) *Shari'ah* governance
Although Islamic banking is considered new to the UK, there is already a well-developed Islamic financial structure and governance framework. Basically, the UK authority implements equal legal treatment and framework for conventional banks and IFIs. With regard to *Shari'ah* governance, there is no legal requirement for IFIs to establish a *Shari'ah* board, either at individual bank or national level. The UK authorities nevertheless are concerned with the issue of *Shari'ah* governance as the FSA mentions that it needs to clarify, from financial and operational aspects, the role of the *Shari'ah* board in IFIs (Briault 2007).

Actually, the major concern of the FSA about *Shari'ah* governance is whether the *Shari'ah* board has an executive or directorial role in IFIs. As long as it does not have an executive role, there will be no significant issue from the FSA's perspective. The practices of the five existing Islamic banks in the UK show that *Shari'ah* governance is managed by the individual IFIs and they are free to adopt their own *Shari'ah* governance without adhering to any national or other higher level of *Shari'ah* board. HM Treasury clearly mentions that the UK government does not intend to follow the *Shari'ah* governance approach of other jurisdictions, since the UK authorities are secular bodies and not religious regulators.

With respect to the composition of the *Shari'ah* board, current practice shows that the Islamic Bank of Britain and the European Finance House have three *Shari'ah* advisors, the Bank of London and the Middle East and the European Islamic Bank have four *Shari'ah* advisors and Gate House Capital one. The variety of *Shari'ah* board composition amongst the IFIs indicates that there are no legal or policy requirements from the FSA or other UK authorities which creates flexibility for the IFIs in the UK to organise and manage their own *Shari'ah* governance.

The FSA is also concerned about the aspect of confidentiality and the shortage of *Shari'ah* scholars. Some of the *Shari'ah* advisors are sitting on more than three different *Shari'ah* boards at one particular time and this position may raise potential issues of confidentiality and conflict of interest. At the moment, the individual IFIs tackle this issue internally as there is no specific guideline for *Shari'ah* boards. HM Treasury has, however, highlighted its concern on this aspect by recommending the standardisation of products and practices of Islamic finance services. In this regard, the UK government supports the roles played by the international standard-setters, such as the AAOIFI, the IFSB and the IIFM (HM Treasury 2008: 19–25). The standardisation of products and practices guarantees the further growth of the Islamic finance industry as it may reduce costs and time, improve documentation and confidence, lessen the burden on *Shari'ah* scholars (HM Treasury 2008: 23) and mitigate the potential of *Shari'ah* risk. In order to address the problem of the shortage of *Shari'ah* scholars in the UK, the Islamic Finance Council, in collaboration with the Securities and Investment Institute (SII), offers a Scholar Development Programme specifically for *Shariʿah* advisors or potential *Shariʿah* scholars. This programme provides a wide range of subjects with knowledge of the conventional system that *Shariʿah* scholars need to be able to practice in the UK or elsewhere (SII 2008).

Even though the UK authorities are silent on many aspects of *Shariʿah* governance, the situation is different in the case of *sukuk*. HM Treasury (2008b: 39) highlights the need for the appointment of internationally recognised *Shariʿah* scholars to ensure *Shariʿah* compliance of the government sterling *sukuk* issuance. Furthermore, there was a suggestion to incorporate British *Shariʿah* scholars onto the board to approve the *sukuk* issuance (HM Treasury 2008b: 24). This position indicates that the UK authorities have started to look into a possible framework of *Shariʿah* governance. It is expected that the growth of the Islamic finance industry, in parallel with the sophistication of its products, may force the UK authorities to consider introducing a comprehensive *Shariʿah* governance framework in the future, which may be a good model for countries with a non-Islamic legal environment.

4.3 Regulatory issues

Regardless of the positive developments on the *Shariʿah* governance framework in the described case countries, it is observed that there are a few significant regulatory issues which are inherently essential to the *Shariʿah* governance system, such as the legal status of the *Shariʿah* pronouncements, court's jurisdiction, addressing issues on differences of *Shariʿah* rulings and the *Shariʿah* board's advisory and executive roles. This section attempts to highlight these regulatory issues in order to enlighten further discussion on the legal framework of *Shari'ah* governance.

4.3.1 *Legal status of* Shari'ah *pronouncements*

One of the debatable issues of *Shari'ah* governance is the status of *Shari'ah* rulings. The issue refers to whether the *Shari'ah* rulings are binding on IFIs, courts or any other related institutions. To illustrate this important issue, we refer to a survey conducted on the perception of *Shari'ah* rulings, which found that only 56.6 per cent of IFIs consider *Shari'ah* rulings to be binding, 20 per cent as merely advisory and 22.4 per cent gave no response (Dawud 1996: 43). The result of this survey indicates that there are loopholes and shortcomings in the *Shari'ah* governance framework, particularly in positioning *Shari'ah* board decisions as binding and mandatory. Ironically, the IFSB survey on *Shari'ah* boards across jurisdictions demonstrates that 60 per cent of respondents agreed that the national *Shari'ah* authority should be the highest authority in Islamic finance, yet only a few jurisdictions have affirmed this practice (IFSB 2008b: 18).

With reference to the existing *Shari'ah* governance framework in some countries, they have already provided clear legal provision on the superiority of *Shari'ah* board decisions. This is in parallel with the AAOIFI governance standard, which stresses that *fatwa* issued by the *Shari'ah* board shall be binding and fully enforceable (AAOIFI 2005a: 4). It is a similar situation in the case of the IAIB *Shari'ah* board as all the board's decisions for *Shari'ah* supervision are binding on the banks which are members of the institute (Wilson 1997: 83–93).

In Malaysia, sections 57 and 58 of the CBA vividly provide clear provision on the status of *Shari'ah* pronouncements issued, which are binding to IFIs, courts and arbitration.

Similarly, in the case of the UAE, Article 5 of Federal Law No. 6 of 1985 provides for the establishment of the Higher *Shari'ah* Authority (HSA) as the final authority in *Shari'ah* matters pertaining to Islamic banking and finance. All determination and decisions made by the HSA are binding and mandatory to all IFIs in the UAE. Paragraph A (ix) of the Instructions for *Shari'ah* Compliance in Islamic Banking Institutions makes it clear that all *fatwa* or rulings issued by *Shari'ah* boards are binding upon IFIs (SBP 2008: 1). While the legal frameworks of Malaysia, the UAE and Pakistan have provided clear positions on *Shari'ah* rulings, the situation is different in other countries such as the UK, Saudi Arabia, Kuwait, Qatar and Bahrain, since the status of *Shari'ah* pronouncements is still ambiguous.

In light of the above, laws and legal arrangements in certain jurisdictions, such as the UAE and Malaysia, seem capable of providing a clear position on the status of *Shari'ah* board decisions to be binding and mandatory, whereas in many other countries the situation is otherwise. With this in mind, there must be a practical solution to resolve the issue by examining and studying the respective countries' legal environments and structures. Proactive efforts and continuous endeavours should be carried out to place *Shari'ah* as the supreme law and authority and to ensure that *Shari'ah* board rulings are binding and mandatory upon the IFIs, the arbitrators and the courts of justice.

4.3.2 Court jurisdiction

Section 4.2 clearly explains that Islamic finance cases often fall under the jurisdiction of non-*Shari'ah* courts, as in the cases of Malaysia, Kuwait, Qatar, the UAE, Bahrain, the UK and the Banking Dispute Settlement (BDS) in Saudi Arabia. Basically, this is not appropriate, since Islamic finance is part of Islamic law and ideally should be under the jurisdiction

of a *Shari'ah* court, which does not happen in some jurisdictions, particularly the UK. In this, two issues might be
significant in respect to the *Shari'ah* governance system:
the judges' ability to decide Islamic finance cases, and to
what extent the judges' attitude is to refer Islamic finance
disputes to a *Shari'ah* board for deliberation.

The significance of the former issue can be illustrated
in the case of *Arab Finance Malaysia Berhad* v. *Taman
Ihsan Jaya and Ors* (2008) 5 MLJ 631, in which the High
Court ruled that the profit derived from the BBA facility
was unlawful and illegitimate as it involved an element of
interest and, therefore, IFIs could only claim the principal
amount of financing. This judgment will seriously affect the
Islamic finance industry in Malaysia as the BBA represents
more than 80 per cent of total financing. By referring to the
inadequate arguments of the learned judge, particularly in
explaining *riba* and elaborating the BBA from a *Shari'ah*
point of view, it indicates that the court may need the deliberation of an expert who specialises in *Shari'ah*, particularly
fiqh al muāmalāt. In this context the *Shari'ah* board is the
ideal institution to be referred to by the court. Hitherto,
after more than a decade of the implementation of Islamic
finance with numerous cases reported, there has been only
one case that the court has referred to a *Shari'ah* board. This
indicates the court's passive attitude towards having the
deliberation of a *Shari'ah* board pertaining to *Shari'ah* matters involving Islamic finance cases, in spite of its limited
knowledge of the subject.

4.3.3 *Addressing issues of differences of* Shari'ah *resolution*

The absence of a comprehensive set of regulatory frameworks on *Shari'ah* governance may cause problems to the
development of Islamic finance. The issue of the differences

of various *fatwa* rulings[15] amongst the *Shariʻah* boards may affect Islamic finance, especially when it involves international entities and cross-border transactions. The IFSB survey indicates the low percentage of reconciled *Shariʻah* issues pertaining to different *Shariʻah* resolutions, in which Bahrain, Bangladesh, Indonesia and Sudan indicate issue resolution of less than 20 per cent, the UAE slightly more than 20 per cent, and Malaysia 40 per cent (IFSB 2008b: 42). This crucial finding denotes that most of the *Shariʻah* issues related to resolution of *Shariʻah* differences are not reconciled in many countries.

The diversity of interpretation of *Shariʻah* may affect the determination of certain rulings on particular issues, where one IFI would accept a new product as being *Shariʻah* compliant while others would decide it is non-compliant (McMillen 2006: 139–40). To tackle this issue, there are a few approaches that can be possibly implemented and these include establishing a *Shariʻah* board at national level, providing legal provision on the final authority of the *Shariʻah* board rulings, allowing interdisciplinary experts to be appointed as *Shariʻah* board members, and issuing universal *Shariʻah* prudential standards.

In the case of conflict of opinions amongst members of the *Shariʻah* boards in Kuwait, the BOD of the designated IFI may transfer the matter to the *Fatwa* Board in the Ministry of *Awqaf* and Islamic Affairs and the *Fatwa* Board shall be the final authority on the matter (Article 93 of CBK Law 32/1968). Similarly, in Malaysia, section 51 of the CBA grants the power to the SAC as the sole *Shariʻah* authority that will be referred to by the court or arbitrator in disputes involving *Shariʻah* issues in Islamic banking, finance and *takāful* cases. In Pakistan, the Instructions for *Shariʻah* Compliance in Islamic Banking Institutions provides that, in the case of difference of opinion arising between *Shari'ah* boards of IFIs, the matter shall be referred to the SBP *Shari'ah* board and any deliberation made by them board shall be final and binding (SBP 2008: 3).

Another possible approach to address the issue of various legal opinions is to allow interdisciplinary experts or professionals to be appointed as *Shari'ah* board members. A combination of interdisciplinary experts in the composition of a *Shari'ah* board may enable the board to come out with more integrated *Shari'ah* rulings. For instance, the *Shari'ah* board of the BNM comprises *Shari'ah* scholars, chartered accountants, lawyers, judges[16] and central bankers. This approach is preferable because any issues discussed by the *Shari'ah* board deal not only with *Shari'ah* matters but also legal and financial aspects.

It is also crucial to see some uniformity, and standards are set to ensure that the differences of legal opinion are addressed effectively. In this respect, the issuance of *Shari'ah* standards is really necessary with the purpose of bringing diverse *Shari'ah* opinions to a universally acceptable practice. The AAOIFI *Shari'ah* standards nevertheless have been adopted by only a few countries since the standards are not made obligatory except in Bahrain, Jordan, Sudan, Qatar and Dubai. The standards are used as guidelines in Saudi Arabia, Kuwait, Malaysia, Lebanon and Indonesia. It is expected that numerous IFIs will adopt the AAOIFI *Shari'ah* standards in order to address any *Shari'ah* issues arising from differences in *Shari'ah* rulings.

4.3.4 *Executive, advisory and supervisory roles of the* Shari'ah *board*

The *Shari'ah* board plays a significant role in ensuring *Shari'ah* compliance in all products, transactions and operations of IFIs. The issue here is whether the *Shari'ah* board has an executive role in exercising its power or whether it is just an advisory authority. This issue is very significant, especially in non-Islamic legal environments such as the UK, where the FSA has a standard requirement to authorise a person to be a director who has an executive role in the company. There are two main consequences if *Shari'ah* board members are seen to have executive power or a directorship role in IFIs in the UK: it is possible that many *Shari'ah* scholars may not meet the fit and proper criteria required by the FSA, and the existing practice of multiple membership of *Shari'ah* boards in various IFIs may be considered as contrary to the rule of conflict of interest (Ainley *et al.* 2007: 13). At the moment, there is no controversial issue on this matter since the FSA's perspective of the role of the *Shari'ah* board is that it is advisory and the board does not interfere in the management of the IFI. It is assumed that potential conflict is likely to exist due to the increasing numbers of *Shari'ah* boards in IFIs and the rapid growth of the Islamic finance industry in the UK[17] and Europe.

On the other hand, if the role and responsibilities of the *Shari'ah* board are considered neither executive nor supervisory but merely advisory, it raises another significant issue as to the actual function of the *Shari'ah* board and to what extent its deliberations bind the IFIs. If it is merely advisory, the IFIs may ignore the decisions made by the *Shari'ah* board since it does not have the authority to enforce its deliberations. This gives the impression that the decisions made by the *Shari'ah* board are not binding upon the court or the respective IFIs or even in alternative dispute resolution such as arbitration. In fact, the absence of a supervisory role for the *Shari'ah* board may negate the efficiency of *ex post* monitoring of *Shari'ah* compliance aspects. This issue hence needs proper deliberation and indeed the *Shari'ah* board must be given full authority to have supervisory and advisory roles that address the *Shari'ah* compliance aspects of IFIs.

4.4 Conclusion

The *Shari'ah* governance system in Malaysia, GCC countries and the UK can be classified into two types: regulated via legal and supervisory requirements, as in the cases of Malaysia, Bahrain, Kuwait, the UAE and Qatar, or through self-regulation, as in the cases of Saudi Arabia and the UK. In terms of classification from a regulatory perspective, Malaysia is identified as a strong proponent of a 'regulatory-based approach', Bahrain, Kuwait, the UAE and Qatar as a 'minimalist approach', Saudi Arabia as a 'passive approach' and the UK as a 'reactive approach'. In view of numerous legal issues involved in the existing *Shari'ah* governance framework, the need to have a comprehensive legal framework and an effective *Shari'ah* governance system is really crucial. Failure to provide efficient *Shari'ah* governance either through law or legislation on the part of regulators and the players would impede the future development of the Islamic finance industry.

In this aspect, the AAOIFI *Shari'ah* standards are an important effort to standardise *Shari'ah* practices, while the IFSB guidelines on governance would be able to guide and promote the best practice of a *Shari'ah* governance system. Referring to the diverse perception and acceptability of the AAOIFI standards and IFSB guidelines, there must be strong mechanisms to guarantee their universal adoption and one of them is through having a proper legal framework. For this purpose, thorough and intense studies need to be conducted to examine, analyse and scrutinise the possible adaptation of the AAOIFI standards and the IFSB guidelines in various markets and legal environments.

The foregoing discussion seems to suggest that the existing regulatory framework of Shari'ah governance needs further enhancement and improvement in order to reinforce the development and growth of the Islamic finance industry. This brings into focus the measures and efforts that need to be taken to strengthen the IFIs through enhancing the Shari'ah governance framework. It is important that some common and fundamental legal elements underlying and promoting good governance and best practices are to be drawn up to facilitate the creation of and optimise a healthy and viable environment for Shari'ah governance without impeding the further growth of the industry.

Notes

1. Paragraph 2 of the *Guidelines on Islamic Private Debt Securities (1 July 2000)*, issued by the SC, requires that the individuals appointed Shari'ah advisors in relation to the approval of the structure of Islamic bonds must be of good reputation and well-versed in *fiqh al muāmalāt* and *usul al fiqh*, having at least three years' experience in Islamic financial transactions (SC 2000).

2. The BNM/GP8-i Shari'ah report's format is lacking several important pieces of information compared to the format of AAOIFI Governance Standard No.1. The AAOIFI requires additional information on the Shari'ah report, which should contain necessary information on Shari'ah compliance matters such as activities, operations and transactions carried out by IFIs (AAOIFI 2005a).

3. This position positively influences the level of compliance of IFIs in Bahrain to the AAOIFI governance standards. A study conducted by Vinnicombe (2010: 61–3) on twenty-six IFIs in Bahrain revealed that the level of compliance was very high with respect to governance standards relating to in-house

supervisory boards and reporting of the Islamic *mudaraba* contract.

4. This was affirmed by the Constitutional Division Bench of the Supreme Court in the case of No. 14, Year 9 (June 1981). The Supreme Court held that Articles 61 and 62 of the Civil Procedure Law of Abu Dhabi No. 3/1970 concerning interest charges were unaffected by Article 7 of the constitution since they were in existence before the application of the constitution, dated 2 December 1971 (Al-Suwaidi 1993: 293).

5. On top of that, the DFSA also issued Islamic-finance-tailored handbooks in five areas of Islamic finance: Islamic Banking, Islamic Insurance, Islamic Investment Business Other than Operating Funds, Islamic Insurance Intermediation and Management and Operation of Islamic Funds (DFSA 2010). These handbooks are designed to create further understanding and awareness of the DFSA's rulebooks pertaining to Islamic finance.

6. The original Commercial Code of Kuwait 1961 was drafted by Al-Sanhouri, an Egyptian jurist, and contained more principles of Western secular law than of the *Shari'ah* (Ballantyne 1988: 317–28).

7. Article 102 of the Commercial Code provides that the creditor has the right to interest in accordance with the terms of contract; in the absence of a specified contract, the interest shall not exceed 7 per cent and if the debtor delays in payment the interest shall then be calculated on the agreed basis rate. In addition, Article 115 further states that interest shall not be paid for a frozen interest.

8. Although *Shari'ah* is considered as the main source of legislation, the other sources of law, such as customary law, world case law and doctrine and jurisprudence, are also acceptable (Ballantyne 1986: 13–14). In the case of *Aramco Arbitration, Saudi Arabia* v. *Arabian American Oil Company* (1958) 27 ILR 117, the arbitrator held that the proper law of the Concession

Agreement was Islamic law, but it is necessary to refer to other laws in order to fill the lacunae in the existing legal frameworks.

9. Unlike the other GCC countries, Saudi Arabia has deliberately avoided the usage of the term 'constitution' as *al-Qur'an* is considered its constitution. *Nizam Asasiy* or the Basic Law of Rule of 1992 is considered as the main law or the constitution of the kingdom (Marar 2004: 111).

10. Despite there being no specific regulation to penalise financial institutions involved in interest-based transactions, any claims for interest are not enforceable. Interestingly, in Saudi Arabia the religious sentiment is so strong it is reported that deposits attracting interest only reached 49 per cent in 1988 compared to 80 per cent in Bahrain and 85 per cent in Kuwait in the same year. This illustrates that there is a significantly strong natural antipathy and awareness of the prohibition of interest amongst Saudi people (Reumann 1995: 218–19). A more recent study by Ernst and Young in 2008 reported that 70–90 per cent of Saudi Arabian mass affluent investors prefer *Shari'ah* investment products over conventional products (Hamedanchi and Altenbach 2009: 58–61).

11. Another Saudi Bank, Bank Al Bilad, has established a *Shari'ah* board, preparatory committee and *Shari'ah* group as its institutional arrangement for *Shari'ah*-compliance purposes. The *Shari'ah* board plays a role as a *fatwa*-issuing body while the preparatory committee acts as a research unit that studies *Shari'ah*-related issues and enquiries before they are forwarded to the *Shari'ah* board for deliberation. Another function emanating from the *Shari'ah* board is the *Shari'ah* group, consisting of the *Shari'ah* secretariat and the *Shari'ah* audit department. The former acts as a *Shari'ah* coordinator and the latter conducts periodic *Shari'ah* reviews (Al Bilad 2008: 13–14).

12. This committee consists of three members; two of them are *Shari'ah* board members (one of them is committee chairman) and the third is the general secretary of the *Shari'ah* board. This executive committee will then have to submit its reports to the *Shari'ah* board (Al Rajhi 2008).

13. Section 6.1.4 of the ISFI requires that records of the assessment of competence of *Shari'ah* Supervisory Board members must include, at a minimum: (a) the factors that have been taken into account when making the assessment of competence; (b) the qualifications and experience of the *Shari'ah* Supervisory Board members; (c) the basis upon which the Authorised Firm has deemed that the proposed *Shari'ah* Supervisory Board member is suitable; and (d) details of any other *Shari'ah* supervisory boards of which the proposed *Shari'ah* Supervisory Board member is, or has been, a member.

14. This subgroup was set up by UK Trade & Investment (UKTI), through their Financial Services Advisory Board, and consists of fifteen practitioners and representatives from UKTI and HM Treasury and four private-sector working groups, set up in another four specific subgroups of Banking and Insurance; Legal; Accountancy; and Education, Training and Qualifications (ETQ; HM Treasury 2008a: 14).

15. Sheikh Mohammed Taqi Usmani claims that there has been near consensus amongst the *Shari'ah* scholars on *Shari'ah*-related issues in Islamic banking and finance and only about 10 per cent of disputed opinions are yet to be resolved (New Horizon 2004: 15). According to the CIBAFI, who sampled about 6,000 *fatwa*, it was found that 90 per cent were consistent across the IFIs (Grais and Pellegrini 2006a: 11).

16. On 1 November 2004 the BNM appointed Tun Abdul Hamid Haji Mohamad, the Chief Justice of Malaysia, as a member of the National *Shari'ah* Advisory Council for Islamic Banking and *Takāful* (New Horizon 2005: 5).

17. Kahf (1999: 454) mentions that the failure of Al Barakah Bank in London to clearly clarify the relationship of its management and *Shari'ah* board to the Bank of England is one of the factors that contributed to its closure in 1995.

CHAPTER 5

THE STATE
OF *SHARI'AH*
GOVERNANCE
PRACTICES IN
ISLAMIC BANKS

5.0 Introduction

Shari'ah governance is peculiarly important to IFIs as part of their corporate governance arrangement. In view of the scarcity of literature on this subject, this book is considered a small effort to contribute to the development of a *Shari'ah* governance system by presenting its current practices across jurisdictions. This chapter hence presents findings derived from the survey that was conducted in 2009. The survey aimed at understanding the extent of current *Shari'ah* governance practices by examining its general approach; regulatory and internal framework; roles of the *Shari'ah* board; attributes of the *Shari'ah* board in terms of independence, competence, transparency and confidentiality; operational procedures; and assessment of the *Shari'ah* board.

It is worth mentioning that the survey was conducted to research the Islamic finance industry's internal perceptions of *Shari'ah* governance. This is significant as the IFIs' perceptions will be able to demonstrate the extent and actual practices of *Shari'ah* governance. For this purpose, the questionnaire was distributed via ordinary mail and email to the selected commercial banks, investment banks, asset management companies and regulatory authorities that offer Islamic financial services in Malaysia, GCC countries (the UAE, Bahrain, Saudi Arabia, Qatar and Kuwait) and the UK. Personal interviews were also conducted in order to get responses from some IFIs.

5.1 Research methodology

Since the availability of secondary data on *Shari'ah* governance practices is very limited, a detailed survey questionnaire (as shown in Appendix 1) was generated in order to source primary data from IFIs, excluding Islamic insurance institutions. The survey was distributed to eighty IFIs in: Malaysia (20), GCC countries (Bahrain 12, the UAE 13, Qatar 10, Kuwait 10 and Saudi Arabia 9) and the UK (6). Table 5.1 and Figure 5.1 illustrate the research sample descriptions.

Table 5.1 *Research sample*

Country	Commercial Bank	Investment Bank/Asset Management Company	Regulatory Authority	Total
Malaysia	18		2	20
Bahrain	8	4		12
UAE	11	2		13
Kuwait	5	5		10
Qatar	6	4		10
Saudi Arabia	5	4		9
United Kingdom	2	4		6
Total	55	23	2	80

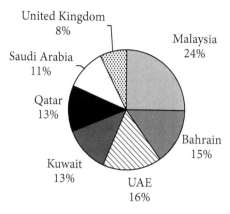

Figure 5.1 *Sample description*

Most of the IFIs sampled are fully fledged Islamic banks (55), followed by investment banks/asset management companies (23) and regulatory authorities (2). Malaysia represents 24 per cent of the overall sample, the UAE 16 per cent, Bahrain 15 per cent, Saudi Arabia 11 per cent, Kuwait and Qatar both 13 per cent, and the UK 8 per cent. The sample of IFIs in this study varied in terms of size and market capitalisation and this enabled the study to evaluate and measure the level of transparency and disclosure of *Shari'ah* governance practices within each individual IFI in various jurisdictions of the case countries.

The response rate of 43.8 per cent out of eighty IFIs is relatively satisfactory and significant. This is affirmed by Sekaran (2003: 237), who considers that a response rate of 30 per cent is acceptable. The survey was launched on 1 April 2009 and ended on 1 June 2009 and the timeline for the survey was extended to 30 December 2009 due to the small response rate. In view of the difficulties in getting responses from the industry players and practitioners due to some inherent factors, the feedback of thirty-five IFIs

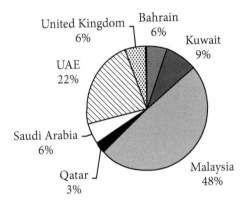

Figure 5.2 *The response rate*

from Malaysia, GCC countries and the UK is considered significant and acceptable for this research.[1] Figure 5.2 illustrates the percentage of the response rate according to the case countries.

5.2 Searching the particularities of *Shari'ah* governance in Islamic banking

5.2.1 Shari'ah *board members*

It is clear from the survey that most of the *Shari'ah* boards in IFIs meet the minimum requirement of the AAOIFI governance standards and IFSB-10 as a majority of them consist of three board members (40%); 22.8 per cent of *Shari'ah* boards comprise four members, 17.1 per cent five members, 5.8 per cent six members, 5.8 per cent ten members, and only 2.9 per cent of IFIs engaged only one or two *Shari'ah* scholars. In Malaysia, the *Shari'ah* board of the BNM and the SC consists of ten members, while the trend at individual-IFI level shows that having three members is the most preferable practice. Significant numbers of *Shari'ah* board members of the BNM and the SC indicate their functional roles and position as being the highest *Shari'ah* authority. On the other hand, in GCC countries, practice shows that there are significant variations in the number of *Shari'ah* board members in IFIs, where the majority of them prefer three or five members. This is similar to the practice of IFIs in the UK, where it was found that their *Shari'ah* boards consist of three or four members.

With regard to female *Shari'ah* board members, only six out of thirty-five IFIs (17.1%) have female board members and all of them are from Malaysia. This indicates that the boardrooms in GCC countries and the UK are still male territory. This book presumes that the issue of the shortage of *Shari'ah* scholars specialised and experienced in Islamic finance and *muāmalāt* may be overcome by liberalising the practice of accepting female *Shari'ah* scholars as *Shari'ah* board members as is the case in Malaysia.

5.2.2 Shari'ah *governance approach*

This section attempts to examine the different approaches of IFIs to *Shari'ah* governance. The majority of IFIs (54.3%) did not adopt the AAOIFI governance standards and some of them (22.9%) were even unaware of the existence of IFSB-10. A total of 57.1 per cent of IFIs claimed that there are *Shari'ah* governance standards set for *Shari'ah* governance at the national level; 68.5 per cent of IFIs showed good commitment to *Shari'ah* governance by having a standard process for *Shari'ah* compliance, audit and review; and 60 per cent of IFIs provided guidelines on *Shari'ah* governance. In general, 71.4 per cent of IFIs indicated that they have a professional code of ethics for their *Shari'ah* board; this demonstrates that 28.6 per cent of IFIs' *Shari'ah* boards are not guided by a code of ethics. More than 85 per cent of IFIs had established their own internal *Shari'ah* board, while

2.8 per cent appointed a *Shari'ah* advisory firm for advisory services and 11.4 per cent had both an internal *Shari'ah* board and used a *Shari'ah* advisory firm. Investment banks preferred to engage a *Shari'ah* advisory firm rather than to have their own *Shari'ah* board.

As a general observation, Malaysia presents a slightly better general framework of *Shari'ah* governance by scoring higher in every question asked as compared to GCC countries and the UK. An interesting observation is that, despite having less interference from regulatory authorities than Malaysia, IFIs in GCC countries and the UK proactively developed their own *Shari'ah* governance framework. In fact, the majority of IFIs in GCC countries have developed their own *Shari'ah* guidelines and standard processes on *Shari'ah* compliance. Although some GCC countries clearly stated in their regulations the adoption of the AAOIFI governance standards, it was found that only 22.8 per cent had implemented them. In spite of the absence of any provision on the AAOIFI governance standards, 22.8 per cent of IFIs in Malaysia had indicated the adoption of the standards based on voluntary practices.

5.2.3 Shari'ah *governance and regulation*

Chapter 4 provides a comprehensive overview of the regulatory framework of *Shari'ah* governance where it classifies Malaysia as the proponent of a 'regulatory-based approach', Saudi Arabia as a 'passive approach', Qatar, the UAE, Kuwait and Bahrain as a 'minimalist approach', and the UK as a 'reactive approach'. This section, hence, tries to explore the general understanding and perception of IFIs of the regulatory and internal framework of *Shari'ah* governance.

Only 37.1 per cent of IFIs indicated that there were separate rules and regulations concerning *Shari'ah* governance. This figure shows that Malaysia is a strong proponent of the regulatory-based approach to a *Shari'ah* governance system while GCC countries prefer less regulator interference. In terms of internal policies or by-laws on the affairs of the *Shari'ah* board, 57.1 per cent of IFIs indicated that they have written policies on it. With regard to jurisdictions on Islamic finance, almost all IFIs (91.4%) indicated that the civil court has jurisdiction pertaining to cases on Islamic finance, 14.2 per cent of IFIs refer cases to the *Shari'ah* court, 51.4 per cent of IFIs to arbitration, and 20 per cent of IFIs to a *Shari'ah* authority such as the central bank or Ministry of *Awqaf.*

All countries put Islamic finance cases under the civil court's jurisdiction and this may lead to some legal and *Shari'ah* issues. While acknowledging this important issue, only a few countries provided other alternative legal avenues, such as arbitration or a national *Shari'ah* board as the highest *Shari'ah* authority. Another important aspect of regulation is the legal status of *Shari'ah* rulings; it was found that almost all IFIs (94.2%) indicated that *Shari'ah* rulings are binding upon them and only 5.7 per cent of IFIs view them as non-binding. It is clear from the findings that IFIs are generally bound by the rulings or pronouncements of their *Shari'ah* board.

5.2.4 Role of Shari'ah board

The ideal roles of the *Shari'ah* board involve *ex ante* and *ex post* aspects of *Shari'ah* governance and these include *Shari'ah* pronouncements, supervision and review. The survey attempts to clarify the actual functions of the *Shari'ah* board in various IFIs in the case countries. The survey illustrates that IFIs had different perspectives on the roles and responsibilities of the *Shari'ah* board.

Around 77.1 per cent of IFIs considered the *Shari'ah* board as advisory, 51.4 per cent as supervisory and, interestingly, 2.8 per cent of IFIs viewed them as having executive power.

The majority of IFIs considered their *Shari'ah* board to have advisory and supervisory powers in which they had responsibility to undertake *ex ante* and *ex post* responsibilities. With respect to advisory functions, all IFIs agreed that the *Shari'ah* board plays a role in issuing *Shari'ah* pronouncements and the declaration of *Shari'ah* compliance. On the other hand, there are different views from IFIs concerning the supervisory function of the *Shari'ah* board, where more than 21 per cent of IFIs asserted that the *Shari'ah* board does not have *Shari'ah* review responsibility and does not oversee the computation of *zakah* payments.[2]

The survey also found an inconsistency in the responses pertaining to *Shari'ah* review or audit. While most *Shari'ah* boards had the function of conducting the *Shari'ah* audit, only 34.2 per cent of IFIs indicated that their *Shari'ah* board undertook *Shari'ah* audit responsibilities. In the event that the *Shari'ah* board did not undertake the *Shari'ah* review task, 74.2 per cent of IFIs granted authority to the *Shari'ah* board to delegate its function of *Shari'ah* review to the internal *Shari'ah* compliance unit. This position demonstrates that numerous *Shari'ah* boards do not conduct *Shari'ah* reviews as they are only concerned with the *ex ante* aspects of *Shari'ah* governance. We can see from this finding that there are shortcomings in the existing practices of *Shari'ah* governance, particularly with regards the clear mandate and authority of the *Shari'ah* board's functions and responsibilities.

5.2.5 *Attributes of* Shari'ah *board members*

5.2.5.1 Appointment criteria for *Shari'ah* board membership

IFIs in the various jurisdictions adopt different processes and fit and proper criteria for *Shari'ah* board members.

This section specifically demonstrates the appointment criteria of the *Shari'ah* board as a mechanism to ensure the competence of the IFIs in the case countries.

Most IFIs (77.1%) indicated that they have clear internal fit and proper criteria to access the competence of *Shari'ah* board members prior to their appointment. These criteria nevertheless vary from one IFI to another. More than 77 per cent of IFIs have the criteria of academic qualification, 74.2 per cent of experience and exposure, and 60 per cent of track record and good character. In terms of academic qualification, IFIs were more concerned with the requirement pertaining to knowledge of *muāmalāt* (74.2%) and Islamic jurisprudence (71.4%). Meanwhile, in the aspect of experience and exposure, they preferred the candidates who have good understanding of *Shari'ah* rules and principles (80%) as well as understanding the impact of *Shari'ah* pronouncements (77.1%). Generally, IFIs agreed that they are also concerned with the requirement of track record, particularly good character (74.2%) and soundness of judgment (71.4%).

While acknowledging the need for expert, experienced and well-known scholars to be part of the *Shari'ah* board, only 51.4 per cent of IFIs provided professional training, especially in the matters of finance and banking, to their *Shari'ah* board. Moreover, more than 42.9 per cent of IFIs do not evaluate or assess the performance of the *Shari'ah* board. This figure illustrates that significant numbers of IFIs do not assess the *Shari'ah* board's contribution and performance, even in the event of renewal of their contracts.

The issue of lack of training and exposure on the part of *Shari'ah* board members has already been highlighted a number of years ago. An earlier study on Islamic banking practices revealed that the majority of *Shari'ah* board members did not have proper training in or exposure to technical aspects of banking and finance; it was found that the majority of *Shari'ah* board members had qualifications in *Shari'ah*, only 8.6 per cent were well-versed in *Shari'ah* and commercial law, and only 11.4 per cent had expertise in *Shari'ah*, law and economics (Bakar 2002: 78). Another earlier study also found that more than 40 per cent of forty-one *Shari'ah* board members had had no exposure to or proper training in banking and finance (Aboumouamer 1989: 226). The findings in this recent study further indicate that improving the competence of *Shari'ah* board members needs serious attention from regulators, supervisors and IFIs. For this purpose, there must be significant effort and continuous endeavour to develop programmes and training for *Shari'ah* boards as well as allocation of funds to produce talented and knowledgeable *Shari'ah* scholars.

5.2.5.2 Independence
There are various ways of ensuring the professional independence of the *Shari'ah* board. The survey identifies four important elements of independence, namely method of appointment, remuneration, *Shari'ah* board mandate and means of mitigating potential conflict of interest.

Despite the AAOIFI governance standards' requirement of appointments being made by the general assembly, more than 74 per cent of the appointments were made by the BOD and only 40 per cent by the shareholders.[3] With regard to the *Shari'ah* board at the national level, the appointments were made by the government in Malaysia. Only 2.7 per cent of IFIs appointed *Shari'ah* board members through its nomination committee. The survey finds inconsistency in the actual practice of appointment of *Shari'ah* board members and the IFIs' perception as to who the *Shari'ah* board should be accountable to. On this point, 51.4 per cent of IFIs thought that the *Shari'ah* board should be accountable to shareholders and 57.1 per cent to the BOD, although the actual practice showed that 74 per cent of the appointments were made by the BOD and 40 per cent by the shareholders. The survey reveals that the majority of IFIs grant authority to the BOD (60%) to determine the *Shari'ah* board's remuneration, whilst a minority of IFIs (5.7% and 2.8% respectively) indicated that the government or the national *Shari'ah* board could exercise such powers.

Although most IFIs acknowledged a potential conflict of interest in the event of *Shari'ah* board members holding numerous positions in various institutions, more than 50 per cent of IFIs do not have a mechanism to mitigate such potential conflict. The survey demonstrates that multiple appointments are a common occurrence in IFIs in GCC countries and this may raise concerns for *Shari'ah* scholars in the aspects of conflict of interest and maintaining confidentiality. In order to manage this kind of potential conflict, 34.2 per cent of IFIs claimed that they would not appoint *Shari'ah* board members who hold numerous board positions, and 48.5 per cent of IFIs made open disclosures on the *Shari'ah* board's composition to the public and made declarations in writing.

Most *Shari'ah* board members served IFIs on a contractual or part-time basis and only 20 per cent of IFIs' *Shari'ah* board members were permanent employees. This position seems to contradict the AAOIFI governance standards, which restrict the appointment of *Shari'ah* board members who work in the same institution. With regard to mandate, more than 37.2 per cent of IFIs did not specify the authority in the letter of appointment and more than 80 per cent of IFIs did not specify it in the articles or memorandum of association. This figure illustrates that there are uncertainties about the actual authority and mandate of the *Shari'ah* board on the part of *Shari'ah* scholars, employees, management, BOD, shareholders and even the public at large.

5.2.5.3 Transparency and confidentiality

The existing literature indicates that *Shari'ah* governance practices in IFIs are less than transparent. The survey attempts to explore the mechanism used by IFIs to ensure transparency and to observe confidentiality on the part of their *Shari'ah* board. The survey included one question on the aspect of confidentiality and three questions on transparency: a written policy on preparation and dissemination of *Shari'ah* information, right to access to all documents and necessary information, and publication of *Shari'ah* rulings.

Surprisingly, more than 49 per cent of IFIs do not have a written policy on preparation and dissemination of *Shari'ah* information. In addition, not all IFIs (80%) grant authority to the *Shari'ah* board to have access to all documents, information and records for the purpose of *Shari'ah* compliance. This is a serious issue, since the *Shari'ah* board is expected to endorse a declaration of *Shari'ah* compliance in the annual report. This position may disrupt the effectiveness of the *Shari'ah* review and its impact is likely to be of material significance to IFIs, particularly with respect to the *Shari'ah* compliance process.

Moreover, more than 68 per cent of IFIs do not publish *Shari'ah* pronouncements, which are of the essence to all organs of governance, customers, depositors and the public. These overall responses demonstrate that IFIs are less than transparent. In the aspect of confidentiality, 74.2 per cent of IFIs indicated that the *Shari'ah* board is fully aware of its fiduciary duty to observe confidentiality and to handle any sensitive information professionally. In spite of this positive finding, it was nevertheless found that more than 25 per cent of IFIs were of the view that their *Shari'ah* board was not aware of such confidentiality issues.

5.2.6 *Operational procedures*

Different IFIs adopt different processes and procedures with respect to the *Shari'ah* compliance process. The survey attempted to discover the state of operational procedures in the context of *Shari'ah* governance practices, particularly standard operational procedures, *Shari'ah* board meetings, the quorum, basis of decisions, voting rights, preparation and dissemination of documents to the *Shari'ah* board, the *Shari'ah* report and its content, and the institutional arrangement for *Shari'ah* review.

The majority of IFIs (54.2%) have standard operational procedures for *Shari'ah* governance; 5.7 per cent of IFIs conduct weekly *Shari'ah* board meetings, 37.1 per cent monthly, 22.8 per cent quarterly, 2.8 per cent twice a month, 2.8 per cent every two months, 14.2 per cent on an ad hoc basis, and 5.7 per cent biannually. Most *Shari'ah* board decisions are made by consensus (45.7%) and 31.4 per cent by simple majority. In the event of a *Shari'ah* board including non-*Shari'ah*-background members, only 20 per cent of IFIs viewed that they should have a voting right in decision-making. The majority of IFIs agreed that those members should not be granted such voting rights.

With regard to *Shari'ah* coordination, the majority of IFIs (74.2%) appointed their internal *Shari'ah* officer to deal with and handle *Shari'ah* governance matters and this includes *Shari'ah* board meetings. Some IFIs employed their company secretary, head of product development, head of the legal department, an officer in the Islamic capital market department or an outsource company to coordinate *Shari'ah* governance-related matters. This position indicates that most IFIs have a proper internal arrangement for *Shari'ah* coordination.

Interestingly, 5.7 per cent of IFIs submit the agenda and documents to the *Shari'ah* board a month in advance and all of them are from GCC countries, while most IFIs (54.2%) do the same thing a week in advance. The *Shari'ah* board meetings are attended by various parties including the executive director, CEO, managing director, board's risk committee, internal auditor and legal advisor. The majority of IFIs (77.1%) indicated that the normal attendees of the *Shari'ah* meeting include the respresentative of the internal *Shari'ah* compliance unit.

According to the survey, 68.5 per cent of IFIs confirmed that the *Shari'ah* board is required to submit a *Shari'ah* report, but the survey also indicated that more than 31 per cent of IFIs do not issue a *Shari'ah* report.[4] With respect to the contents of the report, most IFIs (68.5%) just publish a declaration of *Shari'ah* compliance rather than details of *Shari'ah* compliance activities. This illustrates poor disclosure on the part of IFIs of *Shari'ah*-related information. In spite of the *Shari'ah* report, it is also found that more than 25 per cent of IFIs do not review the *Shari'ah* board pronouncements.

In terms of the *Shari'ah* compliance review, 80 per cent of IFIs set up an independent department, 25.7 per cent delegate the function to the existing internal audit department and 2.8 per cent to an outsource company.[5] A sound *Shari'ah* internal audit mechanism is a tool to deter malpractice and to mitigate *Shari'ah* non-compliance risk. Realising this, most IFIs have set up an independent internal *Shari'ah* review department to conduct a *Shari'ah* compliance review, which is commendable and in line with the best practice of *Shari'ah* governance.

Despite the regulatory requirement to submit a *Shari'ah* report in Malaysia, only 37.1 per cent of IFIs indicated that their *Shari'ah* board is required to submit a *Shari'ah* report. Even in the absence of such a regulatory requirement, 25.7 per cent of IFIs in GCC countries and 2.8 per cent in the

UK indicated that the *Shari'ah* report is part of their internal requirement. In terms of the content of the *Shari'ah* report, 17.1 per cent of IFIs in Malaysia indicated that the *Shari'ah* report contains information on the duties and services of the *Shari'ah* board, 25.7 per cent on *Shari'ah* pronouncements, 17.1 per cent on *Shari'ah* board activities and 37.1 per cent on a declaration of *Shari'ah* compliance. A similar situation is apparent in the case of GCC countries and the UK, by which a majority of IFIs indicated that the content of the *Shari'ah* report is just a declaration of *Shari'ah* compliance.

5.2.7 Assessments of the Shari'ah board

There have been numerous critisms and negative allegations about the roles and functions of the *Shari'ah* board. The problem with all sorts of criticism is that such allegations have not been proven or supported by any empirical evidence or reliable data. The survey included five questions to specifically address this important issue. These questions consist of a general assessment by IFIs of their *Shari'ah* board in terms of organisational accountability, communication with other organs of governance, ability to identify and evaluate *Shari'ah* non-compliance risk, contribution to promotion of Islamic ethics and values, as well as *Shari'ah* control processes.

Regardless of the numerous criticisms of *Shari'ah* boards, the overall responses demonstrate that most IFIs are satisfied with the performance of their *Shari'ah* board. Only 2.8 per cent of IFIs thought that the *Shari'ah* board had failed to identify and evaluate *Shari'ah* compliance risk and to promote continuous improvement of *Shari'ah* control processes and 5.7 per cent had neglected the duty to promote Islamic values and ethics. With understanding that the responses might be biased on the part of IFIs since they engage advisory services from the *Shari'ah* board, the findings on the failure of *Shari'ah* boards to identify and evaluate *Shari'ah* non-compliance risk and to promote Islamic ethics and values is considered slightly significant.

5.3 *Shari'ah* governance index

The survey reveals that significant numbers of IFIs in Malaysia, GCC countries and the UK do not have an adequate framework of the best or ideal *Shari'ah* governance practices as laid down by the AAOIFI governance standards and IFSB-10. Based on the findings from the survey, this book summarises the state of the overall *Shari'ah* governance practices in the case countries by classifying them into five different levels of practice: 'underdeveloped practice', 'emerging practice', 'improved practice', 'good practice' and 'best practice'.

For the purpose of clarity, this book illustrates the extent of the implementation of *Shari'ah* governance in IFIs by constructing specific *Shari'ah* governance indicators using a scoring method. These indicators allow this book to quantify and rank the IFIs according to their *Shari'ah* governance scores. This book has generated fifty key principles for best *Shari'ah* governance practices which are divided into six sections: approach to *Shari'ah* governance (seven indicators); regulation and internal framework of *Shari'ah* governance (four indicators); roles of *Shari'ah* board (five indicators); attributes of *Shari'ah* board with respect to competence (eight indicators), independence (five indicators), transparency and confidentiality (four indicators); operational procedures (twelve indicators); and assessment of *Shari'ah* board (five indicators). These fifty indicators represent the key principles of best practice of *Shari'ah* governance as promoted in the AAOIFI governance standards and IFSB-10, including the existing literature pertaining to *Shari'ah* governance. The overall key principles of best *Shari'ah* governance practices are summarised in Table 5.2.

Based on the fifty formulated key principles of *Shari'ah* governance in Table 5.2, this book ranks IFIs into five levels of *Shari'ah* governance practice. IFIs that score 1–15 key principles of *Shari'ah* governance are ranked as 'under-developed practice', 16–25 as 'emerging practice', 26–35 as 'improved practice', 36–45 as 'good practice' and 46–50 as 'best practice'. This classification will provide a clear illustration of the extent of *Shari'ah* governance implementation as practised by IFIs in the case countries. The ranking process and scoring method used in this book is further explained in Table 5.3.

5.3.1 *The overall score of* Shari'ah *governance*

This book illustrates the overall scores of *Shari'ah* governance in Malaysia, GCC countries and the UK in Figure 5.3. This illustration provides an overview of the extent of *Shari'ah* governance practices in IFIs.

Figure 5.3 demonstrates that the average *Shari'ah* governance score is 30.1 best indicators. The majority of IFIs (40%) fall into the 'improved practice' category, with an average of 32.9 best indicators. Meanwhile 8.6 per cent of IFIs fall into the 'emerging practice' category and 17.1 per cent into 'underdeveloped practice'. This finding indicates that a significant number of IFIs (more than 25%) scored less than 25 of the best indicators of *Shari'ah* governance, indicating very weak practice, and 40 per cent of IFIs show some positive improvements. The survey reveals that only 34.2 per cent of IFIs fall into the 'good practice' category and none of the IFIs were categorised as 'best practice'. This position indicates that only a minority of IFIs are categorised as having

Table 5.2 Shari‘ah *governance indicators*

Key principles of *Shari‘ah governance*	Indicators
Approach to *Shari‘ah* governance	7
P1. IFIs that adopt the AAOIFI governance standards.	
P2. IFIs that are sensitively aware of the development of *Shari‘ah* governance such as IFSB-10.	
P3. IFIs that have standards or guidelines for *Shari‘ah* governance.	
P4. IFIs that develop standard processes for *Shari‘ah* compliance, audit and review of the *Shari‘ah* board's legal rulings.	
P5. IFIs that have a professional code of ethics for the *Shari‘ah* board.	
P6. IFIs that have an internal *Shari‘ah* board.	
P7. IFIs that have at least three *Shari‘ah* board members.	
Regulatory and internal framework of *Shari‘ah* governance	4
P8. IFIs that have specific rules and policies concerning *Shari‘ah* governance.	
P9. IFIs that have written policies or by-laws specifically referring to the conduct of the *Shari‘ah* board.	
P10. IFIs that have good understanding of types of dispute settlement to redress legal matters concerning Islamic finance.	
P11. IFIs that have good understanding of the legal position of the *Shari‘ah* board's rulings.	
Roles of *Shari‘ah* board	5
P12. IFIs that provide clear advisory and supervisory authority to their *Shari‘ah* board.	
P13. IFIs whose *Shari‘ah* board performs *ex ante* and *ex post Shari‘ah* governance processes.	
P14. IFIs that grant authority to the *Shari‘ah* board to oversee the payment and computation of *zakah*.	

Table 5.2 (*continued*)

Key principles of *Shari'ah governance*	Indicators

P15. IFIs whose *Shari'ah* board performs the *Shari'ah* audit function.

P16. IFIs that delegate *Shari'ah* review functions to the internal *Shari'ah* compliance unit to assist the *Shari'ah* board.

Attributes of *Shari'ah* board (competence)   8

P17. IFIs that have policies on the fit and proper criteria for the members of the *Shari'ah* board.

P18. IFIs that put conditions of academic qualification, experience and track record on their *Shari'ah* board members.

P19. IFIs that put requirements of being specialised in *muāmalāt*, Islamic jurisprudence and knowledge of Arabic and English in terms of academic qualifications on their *Shari'ah* board members.

P20. IFIs that put requirements on their *Shari'ah* board members of understanding of *Shari'ah* and general banking law as well as the impact of *Shari'ah* rulings in terms of experience and exposure.

P21. IFIs that put requirements of good character and competence and diligence in terms of track record.

P22. IFIs that allow non-*Shari'ah*-background individuals as members of the *Shari'ah* board who are well-versed in law, economy and finance.

P23. IFIs that organise adequate training for the *Shari'ah* board.

P24. IFIs that have proper assessment of the *Shari'ah* board.

Attributes of *Shari'ah* board (independence)   5

P25. IFIs that appoint the *Shari'ah* board through their shareholders.

P26. IFIs that appoint the *Shari'ah* board on a contractual basis.

Table 5.2 *(continued)*

Key principles of *Shari'ah governance*	Indicators

P27. IFIs that determine the *Shari'ah* board's remuneration through the BOD but subject to the approval of shareholders.

P28. IFIs that have a mechanism in place to mitigate conflict of interest in relation to *Shari'ah* scholars sitting on various boards.

P29. IFIs that clearly provide full mandate and authority to the *Shari'ah* board.

Attributes of *Shari'ah* board (transparency and confidentiality)   4

P30. IFIs that have a written policy in respect to the preparation and dissemination of *Shari'ah* information.

P31. IFIs that grant full authority to *Shari'ah* board to have access to all documents, information and records.

P32. IFIs that publish the *Shari'ah* pronouncements and ensure they are available to the public.

P33. IFIs that ensure their *Shari'ah* board is fully aware of the issue of confidentiality and sensitive information obtained in the course of performing their duties.

Operational procedures   12

P34. IFIs that have standard operational procedures for their *Shari'ah* board.

P35. IFIs that hold a *Shari'ah* board meeting at least once a month.

P36. IFIs that have a requirement of at least three as their quorum for the *Shari'ah* board meeting.

P37. IFIs that have a requirement of a simple majority as a basis for the decisions of *Shari'ah* board meetings.

P38. IFIs that do not grant voting rights to non-*Shari'ah*-background members of the *Shari'ah* board.

Table 5.2 *(continued)*

Key principles of *Shariʿah governance*	Indicators
P39. IFIs that ensure their agenda is prepared and distributed at least a week in advance of *Shariʿah* board meetings.	
P40. IFIs that set up a *Shariʿah* department/unit/ division to coordinate the *Shariʿah* governance process.	
P41. IFIs that require the attendance of management or directors in the *Shariʿah* board meeting.	
P42. IFIs that require their *Shariʿah* board to review the previous rulings.	
P43. IFIs that have a mandatory requirement for a *Shariʿah* report.	
P44. IFIs that detail the contents of the *Shariʿah* report to include information on duties and activities, *Shariʿah* pronouncements and a declaration of *Shariʿah* compliance.	
P45. IFIs that set up independent organisational arrangements for the internal *Shariʿah* audit.	
Assessment of *Shariʿah* board	5
P46. IFIs whose *Shariʿah* board demonstrates effective organisational accountability.	
P47. IFIs whose *Shariʿah* board communicates effectively with other organs of governance, including the BOD, management and auditors.	
P48. IFIs whose *Shariʿah* board properly identifies and evaluates the organisation's exposure to *Shariʿah* non-compliance risk and reputational risk, and effectively communicates that risk information to appropriate bodies in the organisation.	
P49. IFIs whose *Shariʿah* board promotes Islamic ethics and values within the organisation.	
P50. IFIs whose *Shariʿah* board promotes continuous improvement of an organisation's *Shariʿah* control processes.	
Total indicators	50

Table 5.3 Shari'ah *governance scoring method*

Level of practice	Score	Explanation
Underdeveloped practice	1–15	IFIs that have a minimal score of best *Shari'ah* governance practices and need immediate reform.
Emerging practice	16–25	IFIs that have a minimal score of best *Shari'ah* governance practices but indicate positive development.
Improved practice	26–35	IFIs that have a fair score of best *Shari'ah* governance practices and indicate strong improvement.
Good practice	36–45	IFIs that have a good score of best *Shari'ah* governance practices and generally adhere to most of its key principles.
Best practice	46–50	The ideal IFIs that represent the best practice of *Shari'ah* governance.

'good practice' of *Shari'ah* governance, while the remaining majority of IFIs urgently need further enhancement and improvement to their *Shari'ah* governance frameworks and practices. On the whole, the overall scores of *Shari'ah* governance above affirm that there are gaps and shortcomings in the existing frameworks and practices of *Shari'ah* governance in IFIs, in spite of the available international guiding principles and governance standards.

5.3.2 Shari'ah *governance scores for IFIs in Malaysia, GCC countries and the UK*

The overall *Shari'ah* governance scores affirm that more than 65 per cent of IFIs were ranked in the 'improved

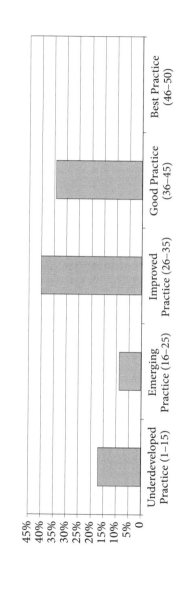

Figure 5.3 *The overall scores of Shari'ah governance*

practice', 'emerging practice' and 'underdeveloped practice' categories, while less than 35 per cent of IFIs were ranked in the 'good practice' category. This section further illustrates a comparative overview of the *Shari'ah* governance scores according to the country's specific behaviour. Figure 5.4 and Table 5.4 demonstrate the different and average *Shari'ah* governance scores for IFIs in the case countries. This comparative perspective is very useful in explaining the effectiveness of diverse *Shari'ah* governance approaches as practised by IFIs.

Figure 5.4 and Table 5.4 illustrate that there are significant differences in the state of *Shari'ah* governance practices in IFIs. Basically, IFIs in Malaysia presented a slightly better score compared to GCC countries and the UK. Most of the IFIs in Malaysia (31.4%) fall into the 'good practice' category and only 17.1 per cent into the 'improved practice' category. This finding demonstrates that the overall score of IFIs in Malaysia is relatively good, with an average of 37.1 best indicators for each IFI, which can be categorised as 'good practice'. The author presumes that the finding of good *Shari'ah* governance practice in IFIs in Malaysia is contributed to by several external and internal factors. With regard to external factors, well-conceived regulation and the proactive approach of the regulatory and supervisory authorities, such as the issuance of the BNM/GPS1, have contributed to better development of the *Shari'ah* governance system. Meanwhile, the internal factors refer to the positive initiative at the individual IFI level to facilitate the implementation of Islamic finance by emphasising the requirements of *Shari'ah* compliance. It was found that the BNM, as well as individual IFIs, have organised training for the *Shari'ah* board and practitioners and allocated a significant amount of funds to develop various programmes pertaining to *Shari'ah* governance.

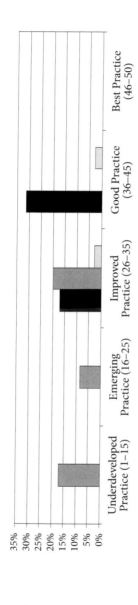

Figure 5.4 *Comparative overview of Shari'ah governance for IFIs in Malaysia, GCC countries and the UK*

Table 5.4 *The average Shari'ah governance scores*[a]

Countries	Scores					Total scores (35x50 =1750)	Average
	Underdeveloped practice	Emerging practice	Improved practice	Good practice	Best practice		
Malaysia (17 IFIs)			202	430		632	37.1
GCC Countries (16 IFIs)	62	66	227			355	22.2
UK (2 IFIs)			32	37		69	34.5
Total	62	66	461	467		1056	30.1

[a] The scores are generated from 50 indicators of *Shari'ah* governance key principles as illustrated in Table 5.2. The total scores of each IFI are 50. IFIs in Malaysia score 632 out of a possible 850 (17x50), GCC countries, 355 out of 800 (16x50) and the UK, 69 out of 100 (2x50). The 'average' is formulated as the scores divided by the number of IFIs.

Unlike Malaysia, the overall finding for IFIs in GCC countries demonstrates that they have a slightly weak *Shari'ah* governance practice with an average of 22.2 best indicators, which can be ranked as 'emerging practice'; 20 per cent of IFIs fall into the 'improved practice' category, 8.6 per cent into the 'emerging practice' category and 17.1 per cent into the 'underdeveloped practice' category. This position indicates that more than 50 per cent of IFIs in GCC countries scored less than 25 best indicators, which demonstrates very weak practice of *Shari'ah* governance. Moreover, it was found that several IFIs have failed to comply with the AAOIFI governance standards as well as the directives or guidelines of their regulatory and supervisory authorities. The author presumes that weak supervision and monitoring by the supervisory authorities as well as less initiative at individual IFI level are amongst the contributory factors that have led to these negative findings.

The author did not expect too much in terms of *Shari'ah* governance scores for IFIs in the UK as the implementation of Islamic finance is within a purely secular legal environment. The findings, on the other hand, surprisingly demonstrate that IFIs in the UK scored slightly better than GCC countries, as 2.8 per cent fall into each of the 'improved practice' and 'good practice' categories with an average of 34.5 best indicators. This phenomenon suggests that strong regulation and supervision is not the sole factor that may positively influence *Shari'ah* governance practice. In the absence of regulations and directives from the FSA, IFIs in the UK have proactively developed their own *Shari'ah* governance system that falls into the 'improved practice' category.

In view of the absence of any specific study to measure and evaluate the extent of *Shari'ah* governance practice in IFIs, this book has introduced *Shari'ah* governance indicators to rank IFIs according to their *Shari'ah* governance scores. With fifty identified key principles of best *Shari'ah* governance practices, this book evaluates and examines the state of *Shari'ah* governance practice based on the feedback from the survey. The overall findings demonstrate that more than 25 per cent of thirty-five IFIs fall into the 'underdeveloped practice' and 'emerging practice' categories, while the majority of them fall into the 'improved practice' category. Only 32.4 per cent of IFIs fall into the 'good practice' category and the majority of these are from Malaysia. In spite of some shortcomings and weaknesses of *Shari'ah* governance practices, the 40 per cent of IFIs that fall into the 'improved practice' category is a positive sign and points to a growing awareness of *Shari'ah* governance. These findings strongly indicate that there is a huge potential for improvement and enhancement on the part of IFIs to develop their *Shari'ah* governance framework.

5.3.3 Shari'ah *governance scores according to year of incorporation*

This section attempts to further demonstrate the extent of *Shari'ah* governance practices in IFIs by classifying them into four different clusters. Unlike section 5.3.2 which presented *Shari'ah* governance scores from a country-specific behaviour perspective, this section highlights the level of *Shari'ah* governance scores on the basis of the year of incorporation. In the case of Islamic windows, this book refers to the year they started offering Islamic financial products and services. The majority of IFIs established their *Shari'ah* board in the same year as their incorporation, and some of them set up their *Shari'ah* board later on, particularly when they started offering Islamic financial products and services. Table 5.5 illustrates the details of the classification.

Table 5.5 *Classification of IFIs' Shari'ah governance scores according to year of incorporation*

IFIs	Malaysia	GCC countries	UK	Total	Percentage
Cluster 1: 1975–1990	1	3		4	11.40
Cluster 2: 1991–2000	7	2		9	25.70
Cluster 3: 2000–2005	8	3		11	31.40
Cluster 4: 2006–2010	3	6	2	11	31.40

The IFIs are classified into four clusters. Cluster 1 refers to the IFIs that were established between 1975 and 1990, cluster 2 between 1991 and 2000, cluster 3 between 2000 and 2005, and cluster 4 between 2006 and 2010. There are 11.4 per cent of IFIs classified as cluster 1, 25.7 per cent as cluster 2, 31.4 per cent as cluster 3 and 31.4 per cent as cluster 4. These figures indicate that the IFIs in clusters 3 and 4 represent the majority of this book sample. Based on the above classification, this book quantifies the *Shari'ah* governance scores and ranks them into 'underdeveloped practice', 'emerging practice', 'improved practice', 'good practice' and 'best practice' categories, as explained in Table 5.3. Details of the findings are illustrated in Figure 5.5.

It is clear from Figure 5.5 that there are significant differences between the *Shari'ah* governance practices in IFIs. IFIs in clusters 2 and 3 have better *Shari'ah* governance scores compared to their counterparts in clusters 1 and 4. The majority of IFIs (40%) fall into the 'improved practice' category, while a minority of them fall into the 'emerging practice' (8.6%) and 'underdeveloped practice' (17.1%) categories. A total of 14.2 per cent of IFIs in cluster 2 fall

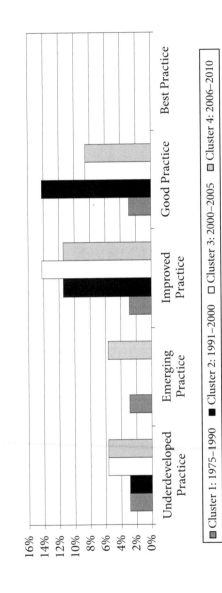

Figure 5.5 Shari'ah governance scores according to cluster

Cluster 1: 1975–1990 ■ Cluster 2: 1991–2000 □ Cluster 3: 2000–2005 ▨ Cluster 4: 2006–2010

into the 'good practice' category, while the majority of IFIs (14.2%) in cluster 3 fall into the 'improved practice' category. IFIs in cluster 1 show slightly lower *Shari'ah* governance scores, with most of them falling into the 'improved practice', 'emerging practice' and 'underdeveloped practice' categories. IFIs in cluster 4 indicated positive improvement in *Shari'ah* governance matters, where a significant percentage of 11.4 per cent are ranked as being in the 'improved practice' category.

The above figures demonstrate interesting findings which are contrary to this book's expectations that IFIs in cluster 1 will have better *Shari'ah* governance scores than IFIs in clusters 3 and 4. IFIs in cluster 1, which are considered pioneers in Islamic finance, indicated weak *Shari'ah* governance practices. The majority of them are ranked in the 'emerging practice' and 'underdeveloped practice' categories. On the other hand, IFIs in cluster 4, which are considered new to the Islamic finance industry, show positive improvement and slightly better *Shari'ah* governance practices than the IFIs in cluster 1. These results affirm that the early establishment of IFIs is not the determining factor for the extent and quality of *Shari'ah* governance practices. The level of *Shari'ah* governance practices is much more influenced by external and internal factors, where the former refers to the regulatory framework and commitment by the regulatory and supervisory authorities and the latter concerns well-conceived by-laws and internal policies on *Shari'ah* governance, as well as voluntary initiatives by the IFIs themselves.

5.4 Conclusion

In view of the lack of available data and information on *Shari'ah* governance practices in IFIs, this book employed the survey research method to investigate and examine the extent of *Shari'ah* governance practices in Malaysia, GCC countries and the UK. The survey responses affirm that IFIs in the case countries have different and diverse *Shari'ah* governance practices and further acknowledge that there are shortcomings and weaknesses to the present governance framework.

To sum up, the *Shari'ah* governance scores of the thirty-five IFIs in the case countries demonstrate that more than 65 per cent of them require significant enhancement and improvement as they are ranked in the 'improved practice', 'emerging practice' and 'underdeveloped practice' categories. With a small percentage of 35 per cent of IFIs falling into the 'good practice' category with an average of 30.2 best indicators, this book concludes that, overall, *Shari'ah* governance practices are still in the development stage and need immediate attention by policymakers and regulatory authorities as well as the internal organs of governance in the IFIs, such as shareholders, the BOD and senior management. The need for the above enhancement of *Shari'ah* governance practice is crucial as it would then strengthen the performance and credibility of IFIs. In this regard, regulatory authorities should take the initiative to establish *Shari'ah* governance standards or to adopt the existing *Shari'ah* governance guidelines for IFIs. In the meantime, IFIs should initiate efforts to create well-conceived by-laws for their *Shari'ah* governance system. A sound *Shari'ah* governance practice would enhance the potential role of Islamic finance in contributing towards corporate reform and mitigating certain types of risk exclusive to IFIs.

Notes

1. This is affirmed by other surveys such as Chapra and Ahmed (2002), where the response rate of the study was only

23.3% (fourteen IFIs out of sixty). A study conducted by Aboumouamer (1989) demonstrated a very minimal response rate where only fifteen IFIs from twenty different countries participated in the survey. In addition, only sixty-nine IFIs from eleven countries responded to the IFSB survey on *Shari'ah boards* of institutions offering Islamic financial services across jurisdictions, despite getting special assistance from the IFSB's full members from fifteen countries (IFSB 2008b).

2. This finding significantly shows the different practices of IFIs in late 1980s. A study conducted by Aboumouamer (1989: 285–8) demonstrates that the majority of *Shari'ah* boards performed *Shari'ah* audit functions, where 78% of the *Shari'ah* board members carried out the pre-audit function, 80.5% the audit work and 6% the post-audit function.

3. Earlier findings in a study carried out by the International Institute of Islamic Thought in 1996 also indicated the same thing, where 80% of the appointments of the *Shari'ah* board were made by the BOD and a survey by Hasan in the same year also discovered that only 39% were made by the shareholders (Bakar 2002: 78).

4. This finding demonstrates a negative indication of IFIs' commitment to *Shari'ah* governance, particularly the preparation of the *Shari'ah* report. Two earlier studies show weak practice with regards the *Shari'ah* report. Maali *et al.* (2006: 285) revealed that 72% of twenty-five IFIs provide the report of the *Shari'ah* board and a survey conducted by Grais and Pellegrini (2006a: 34) found that 30.8% of thirteen IFIs failed to issue a *Shari'ah* report. The findings of the recent survey in this book indicate that there has been no major improvement in *Shari'ah* report practice of IFIs.

5. This is affirmed by the IFSB survey, which showed that more than 90% of sixty-nine IFIs undertook a *Shari'ah* compliance review (IFSB 2008b: 27). This position indicates a positive development in *Shari'ah* governance in IFIs.

CHAPTER 6
SHARI'AH GOVERNANCE DISCLOSURE IN ISLAMIC BANKS

6.0 Introduction

Shari'ah governance favours accurate and true disclosure and transparency as a prerequisite to accountability. The fundamental concept of governance in *Shari'ah* is account-ability and hence it requires IFIs to make true disclosures and to provide accurate and necessary information to all stakeholders. This is in line with the spirit of *al Qur'an* as mentioned in *Surah al Baqarah* verse 282 about the importance of recording and putting in writing any busi-ness dealing and transaction in a very transparent way. In the context of *Shari'ah* governance, Islam promotes greater transparency in *Shari'ah*-related information in order to foster accountability and to strengthen the cred-ibility of IFIs. This chapter is basically aimed at examining the level of disclosure and transparency of *Shari'ah* gov-ernance in IFIs. This is in line with IFSB-4 that provides guidelines for greater disclosure and transparency for IFIs (IFSB 2007b).

6.1 The state of *Shari'ah* governance disclosure practices

The analyses in this chapter are divided into macro- and microperspectives. The macroanalysis provides a general overview of the overall scores for *Shari'ah* governance disclosure and transparency by ranking them into five categories. Meanwhile, the microanalysis illustrates the extent of disclosure and transparency in each of the thirty disclosure indicators, which are divided into six main sections. A sound and good *Shari'ah* governance framework should assure that timely and accurate disclosure is made on all matters regarding *Shari'ah* compliance. Both macro- and microanalyses demonstrate the level of transparency of *Shari'ah* governance in IFIs by looking at the aggregate and country-specific behavioural responses.

6.1.1 *Macroanalysis*

This book attempts to rank IFIs in accordance with the level of disclosure of *Shari'ah* governance practice. For this purpose, this book employs multiple indicator measures to measure the level of transparency of IFIs. There are thirty identified disclosure indicators of best practice of *Shari'ah* governance which are divided into six sections: commitment to good *Shari'ah* governance, *Shari'ah* board information, *Shari'ah* report, *Shari'ah* pronouncements, *Shari'ah* review, and products and services information. This book indicates that these thirty indicators represent the best practice of disclosure for *Shari'ah* governance-related information. The indicators are also able to adequately provide a measure of quantitative and qualitative aspects of *Shari'ah* governance disclosure and transparency in IFIs. Table 6.1 illustrates the overall indicators of *Shari'ah* governance disclosure practices.

Table 6.1 *Disclosure indicators*

Disclosure indicators	Number of indicators
Disclosure of commitment to *Shari'ah* **governance**	3
D1. The existence of guidelines/charter on *Shari'ah* governance	
D2. The existence of fit and proper criteria for the *Shari'ah* board	
D3. Statement of *Shari'ah* compliance	
Disclosure of *Shari'ah* **board information**	15
D4. Method of appointment	
D5. Organisation chart of *Shari'ah* board structure on the website	
D6. The list of *Shari'ah* board members (names)	
D7. Details about *Shari'ah* board members other than name and title	
D8. Details about other employment and position	
D9. When each *Shari'ah* board member joined the board	
D10. A named chairman of *Shari'ah* board listed	
D11. Details about the chairman, other than name and title	
D12. Details about role of the *Shari'ah* board	
D13. *Shari'ah* board performs the *Shari'ah* review	
D14. Board size is no fewer than three	
D15. *Shari'ah* board members sit on more than three other IFIs	
D16. Attendance record of *Shari'ah* board meetings	
D17. Board meets more than four times a year	
D18. Tenure of appointment	
Disclosure of *Shari'ah* **board remuneration**	2
D19. Who determines the *Shari'ah* board's remuneration	
D20. The specifics of the *Shari'ah* board's pay	

Table 6.1 (*continued*)

Disclosure indicators	Number of indicators
Disclosure of *Shari'ah* report	4
D21. *Shari'ah* report published in the annual report	
D22. Information on duties and services	
D23. *Shari'ah* board activities	
D24. Declaration of *Shari'ah* compliance	
Disclosure of *Shari'ah* pronouncements	3
D25. *Shari'ah* pronouncements are made known to the public via website, etc.	
D26. *Shari'ah* resolution only	
D27. *Shari'ah* resolution with detailed *Shari'ah* explanation	
Disclosure of *Shari'ah* compliance review	1
D28. IFIs undertake *Shari'ah* review	
Disclosure of information on products and services	2
D29. List of *Shari'ah*-compliant products and services	
D30. *Shari'ah* concepts and principles of products and services	
Total indicators	**30**

The disclosure indicators in Table 6.1 enable this book to classify the IFIs into five categories of *Shari'ah* governance disclosure practices: 'underdeveloped practice', 'emerging practice', 'improved practice', 'good practice' and 'best practice'. As an explanation to the scoring methodology used in this chapter, Table 6.2 specifically elaborates the description of these five categories.

As a general rule, IFIs that have more transparent disclosure practices are more highly regarded and valued

Table 6.2 Shari'ah *governance disclosure scoring method*

Level of practice	Score	Explanation
Underdeveloped practice	1–5	IFIs that have a very minimal score of Shari'ah governance disclosure and need immediate reform
Emerging practice	6–10	IFIs that have a minimal score of Shari'ah governance disclosure but indicate positive development
Improved practice	11–15	IFIs that have a fair score of Shari'ah governance disclosure and indicate strong improvement
Good practice	16–23	IFIs that have a good score of Shari'ah governance disclosure and generally adhere to key elements of good disclosure practice
Best practice	24–30	The ideal IFIs that represent the best practice of Shari'ah governance disclosure

not only by investors but also by the public at large. IFIs that score 24–30 disclosure indicators are ranked as a 'best practice' and represent the ideal and best practice of Shari'ah governance disclosure. IFIs that fall into the 'good practice' category indicate a good score of Shari'ah governance disclosure while IFIs that have a fair score but show some positive improvements are classified as an 'improved practice'. The 'underdeveloped practice' category refers to IFIs that have a very minimal score that represents very weak Shari'ah governance disclosure practice. This is followed by IFIs that have a minimal score of 6–10 disclosure indicators, which are ranked in the 'emerging practice' category.

6.1.1.1 *Shari'ah* governance disclosure in Malaysia, GCC countries and the UK

As an illustration of the general findings on the level of transparency of *Shari'ah* governance in all eighty IFIs included in this book, Figures 6.1–6.4 demonstrate the significant differences in the extent of *Shari'ah* governance disclosure practices by using frequencies and cross-tabulation techniques. These findings affirm that there are significant differences in the extent of *Shari'ah* governance disclosure practices, where the majority of IFIs fall into the 'emerging practice' category and only 1.3 per cent of IFIs can be ranked in the 'best practice' category.

Figure 6.1 demonstrates the overall disclosure of *Shari'ah* governance-related information by IFIs in the case countries. Most IFIs (37.5%) are ranked in the 'emerging practice' category, followed by 30 per cent in 'improved practice', 16.3 per cent in 'underdeveloped practice', 15 per cent in 'good practice' and 1.3 per cent in 'best practice'. This finding indicates that the overall level of transparency of *Shari'ah* governance practices in IFIs is relatively low. Only 13 per cent out of eighty IFIs fall into the 'good practice' and 'best practice' categories; the remaining 87 per cent fall into the 'improved practice', 'emerging practice' and 'underdeveloped practice' categories. These figures vividly indicate the failure of the majority of IFIs to seriously take into consideration the essence of disclosure and transparency in Islam within the context of *Shari'ah* governance. While Islam promotes transparency to the extreme, the practice demonstrates a negative indication where only 1.3 per cent of IFIs fall into the 'best practice' category. The low percentage of disclosure and transparency of *Shari'ah* governance

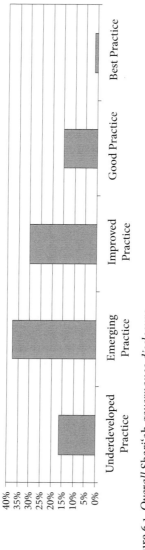

Figure 6.1 *Overall Shariʿah governance disclosure*

practices demonstrates that there are deficiencies and short-comings in the current *Shari'ah* governance framework of IFIs.

Figure 6.2 illustrates the level of disclosure of IFIs in Malaysia. The graph demonstrates that IFIs in Malaysia are generally producing fair and better disclosure compared to GCC countries and the UK. A total of 50 per cent of IFIs are ranked in the 'good practice' category, 30 per cent in 'improved practice', 15 per cent in 'emerging practice' and 5 per cent in 'best practice'. This result indicates that the proactive approach of Malaysian regulatory authorities, who facilitate *Shari'ah* governance practices through comprehensive regulatory frameworks, leads to better disclosure and transparency. In addition, IFIs in Malaysia also demonstrate serious commitment to this aspect of *Shari'ah* governance, where the majority of the *Shari'ah* governance disclosures that have been made were classified as voluntary disclosures and are not mandatory by law or regulation. These two external and internal factors have positively influenced the *Shari'ah* governance practices in Malaysia, particularly in terms of transparency. In spite of these findings, it is worth noting that the level of transparency in the majority of IFIs in Malaysia is still only in the 'good practice' category and this indicates that there are numerous efforts that could be initiated to improve and enhance the *Shari'ah* governance practices to achieve the level of 'best practice'.

The overall level of disclosure of *Shari'ah* governance in GCC countries is minimal (Figure 6.3). The majority of IFIs (46.2%) are ranked in the 'emerging practice' category, followed by 22.2 per cent in 'underdeveloped practice' and 29.6 per cent in 'improved practice'. Only 1.9 per cent of IFIs achieved the level of 'good practice' and none of them fall into the 'best practice' category. This position indicates that

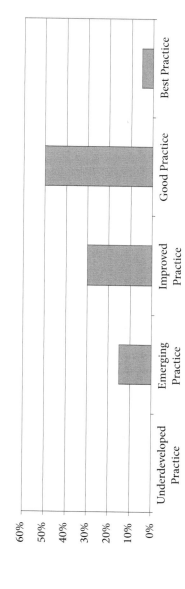

Figure 6.2 Shari'ah governance disclosure for IFIs in Malaysia

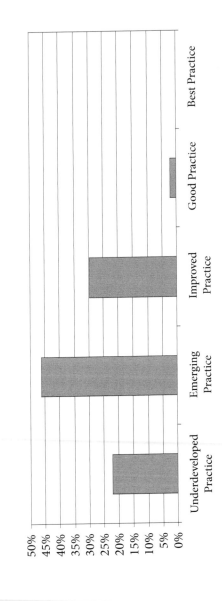

Figure 6.3 Shari'ah governance disclosure for IFIs in GCC countries

less interference from regulatory authorities and the lack of regulatory frameworks on Shari'ah governance contribute to the minimal transparency on the part of IFIs in GCC countries. Although the majority of GCC countries clearly mention the adoption of the AAOIFI governance standards, as compared to Malaysia and the UK, the implementation of these governance standards nevertheless has not significantly increased the level of transparency with regards to Shari'ah governance. In fact, the majority of IFIs only score between six and ten Shari'ah governance disclosure indicators, which demonstrates serious shortcomings and weaknesses with respect to Shari'ah governance transparency in GCC countries.[1]

Figure 6.4 presents the disclosure of Shari'ah governance practices of IFIs in the UK. Although, IFIs in the UK are relatively new, the level of disclosure and transparency is fair and better than GCC countries. The graph shows that 33.3 per cent of IFIs are ranked in the 'emerging practice' and 'improved practice' categories and 16.7 per cent in the 'good practice' category. As compared to IFIs in GCC countries, the fair disclosure practices of IFIs in the UK proves that the regulatory-based approach of Malaysia is not the sole factor in determining the level of disclosure and transparency of Shari'ah governance. The reactive approach of the UK regulatory authorities, with less regulatory interference, lets IFIs develop their Shari'ah governance framework independently. This finding proves that internal factors within the IFIs are far more important than external factors in influencing the level of transparency of Shari'ah governance. The IFI's management's commitment to and awareness of the importance of transparency on Shari'ah governance are actually the significant factors that could improve the extent of Shari'ah governance transparency.

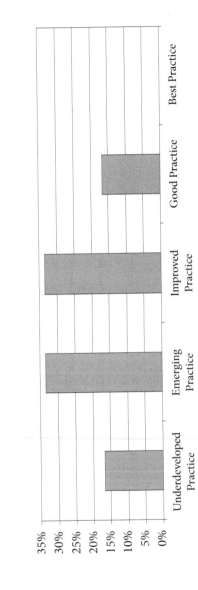

Figure 6.4 *Shariʻah governance disclosure for IFIs in the UK*

Table 6.3 *Classification of IFIs' disclosure scores according to year of incorporation*

IFIs	Malaysia	GCC countries	UK	Total	Percentage
Cluster 1: 1975–1990	1	11		12	15
Cluster 2: 1991–2000	7	8		15	18.8
Cluster 3: 2000–2005	7	16	3	26	32.5
Cluster 4: 2006–2010	5	19	3	27	33.8

6.1.1.2 *Shari'ah* governance disclosure scores according to year of incorporation

The IFIs are classified into four clusters. Cluster 1 refers to the IFIs that established their *Shari'ah* board between the years of 1975 and 1990, cluster 2 between 1991 and 2000, cluster 3 between 2000 and 2005, and cluster 4 between 2006 and 2010. A total of 15 per cent of IFIs are classified as cluster 1, 18.8 per cent as cluster 2, 32.5 per cent as cluster 3 and 33.8 per cent as cluster 4. These figures indicate that IFIs in clusters 3 and 4 represent the majority of this book sample. This reflects the phenomenon from early 2000 until recent years where numerous IFIs were established worldwide because of the tremendous growth and opportunity in Islamic finance. On the basis of this classification, this book quantifies the *Shari'ah* governance scores and ranks them into five categories as illustrated in Figure 6.5.

Figure 6.5 presents an overview of the level of *Shari'ah* governance disclosure practices in the four different clusters. This book's findings show that the majority of IFIs (54%) fall into the 'improved practice' category, 37.6 per cent into the 'emerging practice' category, 16.4 per cent into

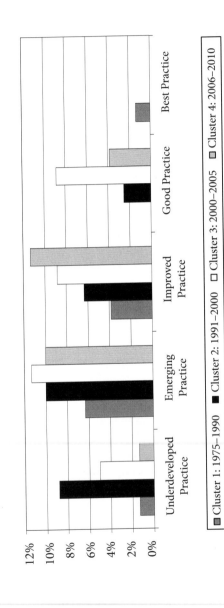

Figure 6.5 Shariʿah governance disclosure scores according to cluster

the 'underdeveloped practice' category, 15.1 per cent into the 'good practice' category and only 1.3 per cent into the 'best practice' category. IFIs in cluster 3 represent better *Shari'ah* governance disclosure scores, where the majority of them are ranked in the 'good practice' category. On the other hand, IFIs in cluster 2 demonstrate weak disclosure practices, where most of them are classified in the 'emerging practice' category. In fact, a significant percentage of IFIs in cluster 2 fall into the 'underdeveloped practice' category. Looking at the emergence of good *Shari'ah* governance disclosure practice, it was nevertheless found that only 1.3 per cent of IFIs meet the ideal criteria for the 'best practice' category as formulated in this book. These findings affirm that the level of *Shari'ah* governance disclosure practice in many IFIs is significantly low. This issue should be taken seriously by IFIs as well as regulators and supervisors because transparency is one of the prerequisites for a good and sound *Shari'ah* governance framework in IFIs.

6.1.2 *Microanalysis2*

6.1.2.1 Commitment to *Shari'ah* governance

This book analyses IFIs' commitment to *Shari'ah* governance by examining the vision and mission, articles of association and memorandum of association, chairman's message on the annual report, CEO's statement, and any other statements indicating the IFIs' commitment and devotion to *Shari'ah* governance-related matters.

The research findings demonstrate poor *Shari'ah* governance practice on the part of IFIs' commitment to *Shari'ah* governance. Only 8.8 per cent of IFIs indicated that they had guidelines or a charter on *Shari'ah* governance and 7.5 per cent on the existence of fit and proper criteria for the *Shari'ah* board. On the other hand, the majority of IFIs

(60%) indicated their commitment to *Shari'ah* compliance. Generally, it is observed that the level of disclosure on the aspect of commitment to *Shari'ah* governance of IFIs is relatively low. The finding that more than 91 per cent of IFIs do not have guidelines for *Shari'ah* governance or fit and proper criteria for their *Shari'ah* board clearly indicates a deficiency in *Shari'ah* governance disclosure practice.

6.1.2.2 *Shari'ah* board information

Shari'ah board information is of the essence to *Shari'ah* governance in IFIs. This book identified fifteen indicators to measure the level of disclosure of *Shari'ah* governance practices on the aspect of *Shari'ah* board information. In terms of disclosure of *Shari'ah* board information, only 16.3 per cent of IFIs disclosed the method of appointment of their *Shari'ah* boards while 11.3 per cent published the organisation chart of the *Shari'ah* board structure on their website. In terms of the list of *Shari'ah* board members, a significant number of 88.8 per cent of IFIs disclosed information on their *Shari'ah* board members. The disclosure on the method of appointment is important in defining their relationship within the organ of governance and to maintain the state of independence of the *Shari'ah* board, while publication of the organisation chart will demonstrate the overall corporate structure of IFIs. The disclosure of the list of *Shari'ah* board members is also significant as it indicates the credibility of IFIs and the legitimacy of the products and services offered.

Looking at the cross-border practice of *Shari'ah* governance disclosure, only 25 per cent of twenty IFIs in Malaysia disclosed the method of appointment of their *Shari'ah* board and 20 per cent published the organisation chart of the *Shari'ah* board structure on their website. All IFIs in Malaysia disclosed the list of *Shari'ah* board members.

A similar practice is found in GCC countries, where 7.4 per cent of IFIs disclosed the method of appointment, 9.3 per cent the organisation chart and 85 per cent the list of *Shari'ah* board members. Unlike Malaysia and GCC countries, all of the IFIs in the UK revealed the list of *Shari'ah* board members and 66.7 per cent disclosed the method of appointment. None of the IFIs in the UK published the organisation chart of the *Shari'ah* board structure either on the website or in the annual report or financial statements.

Information on the background of *Shari'ah* board members provides important insights into the credibility of the *Shari'ah* governance. The public and all stakeholders deserve to know the background and necessary information about the *Shari'ah* board members who are advising and supervising the institutions. The majority of IFIs (52.5%) disclosed details about *Shari'ah* board members, other than name and title, 51.3 per cent of IFIs about other employment and position, and 52.5 per cent about the chairman, other than name and title. Only 10 per cent of IFIs disclosed the date that each *Shari'ah* board member joined the board. A significant number of 88.8 per cent of IFIs disclosed the name of the *Shari'ah* board's chairman; this disclosure is important because he plays an active role in tailoring and determining the direction and effectiveness of the *Shari'ah* board. The normal practice in the industry shows that senior or prominent *Shari'ah* scholars who have more experience and excellent academic qualifications will be appointed as the chairman of the *Shari'ah* board.

With reference to the different levels of disclosure on the details and background of *Shari'ah* board members, all IFIs in Malaysia disclosed the details of *Shari'ah* board members, other than name and title, including the name of the *Shari'ah* board's chairman and the details of the chairman, other than name and title, while only 35 per cent disclosed the date each member joined the *Shari'ah* board. A low level of disclosure is found in GCC countries, where only 33.3 per cent of IFIs disclosed on D7, 31.4 per cent on D8, 33.3 per cent on D11 and 83.3 per cent on D10 (see Table 6.1 for details of disclosure indices). None of the IFIs in GCC countries or in the UK disclosed the date each *Shari'ah* board member joined the board. Fair disclosure practice is found in the UK, in which 83.3 per cent of IFIs disclosed on D7, D8 and D11 and 16.7 per cent on D9. As in Malaysia, 100 per cent of IFIs in the UK disclosed the name of the *Shari'ah* board's chairman.

This research identifies the level of disclosure of *Shari'ah* governance practice on the aspect of roles of the *Shari'ah* board, *Shari'ah* review, size of *Shari'ah* board, meetings and tenure of appointment. The majority of IFIs (53.7%) disclosed the details of the role of the *Shari'ah* board, while 83.7 per cent of IFIs disclosed that the board size is no fewer than three members. Only 36.2 per cent of IFIs revealed that the *Shari'ah* board performs the *Shari'ah* review and 20 per cent of IFIs disclosed that their *Shari'ah* board members sit on the boards of more than three other IFIs. A low level of disclosure is found with respect to the attendance records of *Shari'ah* board meetings (6.3%), whether the board meets more than four times a year (7.5%) and tenure of appointment (6.3%). A significant number of 75 per cent of IFIs in Malaysia disclosed the details of the *Shari'ah* board's role, 50 per cent disclosed that the *Shari'ah* board performs the *Shari'ah* review, 100 per cent that the size of the *Shari'ah* board is not fewer than three members. On the other hand, a low level of disclosure is found on the aspect of *Shari'ah* board members sitting on the boards of more than three other IFIs (35%), attendance record (25%), whether the board meets more than four times a year (20%) and tenure of appointment (20%). A different scenario is found in GCC countries, where 44.4 per cent of IFIs disclosed on D12 and 83.3 per cent on D14. In fact, poor disclosure of *Shari'ah* practice was found on D13 (35.1%), D15 (11.1%), D17 (3.7%) and D18 (1.9%) and none of the IFIs disclosed the attendance records of *Shari'ah* board meetings. In the UK, disclosure was only made for D12, D14 and D15: 66.7 per cent of IFIs disclosed the details of *Shari'ah* board's roles, 100 per cent disclosed that the board size is no fewer than three members and 50 per cent that *Shari'ah* board members sit on boards of more than three IFIs. Furthermore, it was found that only six IFIs disclosed the details of *Shari'ah* board meetings in the annual reports, as illustrated in Table 6.4.

Table 6.4 shows that there are significant differences in *Shari'ah* board meeting practices based on the available information derived from seven IFIs in Malaysia (5), Kuwait (1) and Saudi Arabia (1). The *Shari'ah* board of the BMMB meets twenty-four times per year, followed by Bank Al Bilad seventeen times per year, RHB seven times per year, BIMB six times per year, KIB four times per year, and CIMB and MIB both three times per year. This shows that there is no minimum setting of standard practice for *Shari'ah* board meetings. In view of the standard practice of BOD meetings being held at least four times a year, the above findings show that current *Shari'ah* board meeting practices constitute good *Shari'ah* governance practice, with the exception of the MIB and the CIMB.

The author is nevertheless of the view that a monthly *Shari'ah* board meeting is the ideal practice for *Shari'ah* governance. Unlike the BOD, who are responsible for setting the IFI's direction and general policies, the *Shari'ah* board is expected to perform *ex ante* and *ex post* functions of the *Shari'ah* governance process, which requires more time, effort and due diligence from them. On the face of it, the *Shari'ah* board is also anticipated to inculcate awareness

Table 6.4 Shari'ah *board meetings*

IFIs	*Shari'ah* board members	Meetings	Attendance	
			Shari'ah board members	Percentage
BIMB	6	6	4	100
			1	17
			1	83
Bank Muamalat Malaysia Berhad (BMMB)	4	24	1	92
			1	96
			1	86
			1	71
Maybank Islamic Berhad (MIB)	3	3	1	60
			2	100
RHB Islamic Bank Berhad (RHB)	5	7	2	71
			2	100
			1	86
CIMB Islamic Bank Berhad (CIMB)	7	3	3	100
			3	66.6
			1	33.3
Kuwait International Banks (KIB)	6	4		N.A.
Bank Al Bilad	6	17		N.A.

Sources: BIMB (2008: 40), BMMB (2008: 24), MIB (2008: 23), RHB (2008: 16), CIMB (2007: 41–2), KIB (2008: 12) and Al Bilad (2008).

and to educate the IFIs on *Shari'ah* principles as well as Islamic ethics and values. In this regard, this book suggests the practice of monthly meetings as the best practice for *Shari'ah* board meetings; however, only two out of seven IFIs currently meet this standard.

In terms of attendance, the majority of *Shari'ah* board members attended more than 70 per cent of *Shari'ah* board meetings, 45 per cent attended 100 per cent of the meetings, 17 per cent attended more than 80 per cent of the meetings, 11 per cent attended more than 90 per cent and 70 per cent of the board meetings respectively and 6 per cent of *Shari'ah* scholars attended 17 per cent of the board meetings. It is worth mentioning that five of eighteen *Shari'ah* board members of IFIs in Malaysia have failed to attend more than 75 per cent of *Shari'ah* board meetings. In accordance with the fit and proper criteria of the SHC on disqualification of the SGF, those *Shari'ah* board members may be disqualified unless they give a reasonable excuse for their absence. Despite that, results appear to show that the attendance and commitment of *Shari'ah* board members is in line with what would be conceived as good practice, with 73 per cent of *Shari'ah* scholars attending more than 80 per cent of the *Shari'ah* board meetings.

Table 6.5 summarises the findings on *Shari'ah* board sizes. Basically, an appropriate size for a *Shari'ah* board is important to enable them to hold productive and constructive discussions and make prompt *Shari'ah* decisions. Having three to five *Shari'ah* board members is considered a good *Shari'ah* board practice. There are 169 identified individual *Shari'ah* scholars with eighty-two of them holding *Shari'ah* board positions in twenty IFIs in Malaysia, seventy-six *Shari'ah* scholars in fifty-four IFIs in GCC countries, and eleven *Shari'ah* scholars in six IFIs in the UK. In GCC countries 2 per cent of IFIs have only one *Shari'ah* scholar, 4 per cent have two *Shari'ah* board members, 52 per cent have three, 15 per cent have six, 15 per cent have five and 13 per cent have four. A similar scenario is found in Malaysia where 71 per cent of IFIs have three *Shari'ah* board members, 14 per cent have four, 14 per cent have five, 5 per cent have eight and 5 per cent have ten *Shari'ah* board members. In the UK, 40 per cent of IFIs have three *Shari'ah* board members, 40 per cent have four and 20 per cent have only one *Shari'ah* board member. The overall findings show that *Shari'ah* boards in IFIs generally have the right board size and appear to be in line with the AAOIFI governance standards and IFSB-10 with the exception of three IFIs in GCC countries and one IFI in the UK. Fewer *Shari'ah* board members provide less leverage while a large *Shari'ah* board may increase the IFIs' expenses.

In addition, Table 6.5 also demonstrates that Malaysia has more individual *Shari'ah* scholars with an average of 4.1 compared to the UK (average of 1.8) and GCC countries (average of 1.4). There are eighty-two individual *Shari'ah* scholars for twenty IFIs in Malaysia, while there are only seventy-six *Shari'ah* scholars for fifty-four IFIs in GCC countries and eleven *Shari'ah* scholars for six IFIs in the UK. These figures indicate that GCC countries and the UK experience some degree of shortage of *Shari'ah* scholars. The restriction on multiple appointments of *Shari'ah* board members of IFIs at one particular time is one of the factors determining the number of individual *Shari'ah* scholars and an average *Shari'ah* board in Malaysia is larger than an average *Shari'ah* board in GCC countries and the UK.[3]

In order to illustrate the relationship of *Shari'ah* board size to *Shari'ah* governance disclosure practice, Table 6.6 demonstrates the correlation between these two aspects.

Table 6.6 clearly indicates the positive correlation of the board positions of *Shari'ah* scholars and the extent of

Table 6.5 *Board position and size of* Shari'ah *board*

Country IFIs		Board position	*Shari'ah* scholars	*Shari'ah* board size	Percentage
GCC countries	54	199	76	1	2
				2	4
				3	52
				4	15
				5	15
				6	13
Malaysia	20	90	82	3	55
				4	15
				5	15
				8	5
				10	5
UK	6	15	11	1	20
				3	40
				4	40

Shari'ah governance disclosure practice. Although admittedly there are other factors that contribute to the state of *Shari'ah* governance disclosure, the author considers that the size of the *Shari'ah* board may also lead to better disclosure practices. The average size of *Shari'ah* board in Malaysia is 4.5 (out of ninety board positions and eighty-two *Shari'ah* scholars) and the result indicates that the majority of IFIs in Malaysia fall into the 'good practice' category, which is better than its counterparts in GCC countries and the UK. The situation is different in GCC countries where the average *Shari'ah* board size is 3.6 (out of 199 board positions and seventy-six *Shari'ah* scholars) and the majority of IFIs are ranked in the 'emerging practice' category. The same thing occurs in IFIs in the UK, where the average *Shari'ah* board size is 2.5 (out of fifteen board positions and eleven *Shari'ah* scholars) and most of them fall into the 'emerging practice' and 'improved practice' categories.

Table 6.6 Correlation between the Shari'ah board size and the state of Shari'ah governance disclosure practices

Countries	Average Shari'ah board size	State of *Shari'ah* governance disclosure practice				
		Underdeveloped practice	Emerging practice	Improved practice	Good practice	Best practice
Malaysia	4.5		3.75%	7.5%	12.4%	1.25%
GCC Countries	3.6	15%	31.25%	20%	1.25%	
UK	2.5	1.25%	2.5%	2.5%	1.25%	

This book suggests two main factors that lead to findings of better disclosure practices in Malaysia as compared to GCC countries and the UK. Firstly, having a significant number of *Shari'ah* scholars who can allocate more time and effort to performing their duties is a very important factor in improving *Shari'ah* governance disclosure and transparency. *Shari'ah* scholars are not only expected to approve or disapprove the Islamic financial products and services but also to go beyond that by promoting Islamic ethics and values, including insisting on the aspects of disclosure and transparency. Secondly, the practice of limiting the number of board positions a scholar may hold: allowing *Shari'ah* scholars to hold numerous board positions without limitation may negate the effort and initiative of good disclosure of *Shari'ah* governance. Too many board positions for *Shari'ah* scholars does not enable them to allocate sufficient time and effort to improving and promoting disclosure and transparency in IFIs.

To support the above two propositions, this book illustrates the board and chairman positions of the top ten *Shari'ah* scholars. Based on the information available on the websites, annual reports and financial statements, this book has identified sixteen of the most utilised or top *Shari'ah* scholars in the eighty sampled IFIs in Malaysia, GCC countries and the UK. Those sixteen top *Shari'ah* scholars have 105 *Shari'ah* board positions in IFIs in GCC countries, with an average of 6.5 *Shari'ah* boards for each scholar. This book also finds that the eleven top *Shari'ah* scholars hold thirty-five positions as chairman of *Shari'ah* boards, with an average of 3.1 for each scholar. Ten of those sixteen top *Shari'ah* scholars also have *Shari'ah* board positions in Malaysia and the UK. These figures indicate that *Shari'ah* board positions in fifty-four IFIs in GCC countries and five IFIs in the UK (excluding Malaysia) are shared mainly by only sixteen top

Shari'ah scholars. This finding is supported by the *Shari'ah* scholars' network analysis of Unal and Ley (2009) and Unal (2009; 2010). Table 6.7 illustrates the board and chairman positions of the top ten *Shari'ah* scholars in 2008, 2009 and 2010, based on these studies by Unal and Ley (2009) and Unal (2009 and 2010).

These findings positively affirm that there are deficiencies in the current practice of *Shari'ah* governance, particularly in the aspects of confidentiality, competence and accountability of the *Shari'ah* board. Despite some advantages in serving multiple *Shari'ah* boards, such as knowledge and experience, holding too many *Shari'ah* board positions at one particular time in numerous IFIs may affect the efficiency of *Shari'ah* scholars' performance and raise the potential for conflict of interest.[4] In fact, holding numerous chairman positions on *Shari'ah* boards may raise significant issues of confidentiality and accountability of the *Shari'ah* scholars.

The situation is different in the case of Malaysia where there is regulatory restriction on multiple appointments to *Shari'ah* boards. It is reported that the adoption of this kind of limitation on multiple appointments has produced more than 100 registered and qualified *Shari'ah* advisors that are available to fill in the gap in the industry. Besides this, this book also finds that non-*Shari'ah* experts, such as judges and economists, are appointed as *Shari'ah* board members. Furthermore, there are nine individual female *Shari'ah* scholars holding *Shari'ah* board positions in nine different IFIs in Malaysia, whereas the *Shari'ah* boards of IFIs in GCC countries and the UK are still exclusively male territory. The distinct position of *Shari'ah* board engagement in Malaysia is mainly due to the regulatory framework and moderate *Shari'ah* approach, as well as the market initiative and motivation of having an effective and sound *Shari'ah*

Table 6.7 Board and chairman positions of top ten *Shari'ah* scholars

Shari'ah scholar	Data as of 31.12.2008 467 board positions in 19 countries	Data as of 10.10.2009 956 board positions in 22 countries	Data as of 12.04.2010 1050 board positions in 24 countries	Data as of 12.04.2010 Chairman positions in 24 countries
Sheika Nizam Mohammed Saleh Yaquby	46	77	78	10
Sheikh Abdul Satar Abdul Karim Abu Ghuddah	45	72	77	21
Sheikh Muhammad Ali Elgari	31	64	65	8
Sheikh Abdulaziz Khalifa Al Qassar	22	37	38	9
Sheikh Mohd Daud Bakar	22	35	38	
Sheikh Abdulla Bin Sulaiman Al Manea	20	37	38	20
Sheikh Hussein Hamid Hassan	19	29	32	21
Sheikh Ali Mohyuldin Al Qarradaghi	17	23	31	7
Sheikh Essa Zaki Essa	17	25	25	
Sheikh Ajeel Jasim Al Nashmi	15	24	22	
Average no. board and chairman positions per scholar	25.3	42.3	44.4	9.6

Sources: modified from Unal and Ley (2009) and Unal (2009; 2010).

governance system. These internal and external factors have significantly influenced the *Shariʿah* governance practices of IFIs in Malaysia.

6.1.2.3 *Shariʿah* board's remuneration

The ideal *Shariʿah* governance practice promotes more transparency and disclosure and this includes on the *Shariʿah* board's remuneration. This book explores the disclosure of the *Shariʿah* board's remuneration by IFIs in terms of the authority who determines the amount of remuneration and the specifics of the *Shariʿah* board's pay, as stated in their annual reports and financial statements.

The research demonstrates that only 25 per cent of IFIs disclosed the authority who determines the *Shariʿah* board's remuneration, whether the BOD, management or shareholders in the annual general assembly. Interestingly, 23.8 per cent of the sample disclosed the specifics of the *Shariʿah* board's pay, indicating a growth of transparency and disclosure of *Shariʿah* governance practice by IFIs. Setting an appropriate amount of remuneration is important to safeguard the status of the *Shariʿah* board as well as to mitigate the potential for the unhealthy practice of 'shopping' for *Shariʿah* rulings. The disclosure of the amount of remuneration of the *Shariʿah* board, apart from the BOD and external audit fees, is significant to investors, depositors and the public, particularly to provide an accurate perception of the roles played by the *Shariʿah* board.

In terms of a comparative overview of the disclosure of the *Shariʿah* board's remuneration, Malaysia represents good *Shariʿah* governance disclosure practice, where 85 per cent of twenty IFIs disclosed the authority who determines the *Shariʿah* board's remuneration and 80 per cent of IFIs disclosed the specifics of the *Shariʿah* board's pay. This is in contrast to the disclosure of IFIs in GCC countries and the

UK where only a small percentage of 3.7 per cent of fifty-four IFIs in GCC countries disclosed D19 and D20 and only 16.7 per cent of IFIs in the UK disclosed the same. It is clear from this finding that the level of disclosure of *Shari'ah* governance in GCC countries and the UK is significantly low when compared to Malaysia.

Table 6.8 illustrates the amount of remuneration of the *Shari'ah* board, as stated in the financial statements of sixteen of the eighty sampled IFIs in Malaysia, GCC countries and the UK. The average remuneration for the total sixty *Shari'ah* board members is USD 9834 a year, while the average amount of remuneration for the fifty-two *Shari'ah* board members in Malaysia is USD 9767 a year. The *Shari'ah* board members of IFIs in Bahrain and the UK receive a larger amount of remuneration compared to their counterparts in Malaysia with averages of USD 76,432 and USD 74,553 respectively.

The overall figures are considered relatively small compared to the BOD and management's remuneration. These figures also indicate and clearly prove that the allegation of *Shari'ah* arbitrage by establishing *Shari'ah* boards in IFIs, which increases transaction costs to a certain extent, is not accurate as the amount of *Shari'ah* board remuneration is not significant on an institutional level. Nevertheless, *Shari'ah* board members of IFIs in the UK and GCC countries enjoy the privilege of sitting on the boards of numerous IFIs without any sort of restriction. The insignificant amount of remuneration of *Shari'ah* board members will be very significant if they sit on the boards of numerous IFIs at one particular time.

By using the same logic, inferences can be made for the whole sample. This position can be simply illustrated by referring to the average of 6.5 *Shari'ah* board positions per scholar, which amounts to USD 63,921 annually per scholar.

Table 6.8 Shari'ah *board remuneration*

Country	IFIs	Remuneration (2008)	Size of Shari'ah board	Average per scholar
Malaysia	Affin Islamic Bank Berhad	USD 32,951	5	USD 6,590
	Alliance Islamic Bank Berhad	USD 12,401	3	USD 4,113
	Asian Finance Bank Berhad	USD 40,971	3	USD 13,657
	Bank Islam Malaysia Berhad	USD 60,018	6	USD 10,003
	CIMB Islamic Bank Berhad	USD 106,208	3	USD 35,403
	Hong Leong Islamic Bank	USD 36,187	3	USD 12,062
	KFH Malaysia Berhad	USD 91,792	3	USD 30,057
	Bank Muamalat Malaysia Berhad	USD 38,247	4	USD 9,561
	Al Rajhi Banking and Investment Corporation Malaysia Berhad	USD 119,447	4	USD 29,861
	EONCAP Islamic Bank Berhad	USD 25,007	3	USD 8,836
	Maybank Islamic Berhad	USD 22,947	3	USD 7,649
	RHB Islamic Bank Berhad	USD 76,199	5	USD 15,239
	Bank Simpanan Nasional	USD 15,004	4	USD 3,751
	HSBC Amanah Malaysia Berhad	USD 10,003	3	USD 3,334
GCC Countries	Bahrain Islamic Bank	USD 382,158	5	USD 76,432
United Kingdom	Islamic Bank of Britain	USD 223,659	3	USD 74,553

Sources: AIB (2008: 60), Alliance (2009: 58), AFB (2008: 33), BIMB (2008: 125), CIMB (2007: 126), HLIB (2008: 75), KFH (M) (2008: 61), BMMB (2008: 92), Al Rajhi (M) (2008: 48), EONCAP (2008: 50), MIB (2008: 75), RHB (2008: 81), BSN (2008: 199), HSBC (M) (2008: 50), BIB (2008: 56) and IBB (2004: 27).

In contrast, the global situation can be analysed by examining the surveys of Unal and Ley (2009) and Unal (2009; 2010) of the world's top ten *Shariʿah* scholars. The surveys reveal that more than three *Shariʿah* scholars sit on more than sixty-five *Shariʿah* boards and seven *Shariʿah* scholars sit on more than twenty-four boards. As an indication of the potential amount of remuneration for *Shariʿah* scholars, the top five *Shariʿah* scholars will earn more than USD 582,172 annually if the estimation is based on the average amount of remuneration of USD 9,834 with an average of 59.2 board positions. As shown by this book, the amount will be greater if the calculation is based on the average amount of remuneration in Bahrain (i.e. USD 76,432), by which the top five *Shariʿah* scholars will earn more than USD 4,524,774 annually.[5]

The negative indication from the above finding may repudiate the credibility of *Shariʿah* scholars and hence negate the image of IFIs when there is no limitation on board memberships. Investors as well as the public may lose confidence in the legitimacy of Islamic financial products and services. This requires serious consideration on the part of regulators and IFIs to maintain the confidence of the investors, depositors, customers and other stakeholders by having appropriate mechanisms to limit and govern the practice of *Shariʿah* scholars.

6.1.2.4 *Shariʿah* report

This book analyses the *Shariʿah* reports published in the annual reports and financial statements of 2007 and 2008. There are four indicators for good *Shariʿah* governance disclosure practice pertaining to the *Shariʿah* report: publication of the *Shariʿah* report in the annual report, information on duties and services, *Shariʿah* board activities and the declaration of *Shariʿah* compliance.

The majority of IFIs disclosed the *Shari'ah* report in the annual report (52.5%). With regards to the content of the *Shari'ah* report, 53.8 per cent of IFIs disclosed the declaration of *Shari'ah* compliance while a small percentage of 18.8 per cent of IFIs disclosed information on duties and services, and 6.3 per cent on *Shari'ah* board activities. These findings indicate that significant numbers of IFIs in Malaysia, GCC countries and the UK do not meet the specifications of the AAOIFI format of the *Shari'ah* report as specified in sections 9–26 of the AAOIFI Governance Standard for IFIs No. 1: *Shari'ah* Supervisory Board: Appointment, Composition and Report. In fact, the contents of the *Shari'ah* reports reviewed were very brief and inadequate. This issue should be taken seriously by IFIs as well as regulators since the *Shari'ah* report in the annual report is the main available document and reference for the general public, consumers, investors and depositors.

The majority of IFIs in Malaysia (80%), GCC countries (56%) and the UK (50%) disclosed the *Shari'ah* report by publishing it in the annual report. With regard to the contents of the *Shari'ah* report, only 45 per cent of IFIs in Malaysia disclosed information on the duties and services of the *Shari'ah* board and 11.1 per cent of IFIs in GCC countries. A small percentage (5%) of IFIs in Malaysia and 7.4 per cent of IFIs in GCC countries disclosed *Shari'ah* board activities in the *Shari'ah* report, while none of the IFIs in the UK disclosed the same.

This book has found that the majority of IFIs (80% in Malaysia, 44.4% in GCC countries and 50% in the UK) disclosed a statement of *Shari'ah* compliance in the *Shari'ah* report. This finding indicates the weaknesses of disclosure practices with respect to the contents of the *Shari'ah* report in the IFIs' annual report. While IFIs are expected to at least state the declaration of *Shari'ah* compliance duly endorsed by their *Shari'ah* board, a significant percentage of them have failed to comply with this requirement and, in fact, more than 47 per cent of eighty IFIs have not published a *Shari'ah* report in their annual report. This position requires the immediate attention of IFIs as the *Shari'ah* report or the declaration of *Shari'ah* compliance in the annual report is very important. Since the annual report is the main reference providing financial and non-financial information on IFIs, inclusion of the *Shari'ah* report should be a mandatory requirement.

6.1.2.5 *Shari'ah* pronouncements

Transparency in *Shari'ah* pronouncements would strengthen the stakeholders' confidence in the IFIs' credibility with regards the state of *Shari'ah* compliance. This book explores the extent of transparency of *Shari'ah* governance in the aspect of *Shari'ah* pronouncements. There are three selected indicators to measure the level of disclosure of *Shari'ah* pronouncements: *Shari'ah* rulings are made known to the public, only the content of *Shari'ah* resolutions are disclosed, and *Shari'ah* rulings with detailed *Shari'ah* explanations disclosed.

The research findings indicate a low level of disclosure practice of *Shari'ah* pronouncements. A total of 90 per cent of IFIs have not published or made known to the public their *Shari'ah* rulings. In addition, with regard to the content of the *Shari'ah* rulings, 8.8 per cent of IFIs disclosed the *Shari'ah* resolution only and only 3.8 per cent disclosed the *Shari'ah* rulings with a detailed *Shari'ah* explanation. These findings clearly indicate that the disclosure practice relating to *Shari'ah* rulings in IFIs is still at a very minimal and weak level. The finding that only 10 per cent of eighty IFIs published *Shari'ah* rulings demonstrates serious shortcomings in *Shari'ah* governance disclosure practice. IFIs are expected to provide reliable and appropriate information pertaining to the *Shari'ah* pronouncements issued by their *Shari'ah* board; the declaration of *Shari'ah* compliance in the annual report per se is not adequate or sufficient to educate and create an awareness of the essence of *Shari'ah* rules and principles in the consumers, investors, depositors and general public.

As regard to disclosure practices of *Shari'ah* pronouncements in Malaysia, GCC countries and the UK, the majority of IFIs have neglected the disclosure and transparency aspects of *Shari'ah* pronouncements. In Malaysia, only 15 per cent of IFIs' *Shari'ah* rulings were made known to the public. In terms of the content of the *Shari'ah* rulings, 15 per cent of IFIs disclosed the *Shari'ah* pronouncements only, while 5 per cent disclosed them with a detailed *Shari'ah* explanation. A significantly low level of disclosure practice of IFIs in GCC countries was found, by which only 7.4 per cent of IFIs published the *Shari'ah* rulings, 5.5 per cent disclosed *Shari'ah* rulings only and 3.7 per cent disclosed rulings with a detailed *Shari'ah* explanation. A similar situation is found for IFIs in the UK, where only 16.7 per cent of IFIs disclosed the *Shari'ah* rulings and made them known to the public in the form of the *Shari'ah* rulings only. No IFIs in the UK have published *Shari'ah* resolutions with detailed *Shari'ah* explanations. These findings appear to demonstrate that disclosure pertaining to *Shari'ah* pronouncements is lacking in all of the case countries.

6.1.2.6 *Shari'ah* compliance review

The *Shari'ah* compliance review is of the utmost important to ascertain that all transactions, operations and dealings implemented by IFIs comply with *Shari'ah* principles. Although most of the IFIs have established specific institutional arrangements for the *Shari'ah* compliance review, it is also essential for them to disclose and mention this exercise somewhere, whether in the annual report, financial statement or on their website. In view of the limited information available on the *Shari'ah* compliance review, this book only identified one indicator for the level of disclosure practice with respect to the *Shari'ah* compliance review.

A *Shari'ah* compliance review is adopted by most of the IFIs in all the case countries. Nevertheless, more than 61 per cent did not mention undertaking a *Shari'ah* compliance review exercise. Only 38.8 per cent of the IFIs disclosed their undertaking of a *Shari'ah* review, either on their website or in their annual report or financial statements. This indicates that the depositors, investors and the general public are unaware or uncertain of the *Shari'ah* compliance review process undertaken by most IFIs. While the *Shari'ah* review is crucial to IFIs for the purpose of ensuring the legitimacy of Islamic financial products and services, the finding of no more than 39 per cent of IFIs disclosing their undertaking of a *Shari'ah* compliance review demonstrates their weak disclosure practices of *Shari'ah* governance. A total of 50 per cent of twenty IFIs in Malaysia mentioned undertaking a *Shari'ah* compliance review, while only 37 per cent of fifty-four IFIs in GCC countries and none of the six IFIs in the UK did the same. This finding shows that IFIs in Malaysia are slightly more transparent than IFIs in GCC countries and the UK with respect to *Shari'ah* compliance review disclosure.

6.1.2.7 Information on products and services

This book analyses the level of disclosure of *Shari'ah* governance practices pertaining to information on products and services. Two indicators are identified to demonstrate the extent of disclosure and transparency of information on products and services by IFIs: providing a list of *Shari'ah*-compliant products and services, and providing the details of the *Shari'ah* concepts and principles of products and services.

Significant number of IFIs (91.3%) disclosed the list of their *Shari'ah*-compliant products and services. On the other hand, only 33.8 per cent disclosed or mentioned the details of the *Shari'ah* concepts and principles of products and services on their websites or in the annual reports. The lack of disclosure and transparency on the details of the concepts and structure of products and services demonstrates the low level of initiative on the part of IFIs to educate customers, consumers and the public at large about Islamic financial transactions. It is the duty of each IFI to create awareness, to inculcate understanding and to educate people about specific features of Islamic financial products and services, differentiating them from their conventional counterparts.

With reference to the cross-border disclosure of *Shari'ah* governance practices on the aspect of information on products and services, there is good disclosure and transparency of information on products and services from IFIs in Malaysia (100%), GCC countries (87%) and the UK (100%). Nevertheless, a slightly low percentage of disclosure is found for the details of *Shari'ah* concepts and principles (60% of IFIs in Malaysia, 24% in GCC countries and 33.3% in the UK). These figures indicate that the majority of IFIs in Malaysia have initiated efforts to educate the public and consumers about details of Islamic financial products and services, while these practices are not so popular in GCC countries and the UK. This indirectly demonstrates that Malaysian consumers have better access to information on the Islamic financial products and services compared to consumers in GCC countries and the UK.

6.1.3 *Summary of the overall* Shari'ah *governance scores*

This section provides a summary of the overall findings relating to *Shari'ah* governance scores from a country-specific behaviour perspective as well as according to year of incorporation. Both perspectives demonstrate different indications as to the extent of *Shari'ah* governance disclosure in IFIs in each of the thirty indicators.

6.1.3.1 Country-specific behaviour

This book attempts to highlight the significant differences in the *Shari'ah* governance practices of IFIs in the case countries. Table 6.9 illustrates the state of *Shari'ah* governance disclosure practices by presenting the overall scores of *Shari'ah* governance indicators for each country. The findings suggest that IFIs in Malaysia have better *Shari'ah* governance scores compared to their counterparts in GCC countries and the UK.

Table 6.9 clearly shows the level of practice of *Shari'ah* governance disclosure from a country-specific behaviour perspective. The overall findings reveal that IFIs in Malaysia have the best *Shari'ah* governance disclosure scores, with an average of 16 that falls into the 'good practice' category. This is followed by IFIs in the UK that fall into the 'improved practice' category with an average score of 10.7. IFIs in GCC countries fall into the 'emerging practice' category with an average score of 8.4. The average score of 10.5 across all eighty IFIs indicates that *Shari'ah* governance disclosure practices are still at a minimal level as they only just fall into the 'improved practice' category.

Most of the IFIs (more than 50%) in Malaysia have disclosed information on sixteen indicators, namely D6, D7–D11, D12–D14, D19–D21, D24 and D28–D30. In contrast, most of the IFIs in GCC countries have disclosed

Table 6.9 Shari'ah governance scores according to country-specific behaviour[a]

Section	Disclosure index Indicator	Malaysia	GCC countries	UK	Total score
Commitment to Shari'ah governance	**D1**	3	4	0	7
	D2	5	1	0	6
	D3	9	36	4	49
***Shari'ah* board information**	**D4**	5	7	1	13
	D5	4	5	0	9
	D6	20	47	6	73
	D7	20	19	5	44
	D8	20	18	5	43
	D9	7	0	1	8
	D10	20	47	6	73
	D11	19	19	5	43
	D12	15	24	4	43
	D13	10	19	0	29
	D14	19	43	6	68
	D15	7	6	3	16
	D16	5	0	0	5
	D17	4	2	0	6

		'Good practice'	'Emerging practice'	'Improved practice'	'Improved practice'
Shari'ah board remuneration	D18	4	1	0	5
	D19	17	2	1	20
	D20	16	2	1	19
Shari'ah report	D21	16	24	3	43
	D22	9	6	0	15
	D23	1	4	0	5
	D24	16	25	3	44
Shari'ah pronouncements	D25	3	4	1	8
	D26	3	3	1	7
	D27	1	2	0	3
Shari'ah review	D28	10	21	0	31
Information on products and services	D29	20	48	6	74
	D30	12	13	2	27
Average score		16	8.4	10.7	10.5
Level of practice		'Good practice'	'Emerging practice'	'Improved practice'	'Improved practice'

[a] The scores are generated from 30 *Shari'ah* governance disclosure indicators as illustrated in Table 6.1. The total scores of each IFI are 30. IFIs in Malaysia score 320 out of a possible 600 (20x30), GCC countries, 452 out of 1620 (54x30) and the UK, 64 out of 180 (6x30). The total scores are 836 out of 2400. The 'average' is formulated as the scores divide by the number of IFIs.

Shari'ah-related information on only five indicators: D3, D6, D10, D14 and D29. Interestingly, IFIs in the UK have better disclosure practices compared to IFIs in GCC countries in that most of them have disclosed information on twelve indicators: D3, D6–8, D10–D12, D14–D15, D21, D24 and D29. Generally, all of the IFIs have good disclosure practices for the information pertaining to products and services and very weak practices with respect to the disclosure of *Shari'ah* pronouncements. These findings strongly affirm this book's proposition of there being significant differences in *Shari'ah* governance disclosure practices in the case countries.

6.1.3.2 *Shari'ah* governance score according to cluster

As well as analysing country-specific behaviour of IFIs in relation to *Shari'ah* governance disclosure practices, this book further examines the disclosure practices from the perspective of year of incorporation. Table 6.10 demonstrates the relationship between the ages of the IFIs and the extent of *Shari'ah* governance disclosure practice in each of the thirty indicators. This book finds that IFIs in cluster 3, namely institutions which were incorporated in 2001–2005, have better disclosure practices compared to IFIs in clusters 1, 2 and 3.

Table 6.10 reveals that there is a negative correlation between the age of the IFI, based on year of incorporation, and the extent of *Shari'ah* governance disclosure practice. The findings show that the average scores of the senior IFIs in cluster 1 is eleven, which falls into the 'improved practice' category, while IFIs in clusters 2 and 4 fall into the 'emerging practice' category, with average scores of 9.9 and 9.5, respectively. IFIs in cluster 3 show slightly better disclosure practices with an average of 11.5, which falls into the 'improved practice' category.

IFIs in cluster 4 scored very low on the *Shari'ah* governance disclosure index. In fact, fewer than five IFIs in cluster 4 disclosed information on fifteen indicators, namely D1, D2, D4, D5, D9, D16, D17, D18, D19, D20, D22, D23, D25, D26 and D27. On the other hand, the IFIs in cluster 3 scored slightly better than the rest of the IFIs in clusters 1, 2 and 4. Most of the IFIs in cluster 3 disclosed information on eleven indicators: D3, D6, D7, D8, D10, D11, D12, D14, D21, D24 and D29. These findings affirm this book's proposition of the negative correlation between the age of an IFI based on year of incorporation and the level of *Shari'ah* governance disclosure practice. The early established IFIs in cluster 1 that have more experience compared to IFIs in other clusters have a very minimal score of *Shari'ah* governance disclosure indicators. This is rather a disappointing result as the earlier IFIs were established by those people closer to the aspirational view of an Islamic moral economy.

6.2 Conclusion

Basically, this book specifically explores the level of disclosure and transparency of *Shari'ah* governance practices. Disclosure and transparency in *Shari'ah* governance practices are effective mechanisms for exposing IFIs to market discipline and encouraging them towards a good governance framework and, more importantly, for strengthening the stakeholders' confidence in the IFIs' credibility and in their *Shari'ah*-compliant products and services. This book indicates that there are significance differences in the disclosure and transparency of *Shari'ah* governance practices in Malaysia, GCC countries and the UK. Despite considerable efforts being made by IFIs to improve the level of transparency and disclosure relating to *Shari'ah* governance,

Table 6.10 Shari'ah governance scores according to cluster[a]

Section	Indicator	Cluster 1: 1975–1990 (12 IFIs)	Cluster 2: 1991–2000 (15 IFIs)	Cluster 3: 2001–2005 (26 IFIs)	Cluster 4: 2006–2010 (27 IFIs)	Total score
Commitment to Shari'ah governance	D1	2	2	1	2	7
	D2	2	2	0	2	6
	D3	8	3	16	22	49
***Shari'ah* board information**	D4	3	3	4	3	13
	D5	1	3	4	0	9
	D6	10	14	26	23	73
	D7	10	2	16	16	44
	D8	2	9	16	16	43
	D9	1	3	3	1	8
	D10	10	14	26	23	73
	D11	2	10	16	15	43
	D12	8	4	15	16	43
	D13	7	3	12	7	29
	D14	8	14	24	22	68
	D15	1	3	6	6	16
	D16	1	1	1	2	5
	D17	1	1	2	2	6

		'Improved practice'	'Emerging practice'	'Improved practice'	'Emerging practice'	'Improved practice'
Shari'ah board remuneration	D18	0	2	1	2	5
	D19	3	5	7	5	20
Shari'ah report	D20	3	5	7	4	19
	D21	10	9	15	9	43
	D22	2	1	8	4	15
	D23	1	0	2	2	5
	D24	10	9	16	9	44
Shari'ah pronouncements	D25	1	2	4	1	8
	D26	0	2	3	1	7
	D27	0	1	2	0	3
Shari'ah review	D28	8	4	11	8	31
Information on products and services	D29	12	13	26	23	74
	D30	6	5	9	7	27
Average score		11	9.9	11.5	9.4	10.5
Level of practice		'Improved practice'	'Emerging practice'	'Improved practice'	'Emerging practice'	'Improved practice'

[a] The scores are generated from 30 *Shari'ah* governance disclosure indicators as illustrated in Table 6.1. The total scores of each IFI are 30. IFIs in cluster 1 score 133 out of a possible 360 (12x30), cluster 2, 149 out of 450 (15x30), cluster 3, 299 out of 780 (26x30) and cluster 4, 253 out of 810 (27x30). The total scores are 836 out of 2400. The 'average' is formulated as the scores divide by the number of IFIs.

this book proves that the level of disclosure of Shari'ah governance-related information is relatively low, with 37.5 per cent of IFIs ranked in the 'emerging practice' category, followed by 30 per cent in 'improved practice', more than 16 per centin 'underdeveloped practice', 15 per cent in 'good practice'and only 1.3 per cent in the 'best practice' category. The results further indicate that there are weaknesses and deficiencies in the current system of disclosure of Shari'ah governance practices.

This chapter makes it clear that the current state of disclosure and transparency of Shari'ah governance practices deserves immediate attention, and further reform and improvement, at least in the aspects of commitment to Shari'ah governance, Shari'ah board information, the Shari'ah report, the Shari'ah compliance review, Shari'ah pronouncements and information on products and services. It was observed that IFIs in Malaysia are slightly more transparent than their counterparts in GCC countries and the UK in all six disclosure aspects of Shari'ah governance practices. This position denotes that a proactive regulatory approach to the Shari'ah governance framework, as practised by Malaysia, significantly influences the state of disclosure and transparency of Shari'ah governance practices, as compared to the reactive regulatory approach in the UK and the minimalist regulatory approach in GCC countries. In this regard, undeniably, Malaysia's model of Shari'ah governance has proven that a strong and comprehensive regulatory framework for Islamic finance would be able to drive the market towards more transparent governance practices.

On top of the analysis from a country-specific behaviour perspective, this book also indicates that there is a negative correlation between the ages of IFIs based on year of incorporation and the level of Shari'ah governance disclosure practice. IFIs in cluster 3, which were incorporated in 2001–5, have less experience compared to the IFIs in clusters 1 and 2 yet have a better score on the *Shari'ah* governance disclosure index. This indicates that the level of *Shari'ah* governance disclosure practice is determined by other internal and external factors, such as regulation and well-conceived by-laws and internal policies.

Notes

1. These findings from research conducted by Al-Baluchi (2006) on thirty-four IFIs in Bahrain, Qatar, Jordan and Sudan are contrary to the result found in this book. Al-Baluchi revealed that the implementation of the AAOIFI governance standards had significantly increased the level of voluntary disclosure in IFIs' annual reports with an average of 35% improvement in Bahrain, Qatar and Jordan (Al-Baluchi 2006: 192). This position suggests that the adoption of the AAOIFI governance standards is not the sole factor that may improve the level of transparency of IFIs.

2. It is important to note that the percentages on a comparative overview to illustrate country-specific behavior practices in this section refer to the group of IFIs in the individual jurisdictions.

3. The BNM (2009: 100) reports that the rules on the restriction on individuals sitting on more than one *Shari'ah* board increased the total number of *Shari'ah* experts in the period 2004–9 to more than 100 individual *Shari'ah* scholars.

4. This is highlighted by Jawad Ali who mentions that there were mistakes committed by *Shari'ah* boards due to them merely focusing on the instruments being presented by the IFIs rather than monitoring and meticulously scrutinising the whole implementation of certain Islamic financial products and services (Pasha 2010a).

5. It is worth mentioning that these figures may not represent

the actual amount of remuneration of *Shari'ah* board members in IFIs. Such estimation and simulation of *Shari'ah* board membership attempt to highlight the need for immediate measures to control and govern *Shari'ah* board remuneration practices.

THE WAY FORWARD

7.0 Introduction

Based on its overall research findings, this book summarises the state of *Shari'ah* governance practices in IFIs in Malaysia, GCC countries and the UK by classifying them into five different categories, as illustrated in Table 7.1 (*Shari'ah* governance areas investigated: general approach; regulatory and internal framework; roles of the *Shari'ah* board; attributes of the *Shari'ah* board in terms of independence, competence, transparency and confidentiality; operational procedures; and assessment of the *Shari'ah* board) and Table 7.2 (*Shari'ah* governance disclosure practices).

Tables 7.1 and 7.2 specifically demonstrate the level of *Shari'ah* governance disclosure practice. Both tables reveal that the average level of *Shari'ah* governance practice in IFIs only falls into the 'improved practice' category, showing weak governance practices and indicating the need for major improvement in almost all aspects of *Shari'ah* governance. Within these negative findings, this book demonstrates that IFIs in Malaysia have better *Shari'ah* governance practices when compared to IFIs in GCC countries and the UK. This book suggests three main propositions based on the above research findings. Firstly, a strong regulatory framework leads to better *Shari'ah* governance practices.

Table 7.1 *State of* Shari'ah *governance practices*

Shari'ah governance practices	Underdeveloped practice	Emerging practice	Improved practice	Good practice	Best practice	Average practice
Malaysia (17 IFIs)			35.2%	64.7%		'Good practice'
GCC countries (16 IFIs)	35.2%	18.8%	43.8%			'Emerging practice'
UK (2 IFIs)			50%	50%		'Improved practice'
Overall (35 IFIs)	17.1%	8.6%	40%	32%		'Improved practice'

Table 7.2 State of Shari'ah governance disclosure practices

Shari'ah governance practices	Underdeveloped practice	Emerging practice	Improved practice	Good practice	Best practice	Average practice
Malaysia (20 IFIs)		15%	30%	50%	5%	'Improved practice'
GCC countries (54 IFIs)	22.2%	46.2%	29.6%	1.9%		'Emerging practice'
UK (6 IFIs)	16.7%	33.3%	33.3%	16.7%		'Emerging practice'
Overall (80 IFIs)	16.3%	37.5%	30%	15%	1.3%	'Improved practice'

Secondly, less interference from regulatory authorities and lack of a regulatory framework for Shari'ah governance contribute to weak Shari'ah governance practices. Thirdly, the extent of Shari'ah governance practices is also determined by the attitude of the IFIs' management.

A comprehensive regulatory framework is one of the factors that significantly influences the level of Shari'ah governance practices. Well-conceived regulation and a proactive approach of the regulatory authorities, such as is the case in Malaysia, contribute to the better development of a Shari'ah governance system. Considering the importance of an integrated regulatory approach, this book suggests that having numerous rules and regulations on Shari'ah governance will not guarantee the improvement of Shari'ah governance practices in the industry per se. Supervision and enforcement are essential to ensure compliance with the existing rules, regulations and guidelines. This important point then leads to the formulation of the second proposition.

This book suggests that less interference and the lack of a regulatory framework for Shari'ah governance are factors that impede the development of Shari'ah governance practices. In view of the market immaturity in the Islamic finance industry, and lack of self-initiative on the aspect of governance, we cannot expect that IFIs will develop and portray strong Shari'ah governance practices voluntarily and without proper supervision. This is affirmed by the findings on the state of Shari'ah governance practices in GCC countries. Although regulatory frameworks in Bahrain, the UAE and Qatar clearly mention the adoption of the AAOIFI governance standards, the implementation of these governance standards has nevertheless not significantly or positively influenced the level of Shari'ah governance practice. This position denotes that having an appropriate legal framework without proper supervision and enforcement will not guarantee the betterment of *Shari'ah* governance practices in IFIs.

While the first two propositions refer to external factors of *Shari'ah* governance practices, the third proposition concerns an internal factor in that it denotes the importance of a proactive approach of the individual IFI to facilitate the implementation of Islamic finance by emphasising the requirement for *Shari'ah* compliance. In this regard, the state of *Shari'ah* governance practices in IFIs is greatly dependent on the attitude of IFIs' management, particularly its BOD, senior management and *Shari'ah* board. Full commitment of the IFIs' management to the subject of *Shari'ah* compliance is one of the determining factors for better *Shari'ah* governance practice. Well-conceived by-laws and internal policies on *Shari'ah* governance at IFI or 'micro' level will then complement the rules and guidelines of regulations at the 'macro' level.

In summary, this book concludes that the overall *Shari'ah* governance practices in Malaysia, GCC countries and the UK are still at a very minimal level. Based on all the research analysis and observations, this book suggests that the extent of *Shari'ah* governance practices is greatly dependent on the regulatory frameworks, the proactive approach of regulatory authorities and the positive attitude of the IFIs' management. These three components are the determining factors to ensure better *Shari'ah* governance practices in IFIs. Therefore, any efforts and initiatives at the 'micro' or 'macro' level for the improvement and enhancement of *Shari'ah* governance practices must be supported and facilitated with a comprehensive and integrated regulatory framework, strong support from regulatory authorities and the positive attitude of IFIs' management.

7.1 The way forward

This book offers some recommendations to enhance the existing *Shari'ah* governance framework by promoting the key elements of good *Shari'ah* governance.

7.1.1 *Stakeholder-oriented approach*

The foundational dimension of Islamic corporate governance is rooted in the stakeholder-oriented approach, in which its governance style aims at protecting the rights and interests of all stakeholders rather than maximising the shareholders' profit, as in the shareholder value orientation. Considering the dominant position of the shareholder value model of corporate governance worldwide, particularly in Malaysia, GCC countries and the UK, the author strongly insists that the IFIs depart from this inappropriate system by adopting the stakeholder-oriented approach to corporate governance. The adoption of the stakeholder-oriented approach would enhance the corporate governance dimension of IFIs, where all stakeholders, including the *Shari'ah* board, the BOD, the shareholders, the depositors and the managers, play significant roles in ensuring the realisation of the corporation's goal and fulfilling the *maqāsid Shari'ah*. This will help to bring the IFIs closer to the aspirational position of an Islamic moral economy.

7.1.2 *Regulatory-based approach*

This book reveals that the jurisdiction with the strongest regulatory framework has the best *Shari'ah* governance practices in almost all areas investigated. In view of the infancy of the Islamic finance industry and the numerous challenges that may impede the development of Islamic finance, it is strongly recommended that a *Shari'ah* governance system be systematically regulated. In outlining the appropriate legal framework for Islamic finance, a study by the IMF on prudential and supervision issues in Islamic finance laid down three important key points pertaining to governance in IFIs, namely a legal foundation for supervision of IFIs must be in place, all kinds of risk must be dealt with, and there must be adequate information disclosure (Errico and Farahbaksh 1998: 15).

In this regard, this book strongly recommends that the regulators and policymakers should promulgate specific regulations on a *Shari'ah* governance system by taking into consideration the key points formulated by Errico and Farahbaksh (1998). This regulatory framework should cover the whole process of *Shari'ah* governance by considering the overall market practice and the local legal environment. While regulation is expected to govern and regulate the market effectively, it is worth noting that over-restrictive regulation can also be counter-productive and may impede the development of Islamic finance. With this understanding, the regulators should ensure they take into consideration all these points when tailoring the regulatory framework for *Shari'ah* governance.

7.1.3 *Centralised* Shari'ah *board*

The ideal *Shari'ah* governance system requires a proper structure for the *Shari'ah* board. It is good practice to have two layers of *Shari'ah* board structure, that is, *Shari'ah* boards at both 'micro' and 'macro' levels. The establishment of a *Shari'ah* board at the 'macro' (or national) level is strongly recommended as it may become the highest authority in Islamic finance in a country and may resolve any issues raised by the *Shari'ah* boards within IFIs. The setting up of a national *Shari'ah* board is expected to build and maintain the confidence of various stakeholders in IFIs. As an independent body that operates within non-profitable institutions, the national *Shari'ah* board would be able to play its role to enhance the practice of Islamic finance by promoting the integration of *maqāsid Shari'ah*where all stakeholders' interests and rights are protected.

Another layer of *Shari'ah* board structure at the international level is needed in order to resolve issues involving cross-border jurisdictions and for *Shari'ah* harmonisation purposes. In this respect, the existing AAOIFI *Shari'ah* board may be considered as the main reference *Shari'ah* board for any jurisdiction. However, it is worth noting that this recommendation may not be appropriate to some jurisdictions, particularly to purely secular legal environments. In this instance, the regulatory authorities should have a clear understanding of market practice and identify which model would be appropriate to IFIs under their supervision.

7.1.4 *Composition of the BOD*

The ideal function of the *Shari'ah* board is advisory and supervisory but with the executive power still in the hands of the BOD. The author agrees with the principle in IFSB-10, which requires the BOD and senior management of IFIs to have certain minimum criteria in terms of knowledge and experience pertaining to *Shari'ah*-related matters. The selection of the BOD members and senior management should be based on these additional criteria.

In view of the importance of *Shari'ah* input during the BOD meetings, it is strongly recommended that the BOD has at least one member with a sound knowledge of *Shari'ah* as an independent director. This independent director will be able to provide input, information and views on the aspects of *Shari'ah*, Islamic ethics and values, which are an important base for any decision-making. This representation is also essential as an indication of the stakeholder-value orientation of the IFI to protect the rights and interests of stakeholders, particularly the investment account holders.

7.1.5 Composition of the Shari'ah board

It is clear from this book that different practices with regards the composition of *Shari'ah* board are currently prevailing. It would be good practice for the *Shari'ah* board to have a minimum number of three members. In line with IFSB-10 and the AAOIFI governance standards, it is recommended for IFIs to have mixed members from different *madhahib* and different nationalities without neglecting local expertise. *Shari'ah* rulings coming from the mixed members of a *Shari'ah* board would mitigate any potential inconsistency as well as ensure its acceptability in other jurisdictions.

The practice of appointing non-*Shari'ah* experts, such as scholars and experts in law, finance, banking, economics and accounting, is also acceptable subject to certain limitations. Those members may provide their views and actively participate in the *Shari'ah* board meetings but they should not have voting rights. This is affirmed by findings from the semi-structured interviews, where the majority of *Shari'ah* scholars agreed on such a practice and admitted their limited knowledge on subjects other than *Shari'ah*. It would also be very good *Shari'ah* board practice for the board to have an executive member who would engage and deal with the day-to-day operations. Unlike the regular *Shari'ah* board members, the executive members should be full-time staff in the IFIs and work on a daily basis, providing *Shari'ah* consultancy services from time to time.

7.1.6 Shari'ah advisory firms

This book reveals that some IFIs opt to engage a *Shari'ah* advisory firm as their organisational arrangement for *Shari'ah* governance and this practice is popular for Islamic windows, Islamic investment collective scheme institutions and Islamic fund management companies. Since the *Shari'ah* advisory firm is not one of the internal organs of governance in IFIs, some mechanisms may need to be imposed to regulate such a practice. IFSB-10 seems to fail to adequately address this issue and has only very minor provision stating the position pertaining to *Shari'ah* advisory firms.

The regulators should consider the framework for *Shari'ah* advisory firms and this includes licensing, professional indemnity insurance, mandatory reporting, confidentiality and transparency. Another important aspect that needs to be addressed is the rules on shareholding of *Shari'ah* scholars and advisory services provided by their companies. It would be good practice if the regulators issued licences for the *Shari'ah* advisory firms and put certain conditions on them. This licence could be renewed if the *Shari'ah* advisory firms satisfy all the necessary conditions set by the regulators. It is also necessary for the regulators to require the *Shari'ah* advisory firms to have professional indemnity insurance. In the event that the *Shari'ah* advisory firms have a relationship with particular IFIs, such as common shareholders or directors, they should exclude themselves from doing any business with them. This may help the IFIs to mitigate risk due to negligence or being wrongly advised by the *Shari'ah* advisory firm. Furthermore, the policy for the *Shari'ah* advisory firm must cover the aspects of mandatory reporting, confidentiality and transparency.

7.1.7 *Adoption of IFSB-10 and the AAOIFI governance standards*

The survey clearly indicates that the level of awareness of IFIs regarding the development of *Shari'ah* governance is slightly low, withe more than 22per cent of IFIs not aware of the existence of IFSB-10. In fact, only 45.7per cent of IFIs have adopted the AAOIFI governance standards. This position indicates that numerous IFIs do not have adequate and sound guidelines for their *Shari'ah* governance system. The AAOIFI governance standards lay down key principles, guidelines, standard formats and a code of ethics that are very important for the purpose of *Shari'ah* governance. On top of that, based on the comprehensive study of the issue of *Shari'ah* governance in various countries, IFSB-10 provides guidelines and standards of best practice of *Shari'ah* governance for IFIs.

The key principles of competence, independency, consistency, transparency and confidentiality formulated in IFSB-10 are really important for any *Shari'ah* governance system. Hence, this book strongly recommends the adoption of IFSB-10 by regulators or supervisors as well as IFIs to enhance and strengthen the *Shari'ah* governance framework. Once the documents are adopted, the IFSB, with proper coordination by the AAOIFI, can play a watchdog role to monitor, supervise and revise the implementation of the *Shari'ah* governance system.

7.1.8 *Proactive approach and integrated corporate and* Shari'ah *governance*

In view of the numerous challenges faced by Islamic finance, it is recommended that the industry adopts a regulatory-based framework as explained before. As a prerequisite, *Shari'ah* governance must be one of the concerns of regulators and policymakers. The regulators should proactively monitor the implementation of *Shari'ah* governance and learn from the experience of other jurisdictions in nurturing the *Shari'ah* governance framework. The principle of 'one-size-fits-all' *Shari'ah* governance is not appropriate as the market and local legal environments differ from one place to another.

In designing the *Shari'ah* governance framework, it is a matter of necessity to have an integrated corporate and *Shari'ah* governance framework. These two things must not be segregated as they complement each other. Therefore, the principles or guidelines on corporate governance must take into account the element of *Shari'ah* governance when it involves institutions offering Islamic financial services. This is important because the stakeholder-oriented model of governance in IFIs requires them to protect the rights and interests of all stakeholders.

7.1.9 Supervision and enforcement

The regulators should have a comprehensive framework of the aspects of supervision and enforcement, and these include written guidelines on supervision for supervisors, directives for IFIs issued by supervisors, sufficient resources with adequate knowledge on *Shari'ah* governance-related matters and full authority to carry out the enforcement functions. The supervisors should provide guidelines and make sure that they evaluate the internal policies and procedures as well as the implementation of these procedures. It is also important for the supervisors to consistently inspect the IFIs, having a proper framework in place which allows them to make an assessment of IFIs' *Shari'ah* governance policies and tools to redress any deficiencies.

7.1.10 Dispute settlement

The existing framework for dispute settlement puts Islamic finance cases under the jurisdiction of the civil court, with the exception of Saudi Arabia where they fall under the auspices of the Banking Dispute Settlement. This position raises an issue as to the ability of the court or the judge to hear cases involving *Shari'ah* matters. Therefore, it would be an ideal development if the regulators initiated a special bench for Islamic finance cases as part of the court's structure. To this special bench, the court may appoint judges who are knowledgeable in Islamic finance or the regulators may allocate a certain amount of funds to provide training for those judges. On top of that, a reliable *Shari'ah* litigation system must also be in place. It is understood that in a secular legal environment, such as in the UK, the above arrangement is slightly difficult to implement. Therefore, it is important for the regulators in the secular legal environment to consider a court referral to a *Shari'ah* board or a *Shari'ah* expert to determine cases involving *Shari'ah* issues. Alternatively, a special tribunal for Islamic finance cases may be established to handle disputes involving IFIs in this kind of jurisdiction.

The policymakers should also take into account other legal avenues for dispute settlement, such as arbitration and mediation. At this point in time, there are several institutions for international dispute resolution, such as the Dubai Centre for Arbitration and Conciliation, the GCC Commercial Arbitration Centre, the Bahrain Centre for International Commercial Arbitration Centre, the International Chamber of Commerce's International Court of Arbitration, the London Court of International Arbitration, the Kuwait Centre for Commercial Arbitration, the Kuala Lumpur Arbitration Centre, among others. In view of these numerous arbitration centres, it is recommended that there should be one specific institution that offers alternative dispute resolutions and settlement for Islamic finance cases. Alternatively, the existing arbitration centres should develop and enhance their expertise and capabilities in Islamic finance in terms of resources, frameworks, procedures and facilities to address the need for dispute settlement involving Islamic finance cases.

7.1.11 *Well-conceived by-laws and internal policies*

This book reveals that many IFIs do not have by-laws or internal policies pertaining to *Shari'ah* governance. Well-conceived by-laws and internal policies are prerequisites of effective *Shari'ah* governance. Realising this, IFIs should have appropriate by-laws and policies as guidelines for their own internal use, in terms of meeting procedures, decision-making, preparing reports and dissemination of information, records and reviews. IFSB-10 and the AAOIFI governance standards may be the basis for such by-laws, with some modifications appropriate to implementation within the particular local market and regulatory environment.

7.1.12 *Full mandate and clear definition of duties and functions*

The regulators should define the *Shari'ah* board's duties and functions precisely, including their areas of responsibilities, authority level and reporting lines. The functions of the *Shari'ah* board should be limited to the advisory and supervisory roles. Effectiveness of the *Shari'ah* board functions can only be achieved if the regulators, as well as the IFIs, precisely define the relationship between the *Shari'ah* boards and other organs of governance in IFIs. This is crucial to give full mandate and authority to the *Shari'ah* board, and at the same time other organs of governance such as management, the BOD and employees must respect and comply with the directions and instructions given by the *Shari'ah* board. With regard to IFIs operating in numerous jurisdictions, the *Shari'ah* board should understand the IFI's operational structure. The *Shari'ah* board should constantly review the appropriateness of *Shari'ah* pronouncements and take into consideration all aspects, including the legal environment, difference of *madhhab* and implications of the rulings.

7.1.13 Expanding the scope of duties and functions

The present practice with regards the scope of the *Shari'ah* board's duties and functions mainly emphasises the issuance of *Shari'ah* pronouncements and, hence, their role does not include any proactive approach. It is imperative to stress the need to inculcate Islamic ethics and values as well as the social dimension into the *Shari'ah* board's responsibility. This aspect will truly add value to Islamic finance as a part of the existing financial system. The *Shari'ah* board should play a more active role in the IFIs' operations and activities, such as participating in the design of policies, procedures and training programmes. The regulators should encourage the IFIs, through the *Shari'ah* board, to implement Islamic ethics and values and to give more consideration to the social dimension. Perhaps some incentives in the form of awards to individual *Shari'ah* scholars as well as the institution of a systematic *Shari'ah* board development programme would be a good initiative.

7.1.14 Limitation on multiple appointments

This book reveals that some *Shari'ah* scholars have enjoyed the privilege of sitting on the boards of numerous IFIs without any sort of limitation. This may raise a serious issue of credibility and damage the image of the *Shari'ah* board as well as introducing a potential conflict of interest. While this book claims that sitting on numerous *Shari'ah* boards is an acceptable practice due to market considerations and, to a certain extent, the shortage of qualified *Shari'ah* scholars, it strongly recommends that some limitations be put in place for efficiency and, more importantly, for overcoming any conflict of interest and promoting transparency. In this regard, serving on a maximum of five *Shari'ah* boards at one particular time might be appropriate as a standard practice. In the event that there is a potential conflict of interest, the IFIs or the *Shari'ah* board members themselves must disqualify individuals from being involved in those transactions. In addition, the IFIs are also recommended to monitor and assess the commitment and discipline of the *Shari'ah* board members to check that they allocate sufficient time and effort to performing their duties with due diligence.

7.1.15 *Minimum and high standard of fit and proper criteria*

The findings in this book reveal that there are significant differences in the attributes of *Shari'ah* boards relating to competence and independence. Some IFIs did not even have a clear policy on the requirement of fit and proper criteria for selecting the *Shari'ah* board. In this regard, it would be appropriate for both the regulators and the IFIs to set minimum standards on the fit and proper criteria for selecting the *Shari'ah* board members. Four attributes must be taken into consideration, namely academic qualifications, experience and exposure, track record and good character. Before their appointment, additional measures may be taken requiring the *Shari'ah* board members to make statutory declarations pertaining to all of these criteria. A particularly high standard of fit and proper criteria might be needed in the case of *Shari'ah* boards at the international and national levels, including *Shari'ah* advisory services involving sophisticated Islamic financial products.

It is contended that the effectiveness of the *Shari'ah* board mainly depends on the role played by its chairman. Therefore, it is important to set up different criteria for the chairman of the *Shari'ah* board. Senior *Shari'ah* scholars with vast experience in the industry would be ideal for this position. In addition, it is also important to limit individual scholars to chairmanship of not more than three IFIs at one particular time, as multiple chairmanship positions may raise serious issues of conflict of interest. It is also worth considering a rotation of the chairman of the *Shari'ah* board.

7.1.16 *Corporate governance committee and nomination committee*

In line with the recommendation of the IFSB, it is recommended that the IFIs set up a corporate governance committee. This committee should offer mixed expertise from interdisciplinary members including representatives of the *Shari'ah* board. The function of this corporate governance committee would be to monitor the IFIs' implementation of corporate and *Shari'ah* governance guidelines and principles. The corporate governance committee should also have the function of overseeing and implementing the governance framework that will protect the interest of all stakeholders, particularly investment account holders since they have no right of governance participation. While the corporate governance committee are concerned with the implementation of corporate governance matters, the nomination committee, which selects and nominates the BOD, can also be used to identify and filter appropriate members for the *Shari'ah* board. This nomination committee will have a specific policy on the fit and proper criteria for *Shari'ah* board members.

7.1.17 *Specific funds and continuous training programme*

This book discloses that the majority of *Shari'ah* scholars do not have backgrounds in banking, finance or economics.

This position may hinder their ability to provide sound and solid *Shari'ah* rulings because such knowledge is a tool to understanding and appreciating the whole picture of certain products and services. To overcome this, the *Shari'ah* board should undergo ongoing training in technical and industry-specific knowledge of banking and finance, and any other necessary areas that enhance their professional, ethical and technical skills. It would be good practice for newly appointed *Shari'ah* board members to attend orientation and induction programmes to make them familiar with the operational and technical aspects of IFIs. At the same time, the IFIs should consistently introduce measures for annual training for *Shari'ah* board members.

To these ends, a specific allocation of funds should be established either at national or IFI level. At the national level, the regulators should allocate a certain amount of funds to develop training programmes for *Shari'ah* boards as well as *Shari'ah* auditors. For long-term development, it is also important to consider an academic approach, such as developing a syllabus and academic programme in the institutions of higher learning and any research institutions. At the IFIs' level, an annual financial allocation for a *Shari'ah* training programme should be put in place. This is important for the purpose of ongoing training for employees, *Shari'ah* board members, managers, directors and even shareholders pertaining to *Shari'ah* and its related knowledge.

7.1.18 *Young* Shari'ah *scholar programme*
This book reveals that the top sixteen *Shari'ah* scholars hold more than 100 board positions with an average of 6.5 positions for each scholar. In fact, some individual scholars hold up to seventy-eight board positions and twenty-one chairman positions around the globe (Unal 2010: 6). This may

lead to serious issues regarding independence, conflict of interest and confidentiality, as well as the ability of *Shari'ah* scholars to provide their services with due diligence. Understanding the issue of the shortage of qualified scholars, it is recommended that the regulators, with the cooperation of IFIs, develop a 'young *Shari'ah* scholar programme'. This programme might have a 'mentor–mentee' approach, where potential young *Shari'ah* scholars are allowed to sit on the *Shari'ah* board under the auspices of senior *Shari'ah* scholars. After a certain stipulated time, with the recommendation of the chairman of the *Shari'ah* board, these young scholars will then be admitted and qualified to be full members of the *Shari'ah* board.

7.1.18 *Method of appointment*

This book reveals that there are significant differences in the method of appointment of the *Shari'ah* board between IFIs. It is also found that numerous IFIs did not comply with the AAOIFI governance standards in that their appointments are made by the BOD and not the shareholders. In view of the actual market practice and more practical tools for ensuring independence, this book considers that there are other mechanisms that would be appropriate. Firstly, the appointment must be made either by the BOD or the shareholders. Secondly, the appointment must be subject to the approval of the regulatory authorities. Thirdly, the appointment must not be permanent but rather contractual, subject to renewal. Fourthly, termination and dismissal must also be subject to the approval of the regulatory authorities.

7.1.19 *Code of conduct*

This book clearly indicates that the majority of IFIs do not have a written code of ethics for the *Shari'ah* board. The existing practices seem to presume that *Shari'ah* board members are bound by Islamic ethical principles. In view of the need to have a certain and precise code of ethics specific and exclusive to the *Shari'ah* board, the regulatory authorities as well as the IFIs may prescribe certain acceptable behaviour for *Shari'ah* board members. It is incumbent upon the IFIs to initiate and develop an internal code of conduct for the *Shari'ah* board. This code of ethics should be enforceable and there must be a mechanism within the organisational structure to ensure its strict implementation. Breach of this code of ethics may incur disciplinary action, such as suspension, termination or other kinds of sanctions.

7.1.20 *Professional body*

This book finds that there is no professional body specifically established to set standard practice guidelines for the *Shari'ah* board such as is the case for other professionals, such as lawyers, accountants, medical practitioners and engineers. The establishment of a professional body to set the qualifications of the *Shari'ah* board, to introduce a standard code of conduct, to develop a training programme and to enhance the professionalism of the *Shari'ah* board is consider necessary at this point in time. At the moment, different bodies attempt to provide qualification programmes for *Shari'ah* boards, such as the AAOIFI Certified *Shari'ah* Adviser and Auditor, the Scholar Development Program initiated by the IFC Islamic Finance Council and the SII, and the IBFIM *Shari'ah* Scholars Introduction Program, but such qualifications have not been accepted universally. This book strongly recommends the establishment of an 'Association of *Shari'ah* Advisors' at national and international levels. With this association, the quality of a *Shari'ah* board can then also be rated by an independent agency, similar to a credit-rating agency.

7.1.21 Remuneration policy

This book demonstrates that there are significant differences in the remuneration of different *Shari'ah* boards. The absence of any policy limitation or guidelines on the *Shari'ah* board's remuneration may lead to unhealthy practices. The top ten *Shari'ah* scholars, who dominated the board positions in IFIs around the world, earn a very significant amount. It was found that a chairman of a *Shari'ah* board could earn USD 50,000 to USD 100,000 per board (Pasha 2010b) and a top scholar could even gain up to USD 250,000 on a typical capital markets deal (Devi 2008). This book further estimates that the top five *Shari'ah* scholars may earn up to a million dollars per year for servicing more than a hundred board and chairman positions around the world. While there is no standard benchmark or scale fee for *Shari'ah* advisors, the regulators as well as the IFIs should establish a specific policy for the remuneration of *Shari'ah* board members based on appropriate fee scales. In the context of the internal policy of IFIs, the *Shari'ah* board fee scales should be approved by the shareholders and disclosed in the annual report.

7.1.22 Codification and Shari'ah harmonisation

The ideal approach to ensure consistency is by way of codification of *Shari'ah* standards and a *Shari'ah* harmonisation process. It is worth mentioning that such an approach must be carried out with proper coordination, commitment and the agreement of the industry players. As a good start, adoption of the AAOIFI *Shari'ah* standards should be the first approach to minimising the inconsistency of *Shari'ah* rulings. In view of the different market environments, legal frameworks and local needs, IFIs may adopt the AAOIFI *Shari'ah* standards with some flexibility as to their application.

The issue of inconsistency of *Shari'ah* pronouncements and conflicting views of the *Shari'ah* board can also be resolved by having a central *Shari'ah* body at the national level. In the first instance, the *Shari'ah* boards at IFI level should try to comply with the *Shari'ah* standards and, in the absence of specification of the products in the *Shari'ah* standards, IFIs should adopt the *Shari'ah* pronouncements issued by the central *Shari'ah* board. This will reconcile the issue of inconsistency as the decision made by the *Shari'ah* board at the national level will prevail over any *Shari'ah* rulings at individual IFI level. In the event that both the AAOIFI *Shari'ah* standards and central *Shari'ah* board pronouncements are unable to provide any solution, IFIs then may issue new and fresh rulings. Consistency in *Shari'ah* pronouncements can only be achieved if there is proper coordination and alignment of policy and frameworks from all *Shari'ah* boards at the individual IFI level as well as at national and international levels.

7.1.23 *Proper channel for conflicting views of* Shari'ah *scholars*

Inconsistency may also happen when *Shari'ah* scholars have conflicting opinions in the public forums. This position will confuse the general public as well as the industry players, particularly in the event that different *Shari'ah* rulings are issued upon the same financial products. In view of this issue, it is important for the *Shari'ah* scholars to air their conflicting views in a proper forum and not in the public forum. In this regard, the *Shari'ah* board should have a spokesperson that will make a statement on behalf of the institution. In the event that the individual *Shari'ah* scholars intend to air their own opinion, they must clearly make a declaration as to the opinion being their personal one.

7.1.24 *Full access to information and disclosure policy*

The IFIs need to improve their transparency and disclosure on *Shari'ah* governance as the findings of this book indicate poor disclosure practice overall. *Shari'ah* boards should have access to all information pertaining to *Shari'ah* compliance matters. They must be granted the right and authority to obtain views from the staff, particularly the internal *Shari'ah* auditors, as well as the external auditors. It is important for the *Shari'ah* board to receive adequate resources, information and recognition to carry out their duty.

With respect to the nature of operation and structure of IFIs, information disclosure is more important than in conventional banking. Unlike conventional banking institutions that tend to concentrate on financial disclosure and risk assessment, in addition the IFIs need to disclose necessary information pertaining to *Shari'ah* governance-related matters. The regulators as well as the IFIs should develop suitable information on disclosure requirements within a market-transparency framework. Amongst the types of *Shari'ah* governance information that should be ordinarily disclosed are the *Shari'ah* board information, products and services, corporate governance structure, code of conduct, treatment of *zakah* and corporate social responsibility, and remuneration of the *Shari'ah* board. It is also good practice to disclose, in the annual report, the percentage of profit contributions from activities, products and services that have an element of unlawful and doubtful transactions according to *Shari'ah*.

7.1.25 *Publication of* Shari'ah *rulings*

This book found weak practices in IFIs in the aspect of disseminating *Shari'ah* information, particularly publication of the *Shari'ah* rulings. Practice indicates that only the

Shari'ah board at the regulatory level proactively publishes
and disseminates information on *Shari'ah* pronouncements.
However, it is recommended that the *Shari'ah* board com-
pile and publish the *Shari'ah* pronouncements and makes
them known to the public in a consistent manner. In view
of the commercial nature of IFIs, the author admits that
publication of the *Shari'ah* pronouncements may be considered unfair to the industry players as they have to com-
pete with one another and any disclosure of information on
new products, including new *Shari'ah* rulings, may impede
their business strategy as well as create additional cost to
IFIs. It is recommended that the publication of *Shari'ah* rulings be done annually, with full compilation and details of
their pronouncements, and that this can be via IFI websites.

7.1.26 Shari'ah *governance disclosure index*

The content analysis approach in this book attempts to
introduce a simple *Shari'ah* governance index for IFIs,
which is quite similar to other types of indexes, such as the
Environment, Social and Governance Index. It is strongly
recommended that independent institutions, such as the
IFSB or the AAOIFI, with the cooperation of another
institution, develop and introduce a specific *Shari'ah* governance index for IFIs. The IFIs then can be rated and
ranked in accordance with the *Shari'ah* governance index
score which can be formulated from IFSB-10, the AAOIFI
governance standards and any other *Shari'ah* governance
guidelines. Some incentives, such as an award for the best
IFI for *Shari'ah* governance, may be introduced at national,
regional and international levels. The *Shari'ah* governance
index introduced in this book may in fact be a good model
to develop into a more comprehensive index that would be
accepted by IFIs worldwide. This book considers that such
a *Shari'ah* governance index would directly and indirectly

influence the IFIs to enhance and improve their *Shariʿah* governance practices.

7.1.27 Shariʿah *reporting standards*

Baydoun and Willet (2000) are of the view that IFIs need to have a wider scope of Islamic corporate reporting due to the nature and foundational dimension of Islamic finance as compared to its conventional counterpart. The author positively supports the notion of having a different scope to Islamic corporate reporting of Baydoun and Willet (2000) with some further enhancement to the scope of reporting. In spite of the need for having specific Islamic financial reporting standards, this book also suggests a call for *Shariʿah* reporting standards.

In view of the weak practice of *Shariʿah* reporting, as demonstrated by the sampled IFIs, it is very important for the regulatory authorities as well as IFIs to set a minimum standard for the *Shariʿah* report. The regulatory authorities should issue directives or guidelines on the standard format of the *Shariʿah* report. The IFIs then should use these standard guidelines and format in preparing their *Shariʿah* report, which must be submitted to the BOD with the approval of shareholders before it can be further reported to the respective regulatory authorities. The ideal *Shariʿah* report should contain necessary information on *Shariʿah* compliance. Unlike the financial report, the *Shariʿah* report is classified as non-financial disclosure and therefore requires a different format. Here, it is recommended that the *Shariʿah* report contain activities of the *Shariʿah* board, including training and meetings, details of the meetings, *Shariʿah* pronouncements with detailed explanations, an *ex ante* report pertaining to products and services, an *ex post* internal *Shariʿah* review report and certification of the *Shariʿah* compliance report. In terms of the *Shariʿah* report structure, IFIs are encouraged to prepare a separate chapter on the *Shari'ah* report as part of the annual report or, alternatively, the *Shari'ah* report may form part of the corporate governance report.

7.1.28 Shari'ah *coordination*

This book reveals that some IFIs have not established a *Shari'ah* department to coordinate *Shari'ah* governance matters, or they consider it under the auspices of the company secretary or compliance officer. It would be good practice for IFIs to set up a *Shari'ah* department that may carry out numerous functions within the *Shari'ah* governance process, such as coordinating the *Shari'ah* board meetings, recording the minutes of the meetings, research and development, developing internal policies for *Shari'ah* governance, conducting *Shari'ah* training, publishing the *Shari'ah* pronouncements and coordinating enquiries from employees, consumers or any other parties.

Another important function of *Shari'ah* coordination is to assist the *Shari'ah* board and IFIs in conducting research and development pertaining to *Shari'ah*-related matters. It would be good practice to have a specific unit for *Shari'ah* research and development under the auspices of the head of the *Shari'ah* department. This unit will assist the *Shari'ah* board in terms of *Shari'ah* research and development as well as disseminating information for the purpose of educating IFIs, customers, employees and other stakeholders about *Shari'ah* rules and principles. Appropriate *Shari'ah* coordination is important to ensure the efficiency of the *Shari'ah* board as well as the *Shari'ah* control process. With high market competitiveness, *Shari'ah* coordination will have a considerable impact on the efficiency of IFIs, both in terms of products and services offered and also the quality of *Shari'ah* compliance.

7.1.29 Shari'ah *internal control*

The *Shari'ah* board relies heavily on the internal *Shari'ah* audit and other employees in carrying out its *ex post* functions. With respect to this, it is crucial for the IFIs to enhance the role of internal *Shari'ah* auditors by having a proper policy on documentation, clear segregation of duties, and appropriate fraud prevention and detection controls. To operate this function effectively, IFIs are recommended to establish a *Shari'ah* internal audit department or alternatively to set up a *Shari'ah* internal audit unit under the existing audit department. This is in line with the IFSB-10 recommendation of having an internal *Shari'ah* compliance unit and internal *Shari'ah* review unit as a point of reference for *Shari'ah* compliance issues, to manage the clerical and secretarial matters and to provide *Shari'ah* input for executive decisions (IFSB 2009d: 10).

IFIs should ensure that the *Shari'ah* internal control unit has adequate resources and the capability of doing the audit and review effectively. In addition, IFIs are recommended to have an appropriate policy on *Shari'ah* internal control. These policies should be designed so that *Shari'ah* compliance can be inspected and monitored in daily activities. The role of the internal audit is to evaluate and assess the effectiveness of *Shari'ah* governance and compliance with the *Shari'ah* rulings. Internal *Shari'ah* audit departments should have a specific charter approved by the BOD to guarantee that the review can be made independently, impartially and objectively. In terms of reporting structure, the *Shari'ah* internal audit should report to the *Shari'ah* board and the BOD, not to the audit committee, since the committee does not have expertise in *Shari'ah*. This book offers another alternative approach for *Shari'ah* internal audit reporting lines: the report may be made to the audit committee with the condition that one of the audit committee members must be a representative of the *Shari'ah* board.

7.1.30 *External* Shari'ah *auditors*

There are shortcomings with respect to the *Shari'ah* auditing process and this includes the external audit practices. Chapra and Ahmed (2002: 68–9) propose three options to address the issue of the *Shari'ah* audit and the most preferable one is for the existing chartered audit firm to undertake the *Shari'ah* audit function. In addition, this book considers that *Shari'ah* advisory firms that have the necessary expertise may also undertake *Shari'ah* audit responsibilities.

To regulate and monitor these external *Shari'ah* auditors, appropriate guidelines and directives must be in place. To achieve this, the regulators should issue a policy on their requirements of external *Shari'ah* auditors, including the scope, framework, criteria, conditions, process, qualification, training programme and reporting structure. To address the issue of the shortage of audit firms and *Shari'ah* advisory firms, as well as lack of experts capable of performing the *Shari'ah* audit, the regulators may initiate some incentives and provide support to develop the *Shari'ah* audit programme. Another important aspect of the external *Shari'ah* audit is the method of appointment. Similar to the normal audit practice, the appointment of external *Shari'ah* auditors should be made by the shareholders.

7.1.31 Shari'ah *board meetings*

The majority of *Shari'ah* scholars spend most of their time and effort dedicated to the IFIs during the *Shari'ah* board meetings. This indicates that the *Shari'ah* board should carefully consider the frequency of their meetings in order to enable them to fulfil their responsibility with due diligence. A minimum standard of requirements for the meeting should be implemented and calendar meetings should be mandatory for them. Furthermore, the *Shari'ah* board should proactively plan and arrange quarterly meetings with the BOD to discuss *Shari'ah*-related issues.

In terms of meeting procedures, this book reveals that there are differences in practices with regard to the quorum for the meetings. In parallel with the ideal practice of the *Shari'ah* board, the quorum of a simple majority from the total number of *Shari'ah* board members should be acceptable. With regard to the basis for decision-making, unlike principle 57 of IFSB-10 which requires a consensus decision, the author thinks that the practice of a simple majority vote is acceptable. The practice of unanimous decision-making may create certain issues for IFIs, such as potential for delay and silent disagreement amongst the *Shari'ah* scholars. With the simple majority approach, the dissenting opinion of the disagreeing *Shari'ah* scholars can be evaluated and this may contribute to further healthy discussion. In the event that the *Shari'ah* board consists of non-*Shari'ah* scholars, their votes should not be counted.

7.1.32 Well-defined lines of reporting and proper communication channels

One of the issues highlighted by the *Shari'ah* scholars in the semi-structured interviews was communication barriers and unclear lines of reporting. Therefore, IFIs should have well-defined lines of reporting and establish appropriate communication channels within the organisation as well as with the consumers, regulators and supervisors. In terms of reporting structure, the *Shari'ah* board should report administratively to the BOD and the *Shari'ah* report should be approved of and directed by the shareholders to be included as part of the annual report as recommended by IFSB-10.

With respect to communication, there must be proper coordination between the supervisory authorities and the IFIs' *Shari'ah* board and other organs of governance, particularly senior management and the BOD. In this regard, it is recommended that senior management, such as the CEO, the head of the risk management department and the head of the legal department, attend the *Shari'ah* board meetings. On top of that, some mechanism could also be invoked allowing customers, employees, business partners, suppliers and auditors to indirectly act as agents on the IFIs' actions, relationships and dealings through formal and informal checks, such as via effective consumer enquiries and complaint policies.

7.1.33 Shari'ah *non-compliance risk management*

Shari'ah scholars in the semi-structured interview acknowledge that management of *Shari'ah* non-compliance risk is extremely important. The existing practice puts the *Shari'ah* board as the main organ of governance to address this risk, with the assistance of the *Shari'ah* internal audit team, while other types of risks are under the auspices of the risk management department. Since *Shari'ah* non-compliance risk is one of the operational risks which then constitute systemic risks, the risk management department or unit should have strong coordination with the *Shari'ah* board. A representative of the risk management unit should be a permanent attendee of the *Shari'ah* board meetings. Furthermore, they must have adequate resources and staff who have good knowledge and capabilities in *Shari'ah*-related matters.

7.1.34 *Evaluation of the* Shari'ah *board*

The survey and semi-structured interview affirm that numerous IFIs do not evaluate or assess the performance of their *Shari'ah* board. Assessment of the *Shari'ah* board is important for the purpose of improving its functions by identifying its previous shortcomings and weaknesses. With respect to this, IFIs are recommended to have performance measures for the *Shari'ah* board as a collective assessment as well as individual member evaluations. The assessment report then should be submitted to the BOD for determination and recording. The performance of individual *Shari'ah* board members and the *Shari'ah* board as a whole should be regularly evaluated. Continuous monitoring of *Shari'ah* board competencies must be carried out so that it may function effectively. The IFIs should consistently evaluate their *Shari'ah* board, which should incorporate an assessment of member competencies, and this should be made mandatory.

7.1.35 Shari'ah *pronouncements review*

The scope of the *Shari'ah* review in IFIs only focuses on the compliance aspects of the products and services. Another area which is equally important for review is revision of the *Shari'ah* pronouncements. The *Shari'ah* board, with the assistance of the *Shari'ah* department, should adopt a specific process to ensure the revision of all of the *Shari'ah* rulings. It is recommended that IFIs establish a research and development unit under the *Shari'ah* department to carry out the review process as well as to assist the *Shari'ah* board to conduct necessary research on *Shari'ah*-related matters.

7.1.36 *Key performance indicators*

The semi-structured interviews revealed that some *Shari'ah* scholars are aware of the assessment of their performance but they had no knowledge of the scope of such performance measures. In this instance, it would be good practice for IFIs to set some key performance indicators (KPIs) for the *Shari'ah* board. The KPIs would not be in the form of financial considerations but rather measure factors such as *Shari'ah* compliance, meeting datelines, positive contributions to the organisation, having a proactive approach and assisting the IFIs in setting goals and direction. The set of KPIs, which must be agreed in advance by the individual *Shari'ah* board members, should then be evaluated by the BOD and be subject to the approval of the shareholders.

7.2 Epilogue

This section is a useful point at which to review the overall contents of this book. The discourse on comparative corporate governance between the Western and Islamic models clearly indicates the deficiencies in the literature and the gap which this work is filling. This comparative overview set the initial theoretical framework of corporate governance for the debate and thoughtful discussion. In search of an Islamic perspective on corporate governance through analysing the existing Western models, particularly the shareholder value system and stakeholder value orientation, this book suggests that corporate governance in IFIs is inclined towards the stakeholder value framework. This position is based on the epistemological orientation founded on the fundamental principles of *Tawhīd*, *shura*, property rights and commitment to contractual obligation which enhances the definition of stakeholders.

Since Islamic corporate governance is considered as having a faith-based orientation, *Shari'ah* rules and principles then become part of the corporate governance framework in IFIs. Therefore, corporate governance in IFIs needs a set of institutional arrangements to ensure that there is effective independent oversight of *Shari'ah* compliance. Whilst *Shari'ah* governance is expected to be an effective mechanism to ensure *Shari'ah* compliance, the discussion on the topic of *Shariʻah* governance system in IFIs nevertheless indicates that there are certain deficiencies in the existing *Shariʻah* governance practices, including issues pertaining to regulatory challenges.

This book has yielded substantial findings revealing that there are shortcomings and weaknesses in numerous aspects of the *Shariʻah* governance system as practised by IFIs. There are significant differences in the general approach to *Shariʻah* governance, the regulatory framework and internal policies, the roles and functions of the *Shariʻah* board, the attributes of the *Shariʻah* board in terms of competence, independence, transparency and confidentiality, operational procedures, and performance measures of the *Shariʻah* board. In all these areas, the extent of *Shariʻah* governance disclosure is at a minimal level. With respect to this, this book strongly recommends a continuous and systematic approach to enhancing and improving the existing *Shariʻah* governance practices.

A Survey of *Shari'ah* Governance in Islamic Financial Institutions

Your participation in this survey is greatly appreciated. Most of the questions merely require you to tick the appropriate box. All the information given will be treated in the strictest confidence.

General Instructions and Information

1. The survey aims at providing factual input on the current practice of *Shari'ah* governance system. The present questionnaire is sent to the selected IFIs from Malaysia, GCC countries and the UK. This book may be helpful to increase understanding and to promote best practice of *Shari'ah* governance system in IFIs.

2. Please do not worry about questions that seemingly look alike. If you do not have the exact answer to a question, please provide your best judgement by ticking the appropriate boxes in the questions. **Your answers are very important to the accuracy of this book.**

3. If you wish to make any comment, please feel free to use the space at the end of the questionnaire.

Please return the completed questionnaire via email to z.b.hasan@
durham.ac.uk before

For Office Use Only
Date of Interview/Questionnaire Returned: ___/___/2009   Bank's Branch Code:
Time of Interview: _____ A.M. /P.M.   Respondent Number:

School of Government and International Affairs
University of Durham, United Kingdom.
E-mail: z.b.hasan@durham.ac.uk
Weblog: http://zulkiflihasan.wordpress.com

SHARI'AH *GOVERNANCE IN ISLAMIC BANKS*

GENERAL INFORMATION

Name and Location of the Institution   :

Contact Person   :

Position   :

Composition of the *Shari'ah* Board Members   :

	Number
Male	
Female	

SHARI'AH GOVERNANCE SYSTEM

(Please tick (x) in an appropriate box)

H1:   General Framework for *Shari'ah* Governance

	Yes	No	Comment
Q1. Is the AAOIFI Governance Standards adopted as the guidelines?	☐	☐	
Q2. Are you aware of the recent exposure draft of the IFSB *Shari'ah* governance Guiding Principles?	☐	☐	
Q3. Are there any standards for *Shari'ah* governance set for Islamic financial institutions (IFIs)?	☐	☐	
Q4. Are IFIs required to provide any guidelines for *Shari'ah* governance?	☐	☐	
Q5. Does your institution develop standard processes for *Shari'ah* compliance, audit and review of the *Shari'ah* boards' legal rulings?	☐	☐	

	Yes	No	Comment
Q6. Does your institution have a professional code of ethics and conduct for members of the *Shari'ah* board?	☐	☐	
Q7. What is the organisational arrangement for *Shari'ah* governance? — Internal *Shari'ah* board	☐	☐	
	Shari'ah Advisory Firm	☐	☐	
	Others (Please Specify)	☐	☐	

H2: Regulatory Framework

	Yes	No	Comment
Q8. Are there separate rules and regulations concerning *Shari'ah* governance?	☐	☐	
Q9. Does the bank have any written policies or by-laws specifically referring to the conduct of the *Shari'ah* board?	☐	☐	
Q10. What type of dispute settlement is there to redress legal matters concerning Islamic finance (e.g. conflict of laws)? — Civil Court	☐	☐	
	Shari'ah Court	☐	☐	
	Arbitration	☐	☐	
	Shari'ah authority of the central bank or the ministry of religious affairs	☐	☐	
	Others (Please specify)	☐	☐	

		Yes	No	Comment
Q11. What is the legal position of the *Shari'ah* board's rulings?	Binding	☐	☐	
	Persuasive	☐	☐	
	Non-binding	☐	☐	
	Others (Please specify)	☐	☐	

H3: The Role of *Shari'ah* Board

		Tick (✗)	Comment
Q12. What are the roles of the *Shari'ah* board?	Advisory	☐	
	Supervisory	☐	
	Executive	☐	
	Others (Please specify)	☐	
Q13. Do the functions of the *Shari'ah* board include:	*Shari'ah* pronouncements?	☐	
	Shari'ah review or audit?	☐	
	Endorsing and validating documentations pertaining to the products and services, as well as the internal policies, manuals and marketing advertisements, etc.?	☐	
	Endorsement of *Shari'ah* compliance?	☐	
	Overseeing the computation and payment of *zakah*?	☐	

	Tick (✗)	Comment
Examining any enquiries referred to by the IFIs?	☐	
Developing *Shari'ah*-approved instruments?	☐	
Acting as the *Shari'ah* highest authority pertaining to Islamic finance?	☐	
Approving model agreements of Islamic modes of financing?	☐	
Achieving harmonisation in the concepts and applications amongst the *Shari'ah* boards?	☐	
Others (Please specify)	☐	
Q14. Does the *Shari'ah* board perform the *Shari'ah* audit? Yes	☐	
No	☐	
Q15. Does the *Shari'ah* board have the power to delegate some of its functions to the internal *Shari'ah* compliance unit? Yes	☐	
No	☐	

H4: Mechanism of *Shari'ah* Governance System

H4.1: *Competence*

		Yes	No	Comment
Q16. Does your institution have policies on the fit and proper criteria for the members of the *Shari'ah* board?		☐	☐	
Q17. If yes, what are those criteria?	Academic qualification	☐	☐	
	Experience and exposure (knowledge and skills in financial services industry)	☐	☐	
	Track record	☐	☐	
	Others (Please specify)	☐	☐	
Q18. What are the requirements in terms of academic qualifications?	Specialised in *muāmalāt*	☐	☐	
	Specialised in Islamic jurisprudence	☐	☐	
	Knowledge of Arabic and English	☐	☐	
	Others (Please specify)	☐	☐	
Q19. What are the requirements in terms of experience and exposure?	Understanding of *Shari'ah* rules and principles	☐	☐	
	Understanding of general legal and regulatory framework	☐	☐	

		Yes	No	Comment
	Understanding of the impact of the *Shari'ah* pronouncements?	☐	☐	
	Skills in the financial services industry	☐	☐	
	Others (Please specify)	☐	☐	
Q20. What are the requirements in terms of track record?	Good character	☐	☐	
	Competence, diligence, capability and soundness of judgment	☐	☐	
	Others (Please specify)	☐	☐	
Q21. In the event your institution allows a non-*Shari'ah*-background individual as a member of the *Shari'ah* board, what is the qualification for such appointment?	Well-versed in law	☐	☐	
	Well-versed in economy	☐	☐	
	Well-versed in finance	☐	☐	
	Others (Please specify)	☐	☐	
Q22. Do the *Shari'ah* board members receive adequate training to understand their role in the internal control process?	Yes	☐	☐	
	No	☐	☐	

		Yes	No	Comment
Q23. Is there any evaluation of the *Shari'ah* board?	Yes	☐	☐	
	No	☐	☐	

H4.2: *Independence*

		Tick (✗)	Comment
Q24. Who has the power to approve the appointment and dismissal of the *Shari'ah* board?	Shareholders in the Annual General Meeting	☐	
	BOD	☐	
	Management	☐	
	Government	☐	
	Others (Please specify)	☐	
Q25. How long is the tenure of the appointment?	One year	☐	
	Two years	☐	
	Permanent	☐	
	Others (Please specify)	☐	
Q26. What do you think is the appropriate body for the *Shari'ah* board to be accountable to?	Shareholders	☐	
	BOD	☐	
	Management	☐	
	Others (Please specify)	☐	
Q27. Who determines the *Shari'ah* board's remuneration?	Shareholders	☐	
	BOD	☐	
	Management	☐	
	Others (Please specify)	☐	

		Tick (✗)	Comment
Q28. What mechanisms are in place to mitigate conflict of interest in relation to *Shari'ah* scholars sitting on various boards?	Restriction on multiple appointment	☐	
	Disclosure on *Shari'ah* board's information	☐	
	Declaration in writing	☐	
	Others (Please specify)	☐	
Q29. Is the power and authority of the *Shari'ah* board clearly mentioned in the following documents?	Article of association	☐	
	Memorandum of association	☐	
	Letter of appointment	☐	
	Others (Please specify)	☐	

H4.3: *Transparency and Confidentiality*

	Yes	No	Comment
Q30. Does the *Shari'ah* board have a written policy in respect to the preparation and dissemination of *Shari'ah* information?	☐	☐	
Q31. Does the *Shari'ah* board have access to all documents, information, records, etc.?	☐	☐	
Q32. Are the *Shari'ah* pronouncements published and made known to the public?	☐	☐	
Q33. Is the *Shari'ah* board fully aware of the issue of confidentiality and sensitive information obtained in the course of performing their duties?	☐	☐	

H5: Operational Procedure

		Tick (✗)	Comment
Q34. Is there any standard operational procedure for the *Shariʿah* board?	Yes	☐	
	No	☐	
Q35. Does the *Shariʿah* board hold its meeting regularly?	Weekly	☐	
	Monthly	☐	
	Quarterly	☐	
	Biannually	☐	
	Others (Please specify)	☐	
Q36. What is the quorum for the *Shariʿah* board meeting?	Three	☐	
	Five	☐	
	Seven	☐	
	Others (Please specify)	☐	
Q37. On what basis are decisions made at the *Shariʿah* board meeting?	Simple majority	☐	
	Two-thirds majority	☐	
	Consensus	☐	
	Others (Please specify)	☐	
Q38. In the event of the *Shariʿah* board including non-*Shariʿah*-background members, do they have the right to vote?	Yes	☐	
	No	☐	

		Tick (X)	Comment
Q39. Is an agenda prepared and distributed in advance of *Shari'ah* board meetings?	A week in advance	☐	
	Two weeks in advance	☐	
	A month in advance	☐	
	Others (Please specify)	☐	
Q40. Who is responsible for dealing with the organisation of the *Shari'ah* board meetings?	Internal *Shari'ah* officer	☐	
	Company secretary	☐	
	Head of product development	☐	
	Head of the legal department	☐	
	Others (Please specify)	☐	
Q41. Besides the *Shari'ah* board, who attends the meeting?	Representative from the internal *Shari'ah* compliance unit	☐	
	Representative from risk management department	☐	
	Representative from legal department	☐	
	Representative from product department	☐	

		Tick (✗)	Comment
	Representative from an external legal firm	☐	
	Representative from the IFIs (Example, in the case of *Shari'ah* board at the regulatory level)	☐	
	Others (Please specify)	☐	
Q42. Are the *Shari'ah* pronouncements reviewed whenever necessary?	Yes	☐	
	No	☐	
Q43. Is the *Shari'ah* board required to submit a *Shari'ah* report?	Yes	☐	
	No	☐	
Q44. What are the contents of the *Shari'ah* report?	Information on duties and services of the *Shari'ah* board	☐	
	Shari'ah pronouncements	☐	
	Shari'ah board activities	☐	
	Declaration of *Shari'ah* compliance	☐	
	Others (Please specify)	☐	

		Tick (✗)	Comment
Q45. What is the organisational arrangement for the internal *Shari'ah* review?	Independent division/ department	☐	
	Part of the internal audit department	☐	
	Others (Please Specify)	☐	

H6: General Assessment of the *Shari'ah* Board.

	Strongly Disagree	Disagree	Neutral	Agree	Strongly Agree
Q46. The *Shari'ah* board has demonstrated effective organisational accountability.	☐	☐	☐	☐	☐
Q47. The *Shari'ah* board has communicated effectively with other organs of governance, including the BOD, management and auditors.	☐	☐	☐	☐	☐

	Strongly Disagree	Disagree	Neutral	Agree	Strongly Agree
Q48. The *Shari'ah* board has properly identified and evaluated the organisation's exposure to *Shari'ah* non-compliance risk and reputational risk, and effectively communicate that risk information to appropriate bodies in the organisation.	☐	☐	☐	☐	☐
Q49. The *Shari'ah* board promotes Islamic ethics and values within the organisation.	☐	☐	☐	☐	☐
Q50. The *Shari'ah* board promotes continuous improvement of the organisation's *Shari'ah* control processes.	☐	☐	☐	☐	☐

Thank you for taking the time to complete this questionnaire. Your assistance in providing this information is very much appreciated. If there is anything else you would like to tell us about this survey or other comments, please provide any other insights which you think are relevant to *Shari'ah* governance in the space provided below.

ABBREVIATIONS

AAOIFI	Accounting and Auditing Organization for Islamic Financial Institutions
AASB	Accounting and Auditing Standard Board
AGC	Audit and Governance Committee
BAFIA	Banking and Financial Istitutions Act 1989
BBA	*Al-Bai' Bithaman Ajil*
BCBS	Basel Committee for Banking Supervision
BDS	Banking Dispute Settlement
BMBI	Borneo Merchant Banking Islamic
BNM	Bank Negara Malaysia
BOD	Board of Directors
CBA	Central Bank of Malaysia Act 2009
CBB	Central Bank of Bahrain
CBK	Central Bank of Kuwait
CIBAFI	General Council of Islamic Banks and Financial Institutions
CSBD	Committee of Settlement for Banking Disputes
DFIA	Development Financial Institutions Act 2002
DFSA	DIFC Services Authority
DIFC	Dubai International Financial Centre
FI	Failaka International
FSA	Financial Services Authority
GCC	Gulf Cooperation Council
IAIB	International Association of Islamic Banks
IB	the QCB 'Instructions to Banks'

IBA	Islamic Banking Act 1983
IBFIM	Islamic Banking and Finance Institute of Malaysia
IBSA	Islamic Bank of South Africa
IDB	Islamic Development Bank
IFIs	Islamic financial institutions
IFSB	Islamic Financial Services Board
IFSC	Islamic Financial Securities and Co. of Qatar
IIBI	Institute of Islamic Banking and Insurance
IIFM	International Islamic Financial Market
IIIF	International Institute of Islamic Finance Incorporated
IIRA	International Islamic Rating Agency
IOSCO	International Organization of the Securities Commission
ISFI	Islamic Finance Rule Book 2007
JBIC	Japan Bank for International Cooperation
KPI	key performance indicators
MIFC	Malaysian Islamic Financial Centre
MSFA	Minhaj *Shari'ah* Financial Advisory
OECD	Organisation for Economic Co-operation and Development
OIC	Organization of the Islamic Conference
QCB	Qatar Central Bank
QFC	Qatar Financial Centre
QFMA	Qatar Financial Markets Authority
SAMA	Saudi Authority Monetary Agency
SBP	State Bank of Pakistan
SC	Securities Commission
SGF	*Shari'ah* governance framework for IFIs issued by the BNM
SHC	*Shari'ah* committee
SII	Securities and Investment Institute

TASIS   *Taqwaa* Advisory and *Shari'ah* Investment
         Solutions
YL   Yasaar Limited

BIBLIOGRAPHY

Books

Abdul-Rahman, Y. (2010), *The Art of Islamic Banking and Finance. Tools and Techniques for Community-Based Banking*, Hoboken, NJ: John Wiley & Sons.

Ainley, M., Mashayekhi, A., Hicks, R., Rahman, A. and Ravalia, A. (2007), *Islamic Finance in the UK: Regulation and Challenges*, London: Financial Services Authority.

Al-Faruqi, I. R. (1982), *Al-Tawhīd: Its Implications for Thought and Life*, Herndon, VA: The International Institute of Islamic Thought.

Ayub, M. (2007), *Understanding Islamic Finance*, London: John Wiley and Sons Ltd.

Ballantyne, W. M. (1986), *Commercial Law in the Arab Middle East: the Gulf States*, London: Lloyds of London Press Ltd.

Banaga, A., Ray, G. and Tomkins, C. (1994), *External Audit and Corporate Governance in Islamic Banks: a Joint Practitioner-Academic Research Study*, Aldershot: Avebury.

Becht, M. and Barca, F. (2001), *The Control of Corporate Europe*, Oxford: Oxford University Press.

Berle, A. and Means, G. (1932), *The Modern Corporation and Private Property*, New York, NY: Macmillan.

Bryman, A. (2001), *Social Research Methods*, Oxford: Oxford University Press.

Cadbury, A. (2002), *Corporate Governance and Chairmanship: a Personal Overview*, Oxford: Oxford University Press.

Chapra, M. U. (1992), *Islam and the Economic Challenge*, Leicester: Islamic Foundation.

Chapra, M. U. and Ahmed, H. (2002), *Corporate Governance in IFIs*, Jeddah: IRTI.

Choudhury, M. A. and Hoque, M. Z. (2004), *An Advanced Exposition of Islamic Economics and Finance*, New York, NY: Edwin Mellen Press.

Dar, H. and Azami, T. A. (2010), *Global Islamic Finance Report 2010*, London: BMB Islamic.

Dawud, H. Y. (1996), *Shari'ah Control in Islamic Banks*, Herndon, VA: International Institute of Islamic Thought.

Dignam, A. and Galanis, M. (2009), *The Globalization of Corporate Governance*, Farnham: Ashgate.

El-Gamal, M. (2006), *Islamic Finance, Law, Economics and Practice*, New York, NY: Cambridge University Press.

Freeman, E. (1984), *Strategic Management: a Stakeholder Approach*, Boston, MA: Pitman Press.

Ghazali, S., Omar, S. and Aidit, G. (eds) (2005), *An Introduction to Islamic Economics and Finance*, Kuala Lumpur: CERT Publications.

Greuning, H. V. and Iqbal, Z. (2008), *Risk Analysis for Islamic Banks*, Washington, DC: World Bank.

Hamed, Sayed Mohamed (1979), *The Development of the Central Banking System in the Kingdom of Saudi Arabia*, trans. Hassan Yasseen, Riyadh: General Management Institute.

Haneef, M. A. (1995), *Contemporary Islamic Economic Thought: a Selected Comparative Analysis*, Kuala Lumpur: Ikraq.

Harun, S. (1997), *Islamic Banking, Rules and Regulations*, Kuala Lumpur: Pelanduk Publications.

Ibnu Taymiya (1985), *Public Duties in Islam: the Institution of the Hisbah*, trans. M. Holland, Leicester: Islamic Foundation.

Iqbal, Z. and Lewis, M. K. (2009), *An Islamic Perspective on Governance*, Cheltenham: Edward Elgar.

Iqbal, Z. and Mirakhor, A. (2007), *An Introduction to Islamic Finance: Theory and Practice*, Singapore: John Wiley and Sons (Asia) Pte. Ltd.

Macey, J. and O'Hara, M. (2001), *Solving the Corporate Governance Problems of Banks: a Proposal*, Cornell University Mimeo.

Mallin, C. A. (2007), *Corporate Governance*, Oxford: Oxford University Press.

Mannan, M. A. (1984), *Abstracts of Researchers in Islamic Economics*, Jeddah: International Centre for Research in Islamic Economics.

Marshall, A. (1920), *Principles of Economics*, London: Macmillan.

Mautz, R. K and Sharaf, H. A. (1961), *The Philosophy of Auditing*, Sarasota, FL: American Accounting Association.

Naqvi, S. N. H. (1994), *Islam, Economics and Society*, London: Kegan Paul International Ltd.

Oxford English Dictionary (1989), 2nd edn, Oxford: Oxford University Press.

Ross, T. (2008), *Financial Services Regulation in the Middle East*, Oxford: Oxford University Press.

Sekaran, U. (2003), *Research Methods for Business: a Skill-Building Approach*, Chichester: John Wiley and Sons Inc.

Siddiqi, M. N. (1981), *Muslim Economic Thinking: a Survey of Contemporary Literature*, Leicester: Islamic Foundation.

Smith, A. (1993), *An Inquiry into the Nature and Causes of the Wealth of Nations*, Indianapolis, IN: Hackett.

Vogel, F. E. (2000), *Islamic Law and Legal System: Studies in Saudi Arabia*, Leiden: Brill.

Vogel, F. E. and Hayes, S. L. (2006), *The Islamic Law and Finance, Religion, Risk and Return*, Arab and Islamic Laws Series, Leiden: Brill.

Wilson, R. (1984), *Islamic Business, Theory and Practice*, London: The Economist Publications Ltd.

Wilson, R. (1997), *Islamic Finance*, London: Financial Times Financial Publishing.

Wilson, R. (2009a), *The Development of Islamic Finance in the GCC*, London: London School of Economics.

Articles

Ali, S. Y. (2007), 'Financial distress and bank failure: lessons from closure of Ihlas Finans in Turkey', *Islamic Economic Studies*, 14(1 & 2), August 2006 & January 2007, 1–52.

Al Muhairi, B. S. B. A. (1996), 'The development of the UAE legal system and unification with the judicial system', *Arab Law Quarterly*, 11(3), 116–60.

Al-Suwaidi, A. (1993), 'Developments of the legal systems of the Gulf Arab States', *Arab Law Quarterly*, 8(4), 289–301.

Andrew, K. (2007), 'Tackling the issue of the corporate objective: an analysis of the United Kingdom's "enlightened shareholder value approach"', *Sydney Law Review*, 29(4), 577–612.

Anon. (1987), 'The European Community and the Gulf Co-Operation Council', *Arab Law Quarterly*, 2(3), 323–7.

Asutay, M. (2007), 'Conceptualization of the second best solution in overcoming the social failure of Islamic finance: examining the overpowering of HomoIslamicus by HomoEconomicus', *IIUM Journal of Economics and Management*, 15(2), 167–95.

Azid, T., Asutay, M. and Burki, M. (2007), 'Theory of the firm and stakeholders management', *Islamic Economic Studies*, 15(1), 1–30.

Ballantyne, W. M. (1985), 'The states of the GCC: sources of law, the *Shari'ah* and the extent to which it applies', *Arab Law Quarterly*, 1(1), 3–18.

Ballantyne, W. M. (1987), 'The *Shari'ah*: a speech to the IBA

Conference in Cairo, on Arab Comparative and Commercial Law', *Arab Law Quarterly*, 2(1), 12–28.

Ballantyne, W. M. (1988), 'The Second Coulson Memorial Lecture: back to the *Shari'ah*?', *Arab Law Quarterly*, 3(4), 317–28.

Baydoun, N. and Willet, R. (2000), 'Islamic corporate reports', *ABACUS*, 36(1), 71–90.

Briston, R. and El-Ashker, A. (1986), 'Religious audit: could it happen here?', *Accountancy*, October, 113–27.

Choudhury, M. A. and Hoque, M. Z. (2006). 'Corporate governance in Islamic perspective', *Corporate Governance*, 6(2), 116–28.

Clarkson, M. E. (1995), 'A stakeholder framework for analyzing and evaluating corporate social performance', *Academy of Management Review*, 20(1), 92–117.

Delorenzo, Y. T. (2007), '*Shari'ah* compliance risk', *Chicago Journal of International Law*, 7(2), 397–408.

Donaldson, T. and Preston, L. E. (1995), 'Stakeholder theory of the corporation: concepts, evidence and implications', *Academy of Management Review*, 20, 65–92.

Gerald, J. O. (1991), 'Legal aspects of doing business in Kuwait', *Arab Law Quarterly*, 6(4), 322–30.

Hamzeh, A. N. (1994), 'The duality of the legal system', *Middle Eastern Studies*, 30(1), 79–90.

Haniffa, R. and Hudaib, M. (2007), 'Exploring the ethical identity of Islamic banks via communication in annual reports', *Journal of Business Ethics*, 76(1), 97–116.

Hart, O. (1995), 'Corporate governance: some theory and implications', *The Economic Journal*, 105(May), 678–89.

Hasan, Z. (2010), '*Shari'ah* governance in Islamic financial institutions and the effect of the Central Bank of Malaysia Act 2009', *Journal of International Banking Law and Regulation*, 3, 105–8.

Iqbal, Z. and Mirakhor, A. (2004), 'Stakeholders model of

governance in Islamic economic system', *Islamic Economic Studies*, 11(2), 43–64.

Islam, M. W. (1999), 'Al Mal: the concept of property in Islamic legal thought', *Arab Law Quarterly*, 14(4), 361–8.

Jones, T. M. (1995), 'Instrument stakeholder theory: a synthesis of ethics and economics', *Academy of Management Review*, 20, 404–37.

Kahf, M. (1999), 'Islamic banks at the threshold of the third millennium', *Thunderbird International Business Review*, 41(4–5), 445–60.

Kay, J. and Silberston, A. (1995), 'Corporate governance', *National Institute Economic Review*, 153(1), 84–97.

Keenan, J. (2004), 'Corporate governance in UK/USA boardrooms', *Journal of Corporate Governance*, 12(2), 172–6.

Kettell, B. (2008), 'Despite falling *sukuk* issuances, Islamic finance products are still in demand', *Islamic Banking and Finance*, 6(4) 19, 38.

Khan, M. A. (1985), 'Role of the auditor in an Islamic economy', *Journal of Research in Islamic Economics*, 3(1), 31–41.

Klein, Y. (2006), 'Between public and private: an examination of *Hisbah* literature', *Harvard Middle Eastern and Islamic Review*, 7, 41–62.

Lazonick, W. and O'Sullivan, M. (2000), 'Maximizing shareholder value: a new ideology for corporate governance', *Economy and Society*, 29(1), 13–35.

Lewis, M. K. (2005), 'Islamic corporate governance', *Review of Islamic Economics*, 9(1), 5–29.

Lim, P. K. (2007), 'Corporate governance reforms in Malaysia: the key leading players' perspective', *Journal of Corporate Governance*, 15(5), 724–40.

Maali, B., Casson, P. and Napier, C. (2006), 'Social reporting by Islamic banks', *ABACUS*, 42(2), 266–89.

Macey, J. and O'Hara, M. (2003), 'The corporate governance of banks', *FRBNY Economic Policy Review*, 9(1), 91–107.

Marar, A. D. (2004), 'Saudi Arabia: the duality of the legal system and the challenge of adapting law to market economics', *Arab Law Quarterly*, 19(1), 91–124.

McMillen, M. J. T. (2006), 'Islamic capital markets: developments and issues', *Capital Markets Law Journal*, 1(2), 136–72.

Nathan, S. and Ribiere, V. (2007), 'From knowledge to wisdom: the case of corporate governance in Islamic banking', *Journal of Information and Knowledge Management Systems*, 37(4), 471–83.

Okeahalam, C. C. (1998), 'The political economy of bank failure and supervision in the Republic of South Africa', *African Journal of Political Science*, 3(2), 29–48.

Pepper, W. F. (1992), 'Foreign capital investment in member states of the Gulf Cooperation Council: considerations, issues and concerns for investors', *Arab Law Quarterly*, 7(1), 33–63.

Pesqueux, Y. and Salma, D. A. (2005), 'Stakeholder theory in perspective', *Corporate Governance: International Journal of Business in Society*, 5(2), 5–21.

Rammal, H. G. (2006), 'The importance of *Shari'ah* supervision in IFIs', *Corporate Ownership and Control*, 3(3), 204–8.

Reumann, R. M. (1995), 'The banking system in Saudi Arabia', *Arab Law Quarterly*, 10(3), 207–37.

Safieddine, A. (2009), 'Islamic financial institutions and corporate governance: an insight for agency theory', *Corporate Governance: An International Review*, 17(2), 142–58.

Schachler, M. H., Juleff, L. and Paton, C. (2007), 'Corporate governance in the financial services sector', *Corporate Governance: An International Review*, 7(5), 623–34.

Sfeir, G. N. (1988), 'The Saudi approach to law reform', *American Journal of Comparative Law*, 36(4), 729–59.

Shleifer, A. and Vishny, R. (1997), 'A survey of corporate governance', *Journal of Finance*, 52, 737–83.

Sobri, S. (2008), 'Rocked to the foundations', *Islamic Banking and Finance*, 6(1) 16, 9–10.

Tamimi, H. (2002), 'Interest under the UAE law and as applied by the courts of Abu Dhabi', *Arab Law Quarterly*, 17(1), 50–2.

Vinnicombe, T. (2010), 'AAOIFI reporting standards: measuring compliance', *Advances in Accounting, Incorporating Advances in International Accounting*, 26(1), 55–65.

Wilson, R. (2009b), 'Shari'ah governance for Islamic financial institutions', *ISRA International Journal of Islamic Finance*, 1(1), 59–75.

Wittmann, R. (2006), 'The *Muḥtasib* in Seljuq times: insight from four chancery manuals', *Harvard Middle Eastern and Islamic Review*, 7, 108–28.

Yamak, S. and Suer, O. (2005), 'State as a stakeholder', *Corporate Governance: International Journal of Business in Society*, 5(2), 111–20.

Zuhaida, S. (1990), 'The politics of the Islamic investment companies in Egypt', *Bulletin of the British Society for Middle Eastern Studies*, 17(2), 152–61.

Chapters in books

Bakar, M. D. (2002), 'The *Shari'ah* supervisory board and issues of *Shari'ah* rulings and their harmonisation in Islamic banking and finance', in S. Archer and A. A. K. Rifaat (eds), *Islamic Finance Innovation and Growth*, London: Euromoney Books and AAOIFI, pp. 74–89.

Baldwin, D. and Wilson, R. (1988), 'Islamic finance in principle and practice', in C. Mallat (ed.), *Islamic Law and Finance*, London: Graham and Trotman Ltd, pp. 171–90.

Chapra, M. U. (2007), 'Challenges facing the Islamic financial industry', in M. K. Hassan and M. K. Lewis (eds), *Handbook of Islamic Banking*, Cheltenham: Edward Elgar, pp. 325–57.

Cohen, C. (1981), 'Monetary circulation in Egypt at the time of the Crusades and the reform of Al-Kamil', in A. L. Udovitch (ed.), *The Islamic Middle East, 700–1900: Studies in Economic and Social History*, Princeton, NJ: The Darwin Press, pp. 315–33.

Hasan, Z. (2011), 'Corporate and *Shariʿah* governance in Islamic financial institutions', in A. W. Dusuki (ed.), *Islamic Financial System, Principles and Operations*, Kuala Lumpur: ISRA, pp. 681–733.

Imamuddin, S. M. (1997a), '*Bayt al-māl* and the banks in the Medieval Muslim world', in M. Taher (ed.), *Studies in Islamic Economics*, New Delhi: Anmol Publications, pp. 128–38.

Imamuddin, S. M. (1997b), 'Islamic banking: historical aspects', in M. Taher (ed.), *Studies in Islamic Economics*, New Delhi: Anmol Publications, pp. 139–57.

Iqbal, Z. (2002), 'The development of Islamic financial institutions and future challenges,' in S. Archer and R. A. A. Karim (eds), *Islamic Finance, Innovation and Growth*, Bahrain: Euromoney Books and AAOIFI. pp. 42–63.

Kahf, M. (2004), 'Islamic banks: the rise of a new power alliance of wealth and *Shariʿah* scholars', in Clement M. Henry and Rodney Wilson (eds), *The Politics of Islamic Finance*, Edinburgh: Edinburgh University Press, pp. 17–36.

Keasey, K., Thompson, S. and Wright, M. (1997), 'Introduction: the corporate governance problem-competing diagnoses and solutions', in K. Keasey, S. Thompson and M. Wright (eds), *Corporate Governance, Economic, Management, and Financial Issues*, Oxford: Oxford University Press, pp. 1–17.

Lewis, M. K. (1999), 'Corporate governance and corporate financing in different cultures', in Zeljko Sevic (ed.), *Banking Reform in South East European Transitional Economies*,

London: University of Greenwich Business School, Balkan Center for Public Policy and Related Studies Humanities Research Centre, pp. 33–6.

Macey, J. R. (2004), 'Measuring the effectiveness of different corporate governance systems: toward a more scientific approach', in Joel M. Stern and Donald H. Chew, Jr (2004) (eds), *The Revolution in Corporate Finance*, Oxford: Blackwell Publishing, pp. 579–88.

Macey, J. R. and Miller, P. (2004), 'Universal banks are not the answer to America's corporate governance "problem": a look at Germany, Japan and the US', in Joel M. Stern and Donald H. Chew, Jr (eds), *The Revolution in Corporate Finance*, Oxford: Blackwell Publishing, pp. 552–69.

Peters, R. (2003), 'From jurists' law to statute law or what happens when the *Shari'ah* is codified', in B. Roberson (ed.), *Shaping the Current Islamic Reformation*, London: Frank Cass, pp. 82–95.

Scott, K. (2003), 'The role of corporate governance in South Korean economic reform', in Joel M. Stern and Donald H. Chew, Jr (eds), *The Revolution in Corporate Finance*, Oxford: Blackwell Publishing, pp. 519–34.

Vikor, K. S. (1998), 'The *Shari'ah* and the nation state: who can codify the divine law?', in B. O. Utvik and K. S. Vikor (eds), *The Midlle East in a Globalized World: Papers from the Fourth Nordic Conference on Middle Eastern Studies*, Oslo: Nordic Society for Middle Eastern Studies and Others, pp. 220–50.

Official/professional guidelines and standards

AAOIFI (2003), *Shari'ah Standards*, Bahrain: AAOIFI.

AAOIFI (2005a), *Governance Standard for IFIs, No. 1 Shari'ah Supervisory Board (SSB): Appointment, Composition and Report*, Bahrain: AAOIFI.

AAOIFI (2005b), *Governance Standard for IFIs, No. 2, Shari'ah Review*, Bahrain: AAOIFI.

AAOIFI (2005c), *Governance Standard for IFIs, No. 3, Internal Shari'ah Review*, Bahrain: AAOIFI.

AAOIFI (2005d), *Governance Standard for IFIs, No. 4, Audit and Governance for Islamic Financial Institutions*, Bahrain: AAOIFI.

AAOIFI (2005e), *Governance Standard for IFIs, No. 5, Independence of Shari'ah Supervisory Board*, Bahrain: AAOIFI.

BCBS (1999), *Enhancing Corporate Governance for Banking Organisations*, available at: www.bis.org/publ/bcbs56.pdf. Access date: 21 February 2008.

BNM (2004), *Guidelines on the Governance of Shari'ah Committee for the IFIs*, Kuala Lumpur: Bank Negara Malaysia, available at: http://www.bnm.gov.my/guide-lines/01_banking/04_prudential_stds/23_gps.pdf. Access date: 10 June 2010.

BNM (2009), *Financial Stability and Payment Systems Report 2009*, Kuala Lumpur: Bank Negara Malaysia.

HM Treasury (2008a), *The Development of Islamic Finance in the UK: the Government's Perspective*, London: HM Treasury, available at: http://webarchive.nationalarchives. gov.uk/+/http://www.hm-treasury.gov.uk/d/islamic_finan ce101208.pdf. Access date: 10 June 2010.

HM Treasury (2008b), *Government Stering Sukuk Issuance: a Response to the Consultation*, London: HM Treasury, avail-able at: http://webarchive.nationalarchives.gov.uk/+/http:// www.hm-treasury.gov.uk/d/consult_sukuk141107.pdf. Access date: 10 June 2010.

IFSB (2003), *Capital Adequacy Standard for Institutions (other than Insurance Institutions) offering only Islamic Financial Services*, Kuala Lumpur: IFSB.

IFSB (2005), *Guiding Principles of Risk Management for*

Institutions (other than Insurance Institutions) offering only Islamic Financial Services, Kuala Lumpur: IFSB.

IFSB (2006a), *Guidance on Key Elements in the Supervisory Review Process of Institutions offering Islamic Financial Services (excluding Islamic Insurance (*Takāful*) Institutions and Islamic Mutual Funds)*, Kuala Lumpur: IFSB.

IFSB (2006b), *Guiding Principles on Corporate Governance for Institutions Offering Only Islamic Financial Services (Excluding Islamic Insurance (*Takāful*) Institutions and Islamic Mutual Funds)*, Kuala Lumpur: IFSB.

IFSB (2007a), *Guiding Principles on Governance for Islamic Collective Investment Schemes and Guidance Note in Connection with the Capital Adequacy Standard: Recognition of Ratings by External Credit Assessment Institutions (ECAIs) on Shari'ah-Compliant Financial Instruments*, Kuala Lumpur: IFSB.

IFSB (2007b), *Disclosures to Promote Transparency and Market Discipline for Institutions offering Islamic Financial Services (excluding Islamic Insurance (*Takāful*) Institutions and Islamic Mutual Funds)*, Kuala Lumpur: IFSB.

IFSB (2008a), *Capital Adequacy Requirements for Sukuk, Securitisations and Real Estate Investment*, Kuala Lumpur: IFSB.

IFSB (2008b), *Survey on* Shari'ah *boards of Institutions Offering Islamic Financial Services Across Jurisdictions*, Kuala Lumpur: IFSB.

IFSB (2009a), *Guiding Principles on Governance for Collective Investment Schemes*, Kuala Lumpur: IFSB.

IFSB (2009b), *Guiding Principles on Governance for* Takāful *(Islamic Insurance) Undertakings*, Kuala Lumpur: IFSB.

IFSB (2009c), *Guiding Principles on Conduct of Business for Institutions offering Islamic Financial Services*, Kuala Lumpur: IFSB.

IFSB (2009d), *Guiding Principles on* Shari'ah *Governance*

System in Institutions Offering Islamic Financial Services, Kuala Lumpur: IFSB.

IFSB and IRTI (2007), *Islamic Financial Services Industry Development; Ten Year Framework and Strategies*, Kuala Lumpur: IFSB, available at: http://www.ifsb.org/docs/10_yr_framework.pdf. Access date: 15 April 2010.

IFSB and IRTI (2010), *Islamic Finance and Global Financial Stability*, Kuala Lumpur: IFSB, available at: http://www.ifsb.org/docs/IFSB-IRTI-IDB2010.pdf. Access date: 15 April 2010.

MIFC (2008), *MIFC Human Capital Development*, Kuala Lumpur: Malaysian Islamic Financial Centre.

OECD (1999), *OECD Principles of Corporate Governance*, Paris: OECD, available at: http://papers.ssrn.com/sol3/papers.cfm?abstract_id=174229. *Access date: 25 February 2010.*

OECD (2004), *OECD Principles of Corporate Governance (Revised)*, Paris: OECD, available at: http://www.oecd.org/dataoecd/32/18/31557724.pdf. Access date: 25 February 2010.

Praesidium and DIFC (2007), *Guide to Islamic Finance in or from the DIFC*, Dubai: Praesidium.

QFC (2009), *Instruction to Banks, Part VII-Instructions of Supervision and Control*, available at: http://www.qcb.gov.qa/English/Legislation/Documents/instructionsMar09_Eng/SEVEN.pdf. Access date: 20 August 2010.

SBP (2007), *Fit and Proper Criteria for Shariʻah Advisors of Islamic Banking Institutions.* Annexure-IV to IBD Circular No. 2 of 2004, Revised vide IBD Circular No. 2 of 2007, available at: http://www.sbp.org.pk/ibd/2007/C2_FP_Criteria.pdf. Access date: 3 November 2008.

SBP (2008), *Instruction and Guidelines for Shariʻah Compliance in Islamic Banking Institutions*, available at: http://www.sbp.org.pk/ibd/2008/C2.htm. Access date: 30 October 2008.

SC (2000), *The Guidelines on Islamic Private Debt Securities*

(1 July 2000), Kuala Lumpur: Securities Commission of Malaysia.

Research papers

Arun, T. G. and Turner, J. D. (2003), *Corporate Governance of Banks in Developing Economies: Concepts and Issues*, Development Economics and Public Policy Working Paper Series, available at: http://ageconsearch. umn.edu/bitstream/30551/1/deo30002.pdf. Access date: 9 June 2010.

Errico, L. and Farahbaksh, M. (1998), *Islamic Banking: Issues in Prudential Regulation and Supervision*, International Monetary Funds Working Paper WP/98/30, available at: http://www.imf.org/external/pubs/ft/wp/wp9830.pdf. Access date: 22 March 2010.

Grais, W. and Pellegrini, M. (2006a), *Corporate Governance and Shari'ah Compliance in Institutions Offering Islamic Financial Services*, World Bank Policy Research Working Paper No. 4054, available at: http://www-wds.worldbank. org/external/default/WDSContentServer/IW3P/IB/2006/11 /08/000016406_20061108095535/Rendered/PDF/wps4054. pdf. Access date: 10 June 2010.

Grais, W. and Pellegrini, M. (2006b), *Corporate Governance and Stakeholders' Financial Interests in Institutions Offering Islamic Financial Services*, World Bank Policy Research Working Paper No. 4053, available at: http://www-wds. worldbank.org/servlet/WDSContentServer/WDSP/IB/2 006/10/26/000016406_20061026114415/Rendered/PDF/ wps4053.pdf. Access date: 10 June 2010.

Grais, W. and Pellegrini, M. (2006c), *Corporate Governance in Institutions Offering Islamic Financial Services: Issues and Options*, World Bank Policy Research Working Paper No. 4052, available at: http://www-wds.worldbank.org/external/

default/WDSContentServer/IW3P/IB/2006/10/26/000016
406_20061026114045/Rendered/PDF/wps4052.pdf. Access
date: 10 June 2010.

Unpublished work

Abdallah, A. A. (1994), 'The role of *Shari'ah* supervisory board
in setting accounting policies in Islamic banks', paper presented at Training Workshop in the Development of an
Accounting System in Islamic Banking, London: Institute
of Islamic Banking and Insurance.

Aboumouamer, F. M. (1989), 'An analysis of the role and function of *Shari'ah* control in Islamic banks', PhD, University
of Wales.

Al-Baluchi, A. E. A. (2006), 'The impacts of AAOIFI standards
and other banks characteristics on the level of voluntary
disclosure in the annual reports of Islamic banks', PhD,
University of Surrey.

Al Hajj, A. Y. (2003), 'The usefulness of annual reports
of Islamic financial institutions in GCC countries
to investors: the case of Kuwait', PhD, University of
Glamorgan.

Al-Sadah, A. K. I. (2007), 'Corporate governance of Islamic
banks, its characteristics and effect on stakeholders and
the role of Islamic banks supervisors', PhD, University of
Surrey.

Faizullah, M. (2009), 'Islamic banking: issues of governance, transparency and standardization', PhD, London
Metropolitan University.

Housby, Elaine S. (2005), 'The development of the Islamic
financial tradition in contemporary Britain', PhD, Open
University, London.

Sulaiman Al Mehmadi, F. S. (2004), 'The external reporting
needs of investors in Islamic banks in Saudi Arabia: an

exploratory study of full disclosure', PhD, University of Dundee.

Conference papers

Al Sayari, H. (2004), 'Islamic banks: current situation and future wailings', research presented at the Islamic Banks Conference, Riyadh, 24-25 February 2004.

Caprio, G. Jr and Levine, R. (2002), 'Corporate govern-ance of banks: concepts and international observations', paper presented at the World Bank, IMF, and Brookings Institution Conference, Building the Pillars of Financial Sector Governance: the Roles of Public and Private Sectors, Washington, DC, 5 April 2002, available at: http://icf.som. yale.edu/Conference-Papers/backup_old_iicg/april_5/ CAPRIO.pdf. Access date: 20 April 2008.

Claessens, S. (2003), 'Corporate governance and develop-ment', presented at Global Corporate Governance Forum, Washington: World Bank, available at: http://papers.ssrn. com/sol3/papers.cfm?abstract_id=642721. Access date: 16 February 2010.

Dar, H. (2009a), 'Implementing *Shari'ah* governance: awaiting challenge', paper presented at the Conference on Managing *Shari'ah* Risk through *Shari'ah* Governance organised by ISRA, London, 10 August 2009.

Delorenzo, Y. T. (2000), '*Shari'ah* supervision of Islamic mutual funds', paper presented at the Fourth Harvard Islamic Finance Forum, Cambridge, MA, 6 April 2000, available at: http://www.djindexes.com/mdsidx/downloads/ delorenzo.pdf. Access date: 5 January 2010.

Ilyas, N. (2008), 'Governance in Islamic banks: the Indonesian experience', paper presented at the INCEIF's Intellectual Discourse Series, Kuala Lumpur, 30 June 2008.

Newspaper/magazine articles

Dar, H. (2009b), '*Shari'ah*-based, *Shari'ah*-compliant and *Shari'ah*-tolerated products', *New Horizon*, 172, 10–12.

Hamedanchi, S. and Altenbach, J. (2009), 'Genetics of the Islamic exchange traded funds', *Islamic Finance News*, May, 6.

ISRA (2009), '*Shari'ah*-compliant versus *Shari'ah*-based products', *ISRA Bulletin*, 2, 2.

New Horizon (2004), '*Shari'ah* council finalizes unified standards for Islamic banking', *New Horizon*, November, 143, 15.

New Horizon (2005), '*Shari'ah* scholars: their contributions and limitations', *New Horizon*, December, 144, 5.

Siddiqi, M. N. (2008), 'The future of *Shari'ah*-compliant finance', *Business Islamica*, Dubai: Business Enterprise, 73–6.

The Banker (2009), 'GCC still dominate', *The Banker*, November (Suppl), 26.

Wolfensohn, J. (1999), 'Corporate governance is promoting corporate fairness, transparency and accountability', *Financial Times*, 21 June, 20.

Internet sources

AAOIFI (2008), *AAOIFI Shari'ah Board*, available at: http://www.aaoifi.com/sharia-board.html. Access date: 4 September 2008.

AFB (2008), *Financial Statements 2008*, available at: http://www.asianfinancebank.com/pdf/financial_reports/audited311208.pdf. Access date: 30 August 2010.

AIB (2008), *Annual Report 2008*, available at: http://www.affinbank.com.my/corporate/AFFINISLAMIC-Annual-Report-2008.pdf. Access date: 30 August 2010.

Al-Abduljabbar, A. and Marshal, J. I. (2010), *Saudi Arabia*,

Financial and Corporate: a Changing Legal Environment, available at: http://www.iflr1000.com/pdfs/Directories/13/ Saudi-Arabia.pdf. Access date: 11 May 2011.

Al Bilad (2008), *Annual Report 2008*, available at: http:// www.bankalbilad.com/en/Albilad%20%28Final%29en.pdf. Access date: 30 August 2010.

Alliance (2009), *Annual Report 2009*, available at: http://www. allianceislamicbank.com.my/pdf/finstmt/ar0910/4qresult. pdf. Access date: 30 August 2010.

Al Rajhi (2008), *Shari'ah Group*, available at: http://www. alrajhibank.com.sa/AboutUs/Pages/ShariaaGroup.aspx. Access date: 17 December 2008.

Al Rajhi (M) (2008), *Financial Statements 2008*, available at: http://www.alrajhibank.com.my/_repository/arb/annual_ report/Condensed%20Fin.Stat%20-%203rd%20Qtr%20 30%20Sept%20%2708.pdf. Access date: 30 August 2010.

BIB (2008), *Annual Report 2008*, available at: http://www.bisb. com/pdf/financials/ar_2008.pdf. Access date: 30 August 2010.

BIMB (2008), *Annual Report 2008*, available at: http://www. bankislam.com.my/bimb_pdf/Annual%20Report%2008. pdf. Access date: 30 August 2010.

BMMB (2008), *Annual Report 2008*, available at: http:// www.muamalat.com.my/downloads/corporate-overview/ annual/2008.pdf. Access date: 30 August 2010.

Briault, C. (2007), *London: Centre of Islamic Finance?*, available at: http://www.fsa.gov.uk/pages/Library/Communication/ Speeches/2007...London:CentreofIslamicFinance? Access date: 21 November 2008.

BSN (2008), *Annual Report 2008*, available at: http://www.bsn. com.my/bsn/laporantahunan/BSNAnnualReport2008.pdf. Access date: 30 August 2010.

Cadbury, A. (1999), *Corporate Governance: a Framework for Implementation*, available at: http://www.sovereignglobal.

com/media/framework_for_implemenation.pdf. Access date: 14 January 2010.

CIMB (2007), *Annual Report 2007*, available at: http://www.cimb.com/annual_reports/CIMB_Islamic/2007/index.html. Access date: 30 August 2010.

Dar, H. (2009c), 'Models of *Shari'ah* advisement in Islamic finance', *Al Watan Daily*, available at: http://alwatan daily.alwatan.com.kw/Default.aspx?MgDid=786239&pageId=476. Access date: 27 August 2009.

Devi, S. (2008), 'Experts: scholars and harmony in short supply', *Financial Times*, 17 June, available at: http://www.ft.com/cms/s/0/4b67288c-3c0f-11dd-9cb2-0000779fd2ac,dwp_uuid=282ce812-36c3-11dd-bc1c-0000779fd2ac.html. Access date: 19 December 2008.

DFSA (2010), *DFSA Launches Electronic Islamic Finance Handbooks*, available at: http://www.dfsa.ae/WhatsNew/DispForm.aspx?Id=131. Access date: 14 March 2010.

EONCAP (2008), *Annual Report 2008*, available at: http://www.eonbank.com.my/group/pdf-files/ECB_AR08_Financials.pdf. Access date: 30 August 2010.

Fischel, W. J. '*Djahbadh* (pl. *djahābidha*)', in P. Bearman, T. Bianquis, C. E. Bosworth, E. Van Donzel and W. P. Heinrichs (eds), *Encyclopedia of Islam*, Leiden: Brill, Brill Online available at: http://www.brillonline.nl/subscriber/entry?entry=islam_SIM-1932. Access date: 16 April 2008.

Hasan, A. (2007), *Optimal Shari'ah Governance in Islamic Finance*, available at: http://www.bnm.gov.my/microsites/giff2007/pdf/frf/04_01.pdf. Access date: 27 August 2009.

Hawkamah (2008), *Hawkamah – The Institute of Corporate Governance*, available at: http://www.hawkamah.org/hawkamah/index.html. Access date: 28 July 2008.

HLIB (2008), *Annual Report 2008*, available at: http://www.hlisb.com.my/data/ann2008.pdf. Access date: 30 August 2010.

HSBC (M) (2008), *Financial Statements 2008*, available at: http://www.hsbcamanah.com.my/1/PA_1_1_S5/content/amanah/website/pdf/financial_results/interim4quarter2008.pdf. Access date: 30 August 2010.

HSBC (2009), *Shari'ah Supervision*, available at: http://www.hsbcamanah.com/1/2/ALL_SITE_PAGES/amanah-global/about-hsbc-amanah/amanah-islamic-banking/shariah-supervision. Access date: 8 September 2009.

IBB (2004), *Prospectus*, available at: http://www.islamic-bank.com/investor-relations/company-information/. Access date: 30 August 2010.

IBB (2008), *Article of Association of Islamic Bank of Britain*, available at: http://www.islamic-bank.com/GetAsset.aspx?id=fAA0ADUAMwB8AHwAVAByAHUAZQB8AHwAMAB8AA2. Access date: 16 August 2010.

IFSB (2008c), *Objectives of the IFSB*, available at: http://www.ifsb.org/objectif.php. Access date: 29 October 2008.

IFSB (2009), *The IFSB Council Adopts Three Documents*, available at: http://www.ifsb.org/preess_full.php?id=129&submit=more. Access date: 14 January 2010.

IFSB (2010), *About IFSB*, available at: http://www.ifsb.org/background.php. Access date: 15 January 2010.

IFSC (2009), *Informative Bulletin for the Purpose of Trading Islamic Financial Securities Company's Share on the Doha Security Market*, Doha: Islamic Financial Securities and Co. available at: http://www.islamicbroker.biz/english/company_profile/index.html. Access date: 4 September 2009.

JBIC (2007), 'Recycling petrodollars in Asian markets: the part JBIC plays in Japan's initiative', *JIBC Today*, July, available at: http://www.jbic.go.jp/en/report/jbic-today/2007/07/td_2007july.pdf. Access date: 17 March 2010.

KFH (M) (2008), *Annual Report 2008*, available at: http://www.kfhonline.com.my/bpmapp-upload/download/fstore/0a14d001d033d0c9_78af2b13_12410a53ae2_-77aa?fileKey=/

fstore/0a14d001d033d0c9_78af2b13_12410a53ae2_-77aa/
KFH%28M%29B%20Annual%20Report%20Year%202008.
pdf. Access date: 30 August 2010.

KIB (2008), *Annual Report 2008*, available at: http://www.
kib.com.kw/UserFiles/Reports/English_Annual_2008.pdf.
Access date: 30 August 2010.

Mahdi, W. (2008), 'Most of Islamic financial products are not
Islamic', *Arabian Business*, 28 April, available at: http://
www.arabianbusiness.com/arabic/517729. Access date: 18
April 2010.

MIB (2008), *Annual Report 2008*, available at: http://www.
maybank.com.my/files/Maybank%20Islamic%20AR2008.
PDF. Access date: 30 August 2010.

Morris, M. (2009), 'Seven charged in bank fraud case', *Arabian
Business*, 10 March, Available at: http://www.arabianbusi-
ness.com/549121-seven-held-in-bank-fraud. Access date: 21
August 2009.

Parker, M. (2005), 'Scandal-hit bank Islam Malaysia declares
huge losses', *Arab News*, 19 December, available at: http://
www.arabnews.com/?page=6&section=0&article=74908&
d=19&m=12&y=2005. Access date: 7 September 2009.

Parker, M. (2009), 'Islamic banking special supplement:
Shari'ah governance a challenge to Islamic banking', *Arab
News*, 11 October, available at: http://archive.arabnews.
com/?page=9&section=0&article=127292&d=11&m=1
0&y=2009. Access date: 8 March 2010.

Parker, M. (2010), '*Shari'ah* governance in Islamic finance
industry', *Arab News*, 22 March, available at: http://
arabnews.com/economy/islamicfinance/article33068.ece.
Access date: 23 March 2010.

Pasha, S. (2010a), '*Shari'ah* board face scrutiny amid financial
crisis', Reuters, 11 March, available at: http://www.reuters.
com/article/idUSLDE62AOJ420100311. Access date: 20 May
2010.

Pasha, S. (2010b), 'Islamic finance seeks young scholars to lead growth', Reuters, 1 June, available at: http://www.reuters.com/article/idUSTRE65021U20100601. Access date: 9 June 2010.

QFC (2010a), *About QFC*, available at: http://www.qfc.com.qa/en-US/About-qfc.aspx. Access date: 20 August 2010.

QFC (2010b), *Islamic Finance*, available at: http://www.qfc.com.qa/en-US/About-qfc/Business_case/Islamic_finance.aspx. Access date: 20 August 2010.

Reuters (2009), 'Islamic banks asset to hit USD 1 trillion', 10 December, available at: http://www.arabianbusiness.com/505919-islamic-bank-assets-to-hit-1tn. Access date: 14 January 2010.

RHB (2008), *Annual Report 2008*, available at: http://www.rhb.com.my/corporate_profile/investor_relation/pdf/annual_reports/2008/RHB%20Islamic%20Bank%20Berhad%202008.pdf. Access date: 30 August 2010.

Saeed, Abdullah (2002),'*Ṣarrāf (a.)*', in P. Bearman, T. Bianquis, C. E. Bosworth, E. van Donzel and W. P. Heinrichs (eds), *Encyclopedia of Islam*, vol. 11,Leiden: Brill, Brill Online, available at: http://www.brillonline.nl/subscriber/entry?entry=islam_SIM-8886. Access date: 16 April 2008.

SC (2009), *SC Streamlines Registration of Shari'ah Advisers*, available at: http://www.sc.com.my/main.asp?pageid=379&linkid=2256&yearno=2009&mod=paper. Access date: 10 August 2009.

SII (2008), *Leading Shari'ah Scholars Debate The Credit Crunch*, First Islamic Finance Council UK and Securities & Investment Institute CPD session on 28 October 2008, available at: http://www.sii.org.uk/web5/infopool.nsf/HTML/LBEN-7L3G23?Opendocument. Access date: 1st January 2009.

Stanley, M. (2008), 'Implementing corporate governance

for Islamic finance', *GT News*, available at: http://www.gtnews.com/article/7059.cfm. Access date: 26 August 2009.

Unal, M. (2009), *Shari'ah Scholars in GCC – a Network Analytic Perspective – Updated*, Germany: Funds@Work, available at: http://www.funds-at-work.com/fileadmin/downloads/Sharia-Network_by_Funds_at_Work_AG.pdf.pdf. Access date: 18 January 2010.

Unal, M. (2010), *Shari'ah Scholars – a Network Analytic Perspective*, Germany: Funds@Work, available at: http://www.funds-at-work.com/fileadmin/downloads/Sharia-Network_by_Funds_at_Work_AG.pdf.pdf Access date: 15 April 2010.

Unal, M. and Ley, C. (2009), *Shari'ah Scholars in GCC – a Network Analytic Perspective*, Germany: Funds@Work, available at: http://www.funds-at-work.com/fileadmin/downloads/Sharia-Network_by_Funds_at_Work_AG.pdf. Access date: 14 July 2009.

Za'za, B. (2009), 'Dubai Islamic Bank DH 1.8 billion fraud case brought to the court', *Gulf News*, 9 March, available at: http://gulfnews.com/news/gulf/uae/crime/dubai-islamic-bank-dh1-8b-fraud-case-referred-to-court-1.56801. Access date: 5 February 2010.

Cases

Affin Bank Berhad v. Zulkifli Abdullah [2006] 1 CLJ 447

Arab Malaysian Finance Bhd v. Taman Ihsan Jaya Sdn Bhd & Ors (Koperasi Seri Kota Bukit Cheraka Bhd, third party) [2008] 5 MLJ 631

Arab Malaysian Merchant Bank Berhad v. Silver Concept Sdn Bhd [2005] 5 MLJ 210

Arab-Malaysian Merchant Bank Bhd v. Silver Concept Sdn Bhd [2008] 6 MLJ 295

Dato' Nik Mahmud Bin Daud v. *Bank Islam Malaysia Berhad* [1996] 4 MLJ 295

Malayan Banking Berhad v. *Marilyn Ho Siok Lin* [2006] 7 MLJ 249, 3 CLJ 796

Malayan Banking Berhad v. *Ya'kup bin Oje & Anor* [2007] 6 MLJ 389

Saudi Arabia v. *Arabian American Oil Company* [1958] 27 ILR 117

Tahan Steel Corporation Sdn Bhd v. *Bank Islam Malaysia Bhd* [2004] 6 CLJ 25

Tan Sri Khalid Ibrahim v. *Bank Islam Malaysia Berhad* [2009] 6 MLJ 416

The Investment Dar Company KSCC v. *Blom Developments Bank Sal* (2009) EWHC 3545 (Ch)

Tinta Press Sdn Bhd v. *Bank Islam Malaysia Berhad* (1987) 1 MLJ 474

INDEX